Human–Robot Interaction

Safety, Standardization, and Benchmarking

Human–Robot Interaction

Safety, Standardization, and Benchmarking

Edited by
Paolo Barattini, Federico Vicentini,
Gurvinder Singh Virk, and Tamás Haidegger

CRC Press
Taylor & Francis Group
Boca Raton London New York

CRC Press is an imprint of the
Taylor & Francis Group, an **informa** business

A CHAPMAN & HALL BOOK

CRC Press
Taylor & Francis Group
6000 Broken Sound Parkway NW, Suite 300
Boca Raton, FL 33487-2742

First issued in paperback 2020

© 2019 by Taylor & Francis Group, LLC
CRC Press is an imprint of Taylor & Francis Group, an Informa business

No claim to original U.S. Government works

ISBN-13: 978-1-138-62675-1 (hbk)
ISBN-13: 978-0-367-73022-2 (pbk)

Library of Congress Cataloging-in-Publication Data

Names: Barattini, Paolo, editor.
Title: Human-robot interaction : safety, standardization, and benchmarking /
[edited by] Paolo Barattini, Federico Vicentini, Gurvinder Singh Virk,
Tamás Haidegger.
Other titles: Human-robot interaction (Taylor & Francis : 2019)
Description: Boca Raton, FL : CRC Press/Taylor & Francis Group, [2019] |
Includes bibliographical references and index.
Identifiers: LCCN 2018060976| ISBN 9781138626751 (hardback : acid-free
paper) | ISBN 9781315213781 (ebook)
Subjects: LCSH: Human-robot interaction.
Classification: LCC TJ211.49 .H8658 2019 | DDC 629.8/924019--dc23
LC record available at https://lccn.loc.gov/2018060976

Visit the Taylor & Francis Web site at
http://www.taylorandfrancis.com

and the CRC Press Web site at
http://www.crcpress.com

Contents

Preface, vii

Editor Bios, ix

Contributors, xiii

CHAPTER 1 ▪ The Role of Standardization in Technical Regulations   1

ANDRÉ PIRLET, IR

CHAPTER 2 ▪ The Intricate Relationships Between Private Standards
and Public Policymaking in Personal Care Robots:
Who Cares More?   9

EDUARD FOSCH-VILLARONGA AND ANGELO JR GOLIA

CHAPTER 3 ▪ Standard Ontologies and HRI   19

SANDRO RAMA FIORINI, ABDELGHANI CHIBANI, TAMÁS HAIDEGGER, JOEL LUIS CARBONERA,
CRAIG SCHLENOFF, JACEK MALEC, EDSON PRESTES, PAULO GONÇALVES, S. VEERA RAGAVAN,
HOWARD LI, HIRENKUMAR NAKAWALA, STEPHEN BALAKIRSKY, SOFIANE BOUZNAD, NOAUEL
AYARI, AND YACINE AMIRAT

CHAPTER 4 ▪ Robot Modularity for Service Robots   49

HONG SEONG PARK AND GURVINDER SINGH VIRK

CHAPTER 5 ▪ Human–Robot Shared Workspace in Aerospace Factories   71

GILBERT TANG AND PHIL WEBB

CHAPTER 6 ▪ Workspace Sharing in Mobile Manipulation   81

JOSÉ SAENZ

CHAPTER 7 ▪ On Rehabilitation Robotics Safety, Benchmarking,
and Standards: Safety of Robots in the Field of
Neurorehabilitation—Context and Developments   91

JAN F. VENEMAN

CHAPTER 8 ▪ A Practical Appraisal of ISO 13482 as a Reference for an Orphan Robot Category   103

PAOLO BARATTINI

CHAPTER 9 ▪ Safety of Medical Robots, Regulation, and Standards   123

KIYOYUKI CHINZEI

CHAPTER 10 ▪ The Other End of Human–Robot Interaction: Models for Safe and Efficient Tool–Tissue Interactions   137

ÁRPÁD TAKÁCS, IMRE J. RUDAS, AND TAMÁS HAIDEGGER

CHAPTER 11 ▪ Passive Bilateral Teleoperation with Safety Considerations   171

MÁRTON LŐRINCZ

CHAPTER 12 ▪ Human–Robot Interfaces in Autonomous Surgical Robots   187

PAOLO FIORINI AND RICCARDO MURADORE

INDEX, 201

Preface

STANDARDISATION AND SAFETY are horizontal topics set across any application domain of robotics.

A few years ago, I was involved for the first time in an industrial robotics project. The project, among other relevant technical themes, investigated ergonomics and safety. Sometime thereafter, I participated in the ISO robotics working groups meeting held in Milan. This occasioned the establishment of personal friendships with some of the participants.

Some of the Europeans soon met again at the venues of the euRobotics Association. This is quite a dynamic environment, self-organised in topical groups created spontaneously by the associates on specific areas of interest or domains. Sometimes, they vanish and new ones emerge.

Standardisation and safety are horizontal topics set across any application domain of robotics. My initial idea of creating a topic group on standardisation reflected the interest of an initial bunch of colleagues, among them the editors of this book. The topic group was launched. It grew immediately to over 70 members.

One of the authors, at the time the youngest member, in his late 20s, is now a leading expert in robotics' legal and regulatory matters. Some others quit the quiet of the academy to dive deep into the practical application of the standards in companies developing products for the market.

We created multiple occasions for debate, while each member in their domain was profiting from discussions, workshops, and technical and cultural exchanges. This book originates from the idea of presenting to a wider audience a condensed look at the current issues and outputs of technical experience and developments in safety and standardisation in robotics, issuing from the network of international experts from the ISO Working Groups and the euRobotics Association.

The book sports an Aristotelian set-up, the initial chapters being those of wider general matter, with the final ones being more technical and specific. It pretends to be a small, but dense, representation of safety and standardisation issues by some of their dedicated actors.

Paolo Barattini
Kontor46 s.a.s.
Turin, Italy

MATLAB® is a registered trademark of The MathWorks, Inc. For product information, please contact:

The MathWorks, Inc.
3 Apple Hill Drive
Natick, MA 01760-2098 USA
Tel: 508-647-7000
Fax: 508-647-7001
E-mail: info@mathworks.com
Web: www.mathworks.com

Editor Bios

Paolo Barattini, MD, PhD is an expert in ergonomics, safety, and physical and virtual interfaces. He has worked on sundry European Space Agency contracts and European Commission FP7 and H2020 funded projects. The focus of his activity is the creation of new devices on a solid scientific innovative basis in the area of robotic biomedical devices. He has served as Coordinator of the Topical Group on Robotics Standards of euRobotics, the European robotics association, currently acting as Deputy.

Federico Vicentini, MSc, PhD in mechanical systems engineering, is a National Research Council of Italy researcher at the Institute of Intelligent Industrial Technologies and Systems for Advanced Manufacturing and Group Leader for "Robot Safety and Human–Robot Interaction" in the Robotics Division, Milan, Italy. His research and technology interests range from industrial robotics to automation safety, with special focus on human–robot interaction and collaborative behaviors.

He is currently serving as coordinator of the Italian national standardization group "Robots and Robot Systems" and as member of the international standardization group ISO TC299/WG3 "Industrial Industrial Robot Safety". He is also active in euRobotics and partner of SPARC PPP, with regards to industrial robotics, safety, and standards. He is a regular system architect or principal investigator in international research programs, and regular contributor for scholarly publications and reviews in robotics journals and conferences.

Professor Gurvinder Singh Virk, PhD, DIC, BSc, CEng, FIET, FCIBSE, CMath, FIMA, MIEEE is Chairman and CEO of Endoenergy Systems, focused on developing wearable assistive exoskeletons in service applications involving close human–robot interactions, with bases in the UK and in India. His current research interests are in wearable exoskeleton robots for wellbeing, robot safety standardisation, robot modularity and inter-operability, social robotics, and robot ethics. In addition to his industrial position at Endoenergy, he is visiting professor at London South Bank University, UK. He holds a PhD in control theory from Imperial College, University of London, UK. He has held senior leadership roles in the UK (Universities of Bradford, Portsmouth, and Leeds), Sweden (University of Gävle and KTH Royal Institute of Technology), and New Zealand (Massey University), as well as visiting professor positions in China (Zhejiang University), France (Université Pierre et Marie Curie, Paris), and Germany (Fachochschule Südwestfalen, Soest). In addition, he has had commercial experience as Technical Director at InnotecUK, where he led

R&D activities for realising commercially viable inspection robots for hazardous environments where mobility, climbing, and manipulation capabilities are needed in the robots systems being developed. Throughout his career, Professor Virk has been active in all areas of academia (including commercialisation), and has been a dedicated researcher, teacher, and administrator as well as motivator of others around him. He has produced over 350 refereed publications, filed four patents, supervised 16 successful PhD/MPhil students, created and led research teams at Portsmouth, Leeds, Massey, and Gävle, registered several spin-out companies (and a UK-registered charity), and led many international externally funded projects. He is an excellent networker for research collaborations and is now focusing on commercialisation of robotics.

Professor Virk is Treasurer and Trustee of the UK-registered charity CLAWAR, whose mission is to advance robotics globally for public benefit. For this, he has been a leading international expert since 2005 in international robot standardisation activities on safety and inter-operability. Details of his involvement are as follows:

1. ISO TC299/WG2: Personal care robot safety, Member; Convenor during 2006–2016.

2. ISO TC299/SG1: Gaps and structure, Member, Convenor during 2017.

3. IEC SC62A & ISO TC299/JWG5: Medical robot safety, Member, Convenor during 2011–2018; and

4. ISO TC299/WG6: Modularity for service robots, Convenor 2014–present.

Professor Virk is also coordinator of the euRobotics' topic group on standardisation in Europe as part the Horizon 2020 programme and beyond. He is actively networking and working with stakeholder organisations in Europe, China, South Korea, Japan, the United States, and India on linking international robot R&D with robot standardisation to facilitate the creation of new robot markets.

Tamás Haidegger received his MSc degrees from the Budapest University of Technology and Economics (BME) in Electrical Engineering and Biomedical Engineering in 2006 and 2008, respectively, then PhD in 2011. His main field of research is on medical technologies, control/teleoperation of surgical robots, image-guided therapy, and assistive devices. Currently, he is associate professor at Óbuda University, serving as the director of the University Research, Innovation, and Service Center (EKIK), and as the technical lead of medical robotics research at the Antal Bejczy Center for Intelligent Robotics. He is also a research area manager at the Austrian Center of Medical Innovation and Technology (ACMIT), working on minimally invasive surgical simulation and training, medical robotics, and usability/workflow assessment through ontologies. Tamás is the co-founder of a university spin-off—HandInScan—focusing on objective hand hygiene control in the medical environment, a member of the World Health Organization POPS group. He is an active member of various other professional organizations, including the IEEE Robotics and Automation Society, IEEE SMC, IEEE EMBC, and euRobotics AISBL, holding leadership positions in the IEEE Hungary Section as well. He is a national delegate to the ISO TC299 standardization committee focusing on the safety and performance of medical robots and the ISO TC304 working on hand hygiene and patient safety standards. Furthermore, he is also involved in the IEEE Global Initiative on Ethics of Autonomous and Intelligent Systems. Tamás is the author and co-author of over 150 books, articles, and scientific papers across the various domains of biomedical engineering, with over 900 independent citations of his work. He has been running a professional blog on medical robotic technologies for 12 years: surgrob.blogspot.com.

Contributors

Yacine Amirat
Laboratoire Images, Signaux et Systèmes
 Intelligents (Lissi)
Université Paris-Est Créteil
Paris, France

Noauel Ayari
Laboratoire Images, Signaux et Systèmes
 Intelligents (Lissi)
Université Paris-Est Créteil
Paris, France

Stephen Balakirsky
Georgia Tech Research Institute
Atlanta, Georgia

Sofiane Bouznad
Laboratoire Images, Signaux et Systèmes
 Intelligents (Lissi)
Université Paris-Est Créteil
Paris, France

Joel Luis Carbonera
Institute of Informatics
Federal University of Rio Grande do Sul
Porto Alegre, Brazil

Abdelghani Chibani
Laboratoire Images, Signaux et Systèmes
 Intelligents (Lissi)
Université Paris-Est Créteil
Paris, France

Kiyoyuki Chinzei
Health Research Institute
National Institute of Advanced Industrial
 Science and Technology (AIST)
and
School of Engineering
Tokyo Denki University
Tokyo, Japan

Paolo Fiorini
Department of Computer Science
University of Verona
Verona, Italy

Sandro Rama Fiorini
Laboratoire Images, Signaux et Systèmes
 Intelligents (Lissi)
Université Paris-Est Créteil
Paris, France

Eduard Fosch-Villaronga
Center for Commercial Law Studies (CCLS)
Queen Mary University of London
London, United Kingdom

Angelo Jr Golia
School of Law
University of Salerno
Fisciano, Italy
and
International Human Rights Law Clinic
University of Aix-Marseille
Marseille, France

Paulo Gonçalves
DMEC, IST
Instituto Politecnico de Castelo Branco
Castelo Branco, Portugal

Howard Li
Collaboration Based Robotics and
    Automation (COBRA)
University of New Brunswick
Fredericton, Canada

Jacek Malec
Department of Computer Science
Lund University
Lund, Sweden

Márton Lőrincz
Department of Electrical Engineering
Sapientia Hungarian University of
    Transylvania
Miercurea-Ciuc, Romania

Riccardo Muradore
Department of Computer Science
University of Verona
Verona, Italy

Hirenkumar Nakawala
Politecnico di Milano
Milan, Italy

Hong Seong Park
Department of Electrical and Engineering
Kangwon National University
Chuncheon, South Korea

André Pirlet, Ir
NCP Wallonie
Wavre, Belgium

Edson Prestes
Institute of Informatics
Federal University of Rio Grande do Sul
Porto Alegre, Brazil

S. Veera Ragavan
Monash University
Subang Jaya, Malaysia

Imre J. Rudas
University Research, Innovation and
    Service Center (EKIK)
Óbuda University
Budapest, Hungary

José Saenz
Business Unit Robotic Systems –
    Fraunhofer IFF
Magdeburg, Germany

Craig Schlenoff
National Institute of Standards and
    Technology
Gaithersburg, Maryland

Árpád Takács
University Research, Innovation and
    Service Center (EKIK)
Óbuda University
Budapest, Hungary

Dr. Gilbert Tang
Cranfield University
Cranfield, United Kingdom

Jan F. Veneman
Tecnalia Research and Innovation
San Sebastian, Spain
and
Hocoma AG
Volketswil, Switzerland

Phil Webb
Cranfield University
Cranfield, United Kingdom

CHAPTER 1

The Role of Standardization in Technical Regulations

André Pirlet, Ir

CONTENTS

1.1 Standardization: The Main Characteristics, the Benefits of Standardization, and the Choice of the Best Procedure 1
1.2 Improving a Given Situation through Project Approaches and Implementation 3
1.3 The Context of Technical Legislation 5
1.4 Conclusions 7
References 7

1.1 STANDARDIZATION: THE MAIN CHARACTERISTICS, THE BENEFITS OF STANDARDIZATION, AND THE CHOICE OF THE BEST PROCEDURE

Standards are formally defined as documents established by consensus that provide, for common and repeated use, rules, guidelines or characteristics for activities or their results, aimed at the achievement of the optimum degree of order in a given context. Standards should be based on consolidated results of science, technology and experience, and aimed at the promotion of optimum community benefits. Standards contain unambiguous requirements, but also, when needed, definitions and testing methods, to assess whether the prescribed requirements are fulfilled, facilitating certification. As they are built on consensus, groups of experts need to meet and communicate. This calls for management, rules and procedures, which form a standardization framework. Non-formal standards can be written by consortia, whether national, European or worldwide (IEEE, GS1, OASIS, etc.). Formal standards can be defined as standards prepared using formal procedures of openness and transparency and published by permanent and not-for-profit recognized standardization organizations. Most of the countries worldwide have a national standards body. At European level, three European standardization bodies can be found:

- CENELEC for Electro-technical Standardization

- ETSI for Telecommunications

- CEN for the rest

At worldwide level, we have similarly:

- IEC for Electro-technical Standardization
- ITU for Telecommunications
- ISO for the rest

It is essential for standards to be written in such a way that they allow evolution and progress, and do not block innovation. There should be flexibility for meeting the requirements specified in the standards, therefore the modern emphasis on "performance standards". Similar possibilities are offered by CEN and CENELEC, while the ETSI standardization system is rather different and focuses only on telecommunications.

- An EN is a European Standard and enjoys the highest status. The acronym EN comes from "die Europäischen Normen", in German. A very important aspect of CEN-CENELEC Internal Rules is that, when an EN is adopted by CEN or CENELEC, their members, who are national standardization bodies, are forced to adopt the full EN as one of their national standards and also to withdraw any conflicting national standard. An EN is issued by CEN-CENELEC in three official languages (French, English and German), but the national standardization bodies in Europe generally issue these standards in their national language(s), and this is a key advantage which is frequently overlooked.

- A Technical Specification (TS) is a prospective standard for provisional application. It is mainly used in fields where the innovation rate is high, or when there is an urgent need for guidance, and primarily where aspects of safety for persons and goods are not involved. Conflicting national standards may be kept in force in parallel with the national implementation of the TS.

- A Technical Report is a non-normative CEN (or CENELEC) publication authorized by the CEN (or CENELEC) Technical Board.

- A CEN Workshop Agreement (CWA) is a document prepared rapidly by experts, without formal consultations (Enquiry, Formal Vote) at national level. It is a frequent standardization deliverable from research projects, and in the case of European R&D projects, a large part of the cost of producing the CWA can frequently be publicly supported. This type of publication aims at satisfying market demands for a more flexible and timelier alternative to the traditional EN, but it still possesses the authority derived from the openness of participation and agreement inherent in the operations of CEN. These CWAs are produced in flexible structures called CEN Workshops, where the registered participants are in charge of both the drafting and the management. CWAs are particularly suited for the exploitation of results of Research Projects and that approach is much appreciated by research consortia.

- Similarly at ETSI, you find ISGs, the Industry Specification Groups.

Formal standardization takes place in technical committees (TCs), where national delegations are in charge of the management, while the drafting of standards is made by experts sitting in working groups (WGs), reporting to their relevant TC. The national delegates at TC level need to reflect national positions, obtained by consensus, while the experts in the WGs are allowed to speak in their own name.

The cross-fertilization nature of standardization committees, due to the involvement of researchers and the various stakeholders, is felt as an additional benefit.

Whenever possible, preference should be given to the drafting of performance standards, which are defined as standards where requirements allow evolution and progress, and do not block but rather enhance innovation. They offer flexibility for meeting the requirements.

The aforementioned deliverables are quite similar to those found in the international standardization organizations ISO and IEC. The rapidly increasing globalization of the economy is concomitant with an increased preference for worldwide standards. The most important difference is that there is no mandatory national implementation of the standards published by ISO and IEC.

When wishing to initiate a new standardization activity, it is important to take into account the pros and cons of these deliverables, and subsequently choose the most relevant procedure in a tailored manner.

Some standards are jointly produced by two bodies, like CEN-CENELEC standards or ISO-IEC standards. Coordination groups exist also sometimes between three bodies, like CEN-CENELEC-ETSI or ISO-IEC-ITU. Other famous standards are those produced by NATO, the STANAGs, including the so-called "dual use" standards.

1.2 IMPROVING A GIVEN SITUATION THROUGH PROJECT APPROACHES AND IMPLEMENTATION

Imagine that you wish to improve an existing industrial situation or to address a societal challenge. It is important to realize that large scale beneficial changes rarely happen by chance, but result from a set of well-planned moves and actions. The "driving" forces for leading and carrying the actions should logically be the groups penalized by a given situation and who could expect substantial improvements by taking the right steps. To really "solve" a problem, there is therefore a need to use a *Project Approach* which should encompass the following steps:

- The starting point should be to clearly define the difficulties and the challenge(s) one wishes to address.

- Then there is a need for that "driving" group to express a clear objective, which should logically be to minimize or to entirely suppress the difficulty.

- Once there is a consensus within the group on the objective to be reached, the necessary time must be allocated to the careful drafting of the corresponding "business plan", which explains in sufficient detail what needs to be reached and why, and then how this could be reached. To reach an ambitious objective, a multi-faceted approach should frequently be used.

- Some results of research might be needed, whether from already carried research or from current research projects or already planned research. The CORDIS system enables a rather good view on collaborative European research. In certain cases, it will be necessary to initiate specific new research activities.

- Then comes the issue of legislation. Current legislation might apply and the stakeholder group should examine how to adapt to any new legislation, but also whether amendments are needed (or are desirable) for reaching their objective. Alternatively, no legislation may yet exist, but is nevertheless needed and should be put in place (for example, a European-wide legislation).

- Similarly, amendment of existing standards or drafting of entirely new standards might be a necessity. This would take place rarely at a purely national level, but more and more frequently at the European or worldwide level.

- As a last step, but quite importantly, there are "complementary measures". Here we find additional actions like marketing, education, training, promotion, protection of "Intellectual Property Rights" and so on, in order to have a comprehensive approach, also called an integrated approach. Again, most of the efforts will come from the "driving forces" mentioned above, and these "driving forces" need to include, for all important steps, a risk analysis and potential corrective measures.

- It is useful to take the analogy of a puzzle: You need to have all the pieces to get a nice picture! The same applies for reaching an ambitious objective.

- Using such an "Integrated Approach" will give the confidence that the goals can be reached in practice in an efficient way.

Standards can provide clarity on issues of terminology and definitions, durability, recyclability, sharing and comparing data, warranties, counterfeiting, and they can enable interoperability and economies of scale. They can also form the basis for rules of best practice. Standardized protocols and improved information technology compatibility are bringing more progress and efficiency, as explained by Pirlet [1]. The methodology of the "Integrated Approach" can now be summarized through the diagram shown in Figure 1.1.

Of course, having the right business plan, using this integrated approach concept, is a good start, but the "driving forces" need to select the right people to ensure the best implementation of the plan, within the decided timeframe. This also calls for careful monitoring of the implementation, in general, by these so-called "driving forces"; possibly some amendments and contingency measures will be decided by these forces and take place, anticipated as much as possible through regularly updated risk assessment.

At this stage, it is good to briefly address the "motivation" factor. In research activities, people are frequently "highly motivated", even passionate, this "comes with the territory". Motivating legal experts to work on new pieces of legislation is in general not too difficult. On the other hand, it is important to use a careful message in order to ensure a long-term commitment in a standardization activity, frequently characterized as "technical,

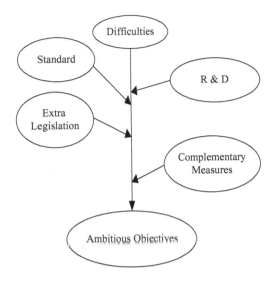

FIGURE 1.1   The integrated approach.

convoluted, long lasting and dull!" People need first to be convinced by the intrinsic importance of the end goals, and second, need to be convinced that a "support through standards" is vital to help reach these goals. The importance of these goals will then generate the necessary motivation. It is, however, harder and harder to find the right kind of people for writing new standards: they must combine solid technical experience with the necessary patience, pragmatism and tenacity, while also being at ease with wordings to formulate precise requirements and explain in all necessary details the most relevant testing methods. To compound the difficulties, these individuals should generally be multi-skilled and might be asked at some point by their company to relinquish their standardization tasks to instead fulfill a set of shorter-term goals, as decided by their hierarchy. That difficulty is compounded by the fact that standardization provides large benefits each time only at medium or long term! The ever-larger reliance on outsourcing and subcontracting in manufacturing industries also complicates the drafting of standards, on the other hand, it reinforces the benefit which can be reached through these new standards. In terms of spent resources, we should, however, stress that, compared with some large expenses like research or marketing, standardization is relatively cheap. The standardization costs could then be easily envisaged, even in the absence of financial support (from the European Commission or other third party).

1.3 THE CONTEXT OF TECHNICAL LEGISLATION

With the acceleration of technical progress after the Second World War, it became evident that there was a real challenge to ensure that legislation related to technical products or issues would remain up to date. A nice solution was found in Europe in the 1980s when some EU Directives were streamlined to contain only "Essential Requirements", while leaving to standardization committees the task to produce the necessary supporting standards, called "harmonised standards". Therefore, since these Essential Requirements were very "stable", there was no need to continuously amend the legislation, while the standards could more rapidly and more easily be improved and adapted to technical innovation. Experience has shown the great benefit of such a procedure, which could/should usefully be expanded to cover new fields, whenever applicable! The fact that all stakeholders can have an input in the drafting of such standards enhances both the practicability of these standards and the acceptability of these directives and regulations. All relevant details about the EU "New Approach" described here are to be found in a comprehensive recent EC Guide [2].

Let us just concentrate briefly on some important aspects: the use of these "harmonised standards" give a "presumption of conformity" to the relevant legislation, though a third-party certification is sometimes made mandatory, in accordance with the modalities applicable to the manufactured product. The EC Guide gives also guidance for the implementation of the provisions and concepts laid down in the "New EU Legislative Framework". Where there are product-specific deviations or provisions, the Guide refers to sectoral guides, which exist for almost all sectoral Union harmonization legislation.

Robotics is a multi-faceted field, encompassing electro-mechanics and IT, plus the specific fields of their applications, but it is mainly mentioned under IT, and it is an essential part of the Industry 4.0 paradigm. In the ICT sector, the Commission has proved its interest for efficient standardization [3] and is regularly updating a useful guide on ICT standards [4]. Since robotics is also, in a way, a part of the Internet of Things, we can usefully highlight chapter 6 "IoT Standards Landscape-State of the Art Analysis and Evolution" in a recent book [5].

The relevant EU legislation for robotics is composed principally of — The restriction of the use of certain hazardous substances in electrical and electronic equipment (Directive 2011/65/EU) — Eco-design requirements for energy-related products (Directive 2009/125/EC) — Electrical equipment designed for use within certain voltage limits (Directive 2006/95/EC and Directive 2014/35/EU) — Machinery (Directive 2006/42/EC) — Electromagnetic compatibility (Directive 2004/108/EC and Directive 2014/30/EU) — Radio equipment and telecommunications terminal equipment (Directive 1999/5/EC and Directive 2014/53/EU) — Active implantable medical devices (Directive 90/385/EEC) — Medical devices (Directive 93/42/EEC) — In vitro diagnostic medical devices (Directive 98/79/EC) — Equipment and protective systems intended for use in potentially explosive atmospheres (Directive 94/9/EC and Directive 2014/34/EU) — Regulation on the labelling of tyres (Regulation (EC) No 1222/2009) — Marine equipment (Directive 96/98/EC and Directive 2014/90/EU) — Noise emission in the environment by equipment for use outdoors (Directive 2000/14/EC) — Emissions from non-road mobile machinery (Directive 97/68/EC as amended) — Energy labelling (Directive 2010/30/EU). For those interested in person carrier robots, we can certainly point out a specific publication [6].

Let us not forget EU Directive 2001/95/EC (19) on general product safety (GPSD), which is intended to ensure a high level of product safety throughout the EU for consumer products that are not covered by sector-specific EU harmonization legislation. The GPSD also complements the provisions of sector legislation in some aspects. The key provision of the GPSD is that producers are obliged to place on the market only products which are safe.

The GPSD also provides for market surveillance provisions aimed at guaranteeing a high level of consumer health and safety protection. And new legislation keeps coming: the regulation on cyber-security (the NIS Directive on security of networks and information systems) and the all-important GDPR (General Data Protection Regulation).

Where a harmonized standard covers only part of the essential requirements identified as applicable by a manufacturer or only certain aspects thereof, she/he additionally has to use other relevant technical specifications or develop solutions in accordance with general engineering or scientific knowledge laid down in engineering and scientific literature in order to meet the essential requirements of the legislation in question. In a similar way, when a manufacturer chooses not to apply all the provisions given in a harmonized standard, and which normally would provide presumption of conformity, she/he needs, on the basis of his own risk assessment, to indicate in his technical documentation how the compliance is reached or that specific essential requirements are not applicable for his product.

Finally, there is the CE marking issue. By affixing the CE marking to a product, the manufacturer declares on his/her sole responsibility that the product is in conformity with the essential requirements of the applicable EU harmonization legislation providing for its affixing and that the relevant conformity assessment procedures have been fulfilled. Products bearing the CE marking are presumed to be in compliance with the applicable Union harmonization legislation and hence benefit from free circulation in the European Market.

1.4 CONCLUSIONS

This concise chapter has been an introduction to the main characteristics of standardization and its potential benefits. Standardization is indeed frequently overlooked, in spite of its large impact. We have shown the need for quality procedures (and therefore standards) to ensure smooth and economical operation. A message has been passed here, that main stakeholders in the "real world" should feel encouraged not only to examine how to use existing standards, but also to consider the needs for new standards and to be ready to initiate their drafting. This is feasible, even if this is rarely straightforward. And you should regularly connect with [3] and [4] to keep up with the latest ICT standardization developments. Second, we hope to have been convincing on the interest to use an "Integrated Approach" to reach ambitious complex objectives, with much greater chances of success! Finally, we have shown all the benefits obtained when technical legislation relies as much as possible on well-maintained standards.

REFERENCES

1. Pirlet A., 2009, Standardization as an ICT implementation enabler, *2nd European Conference on ICT for Transport Logistics*, 29–30 October 2009, San Servolo, Venice; http://www.ecitl.eu/downloads/ECITL_Programme_Print.pdf.
2. European Union, 2016, The "Blue Guide" on the implementation of EU products rules, *Official Journal of the European Union, C 272*, Vol. 59, 26 July 2016, pp. 1–147; http://eur-lex.europa.eu/legal-content/EN/TXT/?uri=OJ%3AC%3A2016%3A272%3ATOC.
3. European Commission, 2017, Rolling Plan on ICT Standardization; https://ec.europa.eu/growth/sectors/digital-economy/ict-standardisation_en.

4. European Commission, 2017, European Catalogue of ICT Standards for Procurement; https://joinup.ec.europa.eu/community/european_catalogue/news/eu-catalogue-ict-standards-draft-contents-and-consultation-launche.

5. Vermesan O. and Bacquet J., 2017, *Cognitive Hyperconnected Digital Transformation: Internet of Things Intelligence Evolution*, Gistrup, Denmark: River Publishers, p. 310.

6. Villaronga E.F. and Roig A., 2017, European regulatory framework for person carrier robots. *Computer Law & Security Review*, Vol. 33, Issue 4, August 2017 (Elsevier), p. 32.

CHAPTER 2

The Intricate Relationships Between Private Standards and Public Policymaking in Personal Care Robots: Who Cares More?

Eduard Fosch-Villaronga and Angelo Jr Golia

CONTENTS

2.1	Introduction	9
2.2	Theoretical Basis	10
	2.2.1 The Concepts of "Standard" and "Standardization"	10
	2.2.2 Differences Between Standard-Setting and Lawmaking	11
	2.2.3 Intertwinement	12
2.3	Standard-Setting and Public Policymaking in the Case of Robot Technology	12
	2.3.1 Personal Care Robots' Private Setting	12
	2.3.2 Public Policymaking for Robots	14
2.4	Hybrid Model Proposal	15
2.5	Conclusions	16
	References	17

2.1 INTRODUCTION

One of the consequences of the inability to keep up with technology is that industry, and more generally, private actors, usually take the lead and develop their own standards. This has happened in many regulatory fields. In the case of robot technologies, there are already available standards addressing the ELSI of these technologies. Both the British Standard Institute (BSI) and the Institute of Electrical and Electronics Engineers (IEEE) have developed standards governing the ethical design of robot technologies. Among other consequences, these standards cause a decentralization of regulation (Guihot et al. 2017).

Although belated, public regulatory bodies have also pronounced on technological advances. Early in 2017, the European Parliament released the Resolution on Civil Law Rules on Robotics 2015/2103(INL). The resolution was pioneering and unique because it was the first time that the European Parliament (EP) called the European Commission (EC) considered initiating a legislative procedure governing emerging robot technologies. Specifically, the European Parliament requested the Commission, on the basis of Article 225 Treaty on the Functioning of the European Union (TFEU), to submit a proposal for a directive on civil law rules on robotics on the basis of Article 114 TFEU (ex 65 Resolution 2015/2103(INL) 2017). Far from being a binding document, the resolution lacks technical awareness (Fosch-Villaronga & Heldeweg, 2018) and, thus, contains provisions that may be "morally unnecessary and legally troublesome" (Bryson et al. 2017).

In this context of multiple regulatory bodies with mismatching interests – one general and public; one specific and private – neither the regulator nor the addressees seem to exactly know what needs to be done (Sabel et al. 2017), although users' rights might be at stake in any case. This becomes particularly interesting when robots not only interact in sensitive contexts involving children, the elderly or disabled but also because robots may have moral implications at large (Salem et al. 2015).

This chapter first briefly explains the distinction between two different modes of regulation, i.e. standard-setting and lawmaking, highlighting their respective features and their reciprocal interrelationships. The much-debated theoretical issue of the normative and legal nature of standards adopted by private/hybrid organizations – such as the International Standardization Organization (ISO) – is brought to the fore to comparatively analyze advantages and disadvantages of these different modes of regulation.

Building on recent robot standards (ISO Standard 13482:2014 on Safety Requirements for Personal Care Robots) and a recent robot regulatory initiative (the European Parliament released the Resolution on Civil Law Rules on Robotics 2015/2103(INL), this paper addresses the impacts and challenges of overlapping public/private regulatory initiatives that govern robot technologies. The paper questions the sole use of standards – and its consequent *mere* harmonization – to govern robot technologies, as these may not provide sufficient protection to end users; but it also questions the technical understanding of public regulatory initiatives, which could risk making them ineffective.

In the light of the considerations argued in this chapter, the authors put forward a proposal for a hybrid approach. Section 5 includes the conclusions and final remarks.

2.2 THEORETICAL BASIS
2.2.1 The Concepts of "Standard" and "Standardization"
From a subjective perspective, i.e. that of the actor producing and/or adopting the norm, the concept of "standard-setting" is a form of regulation put in place by organizations that, from an institutional standpoint, do not act as politically legitimated bodies, but as either private or hybrid actors, whose legitimation is mainly based on their expertise

(Cafaggi 2011). Besides the ISO, at international/transnational level, other relevant standard-setting organizations are the International Accounting Standards Board (IASB); the Basel Committee on Banking Supervision (BCBS); the Codex Alimentarius Commission (CAC); and the Internet Corporation for Assigned Names and Numbers (ICANN).

From an objective perspective, "standardization" can be generally defined as any "activity of establishing, with regard to actual or potential problems, provisions for common and repeated use, aimed at the achievement of the optimum degree of order in a given context"; while "standard" can be referred to as any "document, established by consensus and approved by a recognized body, that provides, for common and repeated use, rules, guidelines or characteristics for activities or their results, aimed at the achievement of the optimum degree of order in a given context" (ISO/IEC 2004).

2.2.2 Differences Between Standard-Setting and Lawmaking

Since the emergence of the state as a dominant political actor, law has been conceived as a product of politically (not necessarily democratically) legitimated bodies, which gained the monopoly of legitimate force in a given territory. In other words, only political processes give institutions the legitimation to adopt rules, valid and enforceable in respect to all members of a community.

Lawmaking does not necessarily relate to "the achievement of the optimum degree of order in a given context," but rather to the achievement of consensus and agreement among the relevant (i.e. hegemonic) members of the community on the substantive content of the rules themselves. This consensus, and only this consensus, legitimates their overall validity, enforceability and binding nature.

Since the first half of the twentieth century at least, legal systems have undertaken fragmentation based on functionally differentiated units, including the economy, sports, science or religion (Luhmann 1971). First in the form of "social norms" but now as proper specific-sector legal systems in different forms and to different extents concerning these domains: *lex mercatoria*, *lex digitalis*, *lex scientifica*, *lex sportiva* and so on. These systems have become transnational, partially freeing themselves from the limits imposed by states' control of territories (Snyder 2003; Fischer-Lescano and Teubner 2004; Catà Backer 2007, 2014).

In short, the functional differentiation, together with the processes of globalization, has generated over these years a plurality of de-centered transnational legal systems, with their own sources of legitimation, which does not only deprive politically legitimated law of its effectiveness, but of actual regulatory domains. Standard-setting is part of these de-centralized legal systems. From this perspective, the fact that compliance with standards remains formally voluntary – though we will further investigate this claim – is considered as a demonstration that they do not set legally binding rules, and somehow contributes to their confinement to the blurred domain of the so-called *soft law*, an a-technical phrase generally indicating any type of regulation considered as not directly enforceable, either for the absence of genuine sanctions or for its lack of precision (Delmas-Marty 1986, 1998).

2.2.3 Intertwinement

Setting a clear distinction between soft law and hard law, between standard-setting and lawmaking, is today quite problematic. This is further shown by their intertwinement and reciprocal cross-references, justified by factual and technical needs.

Indeed, standardization is necessary to both private actors (especially enterprises) and states. Transnational enterprises (TNEs) increasingly externalize, so to say, the functions of self-regulation and self-organization to hybrid institutions for several reasons. First, they gain credibility in the eyes of consumers and, more generally, legitimation towards external actors. Second, compliance with standards is often a condition to access specific or protected markets, or to take part in public procurements. Third, and most importantly, standardization enables more efficient coordination and cooperation by reducing uncertainty and transaction costs and allowing a high degree of technological and/or productive interoperability (Howard-Grenville et al. 2008; Gunningham et al. 2004; Vesting 2004).

However, in contemporary economic and social context, standardization is even more necessary to states. Indeed, standards perform the fundamental function of regulating transnational phenomena (from finance to fishery, from corporate social responsibility to clinical and technological trials) where states do not manage to reach political agreements through the traditional forms of binding international law (Fenwick et al. 2014; Kjaer 2013; Renner 2013). Thus, also from the perspective of states, standardization constitutes an example of externalization of functions once exclusively held by them (De Londras 2011). An example is the recent call of the EP to the EC on harmonizing technical standards for robot technology (*ex 22*, Resolution 2015/2103(INL) 2017), where one can read:

> Standardization, safety and security: Highlights that the issue of setting standards and granting interoperability is crucial for future competition in the field of AI and robotics technologies; calls on the Commission to continue to work on the international harmonization of technical standards, in particular together with the European Standardization Organizations and the International Standardization Organization, in order to foster innovation, to avoid fragmentation of the internal market and to guarantee a high level of product safety and consumer protection including where appropriate minimum safety standards in the work environment; stresses the importance of lawful reverse-engineering and open standards, in order to maximize the value of innovation and to ensure that robots can communicate with each other; welcomes, in this respect, the setting up of special technical committees, such as ISO/TC 299 Robotics, dedicated exclusively to developing standards on robotics.

2.3 STANDARD-SETTING AND PUBLIC POLICYMAKING IN THE CASE OF ROBOT TECHNOLOGY

2.3.1 Personal Care Robots' Private Setting

In view of the rapid evolution of personal care robots, a technical framework was presented in February 2014 – the ISO 13482:2014 Robots and Robotics Devices, Safety Requirements for Personal Care Robots. According to it, personal care robots are "service robots that perform actions contributing directly towards improvement in the quality of life of humans, excluding medical applications [...] might include physical contact with the human to perform the task." Instead of fencing the robots off from humans to ensure safety, this standard addresses the physical human–robot interaction hazards by stipulating safety requirements on several design factors such as robot shape, robot motion, energy supply and storage or incorrect autonomous decisions (Fosch-Villaronga and Virk 2016).

The standard is, however, a bit confusing (Fosch-Villaronga 2015). First, the protected scope is not clear, as "personal care" is not defined throughout the standard. Instead, some examples of personal care robots are presented: person carrier, physical assistant and mobile servant. Another aspect is the statement "future editions of this International Standard might include more specific requirements on particular types of personal care robots, as well as more complete numeric data for different categories of people (e.g., children, elderly, pregnant women)." With no other information throughout the standard, this statement conveys the impression that there should be in place special requirements for different types of users. This means that a personal care robot can be certified under ISO certification without having taken into consideration special safety requirements for different types of user. Without going any further, exoskeletons are not expected to support overweight users (most of them have a maximum weight limit) or it is not sure whether pregnant women can use them.

Connected to this, the safety requirements enshrined in the corpus do not match with the different types of human–robot interaction these robots entail – physically passive or active (including attached to the body) and cognitive (if robots are meant to interact with the user socially). If "mental communication and emotional contact are established between the robot and the person" (Rodić et al. 2016), and the robots may cause psychological harm (Resolution 2015/2103(INL) 2017), physical safeguards might be important but may not suffice. Indeed, there is little research on cognitive or psychological harm, although it seems to be logical if the main channel of interaction between the user and the robot happens at the cognitive level (Fosch-Villaronga 2016).

In fact, the cognitive side of robotics is often disregarded. For instance, certified safety is the one guaranteed by standards or the CE marking, but perceived safety – the perception of the subject/user of the device – is not considered. Certified and perceived safety are two different aspects (Salem et al. 2015). This perceived safety can happen at the physical level, for instance, in the fear of falling during rehabilitation with an exoskeleton (which completely constraints the correct performance of the device); but also at the cognitive level, for instance, long-term robot use in the neurodevelopmental process of typical or non-typical neuro-developed children. This will gain importance after the EP highlighting that every user should have the right to use a robot without fear.

Semantic confusions are also present in the standard. For instance, the use of the term "wheeled passenger carrier" is misleading and creates confusion with the already existing "wheelchairs," which are medical devices. (Fosch-Villaronga and Roig 2017). This is because wheelchairs are medical devices. Concerning to this, the new regulation for medical devices may overrule the standard, as devices that present similar characteristics – in the example of the regulation, contact lenses and colour contact lenses – may have to cumulatively comply with the medical device regulation. And this refers to physical assistant robots too.

While ISO 13482:2014 is concerned with (physical) safety requirements, the legislative system includes many other fundamental rights to be protected. The euRobotics projects on the legal and ethical aspects since 2010, and the European Robolaw project, have repeatedly highlighted five legal themes that any robot regulation should concern: (1) health, safety, consumer and environmental regulation; (2) liability; (3) intellectual property rights; (4) privacy and data protection; and (5) capacity to perform legal transactions.

All these aspects – undefined protected scope, acknowledging the importance of user-specific requirements but not developing them, semantic confusions, focus on (only one type of) safety – make the standard vague and incomplete, as it does not provide any comprehensive framework for the appropriate development of robot technology.

2.3.2 Public Policymaking for Robots

In February 2017, the European Parliament released the pioneering Resolution on Civil Law Rules on Robotics 2015/2103(INL). The resolution included general remarks on legal issues such as liability, insurance, intellectual property, safety and privacy; different types of robot applications such as care robots, medical robots, drones and autonomous cars; and it also covered different contexts of use and social aspects, for instance, unemployment, environment, education, social division and discrimination.

The EP postponed defining "smart robot" in the legal domain, although suggested to the EC the following aspects to take into consideration: (1) the capacity to acquire autonomy through sensors and/or by exchanging data with its environment (inter-connectivity) and the analysis of the data; (2) the capacity to learn through experience and interaction; (3) the form of the robot's physical support; and (4) the capacity to adapt its behaviors and actions to its environment. In the follow-up document, the EC responded by saying that, in the first place, it is crucial to understand whether the definition of concepts such as "cyber physical system," "autonomous system," or "smart autonomous robot" is necessary "for regulatory purposes" (EC Response to the Resolution 2015/2103(INL) 2017).

Some of the most controversial points arisen by such *lege ferenda* are:

- a reference to the Isaac Asimov's Laws of Robotics, as mandatory rules "directed at the designers, producers and operators of robots, since those laws cannot be converted into machine code"

- the proposal for the creation of a special legal status for robots (i.e. electronic personality)

- the emphasis on establishing testing robots in real-life scenarios to identify and assess the risks robots might entail

- the strong belief that care robots may be the cause of human–human interaction decrease

- the introduction of the concept of reversibility

- the creation of an insurance schema revolving around robot technologies

To our understanding, references to science fiction novels as binding norms of conduct for roboticists are a bit problematic and not serious. They offer a disconnection with reality, are not adequately legitimate and are not generally applicable. The second proposal suggests the existence of a gap in the responsibility framework. If in the end robots have a legal personality, this will not be a natural consequence/evolution of the technology, but rather an agreement between the relevant and (legitimate) actors (Johnson 2015). The test in real-life scenarios to identify and assess the risks posed by robots might be a bad idea; instead, testing zones and living labs prior to market entrance may offer valuable knowledge of such risks, which could be then used to feedback the design process accordingly.

Inserting care robots may decrease human–human interaction if in the first place the human was interacting with other humans and now s/he only interacts with the robot. The reality often tells us that the elderly, especially, are not as accompanied as they should be, that not all humans deliver good care (because they cannot, they lack the skills or simply because they are not there), that at the current state-of-the-art robots are not at the stage to fully replace a human (excepting, perhaps, only certain tasks) and that technology can be an enabling technology in many senses, physically and socially.

In relation to the insurance schema, as in the robot personhood discussion, it is often not clear what kind of robots may deserve such insurance nor what type of insurance (Tavani 2018).

The European Commission responded to the resolution, mainly stating that much more analysis is needed. The EC agrees on the fact that legal uncertainty concerning civil law liability may affect negatively the development of robot technology and that not only do they want to work together with the EP on it, but that they have also launched an evaluation of Directive 85/374/EEC on Liability for Defective Products. The Commission argues that because robots involve both the physical/machinery part and complex software systems, determining who is liable is difficult (EC Response to the Resolution 2015/2103(INL) 2017).

The Commission pushes towards the creation of new testing regimes including piloting, modelling, simulation and virtual testing because old tests might not be sufficient to determine whether a robot is safe or not. The problem with such testing regimes is that they are conceived under the idea that new technology may need new testing zones, obviating the fact that machine learning capabilities and much more "real" robots may challenge that. First, machine learning capabilities may create, over time and depending on the "learning from experience" mechanism, unique robots. This challenges certification processes. Second, together with this uniqueness, robots start using imperfect behaviors, which means that they are not 100 percent compliant to their pre-set rules (Konok et al. 2018). The robots may end up being unique, disobedient and imperfect, which can affect trust and reliability. This may pose the question whether we, as a society, want to have non-compliant robots to make them more real or alive, so that engagement with machines is ensured.

2.4 HYBRID MODEL PROPOSAL

In the previous sections, we have recalled the main features of the different types of regulation in the field of robot technologies – private setting and policymaking. Further, we have highlighted the shortcomings via two practical examples, the case of personal care robot technology in a private setting and the recent regulatory initiative of the EP governing robotic technology in general. As we have seen, standards that govern robot technologies may not provide sufficient protection to end-users. At the same time, due to low understanding of what robots are capable of doing and the fear of robots taking over, current regulatory initiatives governing robot technology risk being ineffective.

We propose a hybrid approach where both ways of regulating could benefit from each other. We identify different moments in time where public and private regulatory actors could "talk" to inform each other accordingly:

1. First, we suggest using accountability tools as data generators for policymaking purposes. Nowadays, the simple fulfilment of the accountability requirement (soon through the privacy impact assessment after the General Data Protection Regulation [GDPR]) does not give feedback to the legal system *per se*. In this sense, there is no data collection mechanism oriented towards a repository format that could be used for policymaking. In other words, the law is not (easily) updated with the information generated through the accountability compliance mechanisms that are soon going to be binding; they are just a simple standalone and static instrument. A mechanism that could extract relevant knowledge from these accountability tools (from the private actors) could help build evidence of what technologies are being used, what the identified risks are and how companies are mitigating them (Fosch-Villaronga and Heldeweg 2017).

2. Second, we suggest including private actor participation in ex post legislative evaluations to increase lawmaking efficacy. These evaluations are critical evidence-based judgments of the extent to which an intervention has been effective and efficient, relevant given the needs and its objectives, coherent both internally and with other European policy interventions, and European added value has been achieved (Communication on Smart Regulation*; Radaelli & Meuwese 2009). The inclusion of private actors in this process could help the "learning and evidence utilization" that is carried out in the policy appraisal (Adelle et al. 2012).

3. Third, we propose making binding codes of conduct for robot developers via the inclusion in regulation, in private contracts or via a shaming list. Instead of this code of conduct remaining merely voluntary – as suggested by the EP – and vague – in the words of the EP, "a set of general principles and guidelines for actions to be taken by all stakeholders" – it should make them binding. This could be achieved by means of creating a regulation that can enforce such a right; including such a code of conduct in general clauses of private contracts and criminal law provisions; or by publishing shaming lists and/or advertisements at the addressee's expenses.

2.5 CONCLUSIONS

Due to their specific nature of private soft-law, current standards governing robot technology tend to be single-principle-based – in this case, safety – and tend to disregard other legal principles and values deeply embedded in the social environment where they

---

* See http://europa.eu/rapid/press-release_MEMO-12-974_en.htm

are implemented, i.e. in the social systems where humans and robot technology operate. In other words, standard-based regulations, especially in the field of robot technology, tend to lack a broader legal dimension. Furthermore, these standards lack social legitimacy and accountability.

On the other side, while the importance of a policymaking approach to provide a comprehensive protection to robot users is sustained throughout the article – also highlighted by recent European institutions (Resolution 2015/2103(INL) 2017 and EC Response to Resolution 2015/2103(INL)) – the article also acknowledges the fact that current hard-law sources and prospective lawmaking processes might not be either well-suited for governing emerging robot technologies, as this is an extremely volatile field that evolves and transforms incredibly over time, which makes it difficult to anticipate and know the impact of their applications. Some examples concerning dissonant provisions in the law have also been provided in this regard.

Although the "better regulation" approach of the European Union may increase the use of evidence to inform policy and lawmaking and the involvement of different stakeholders, current hard-lawmaking instruments do not appear to take into consideration the achievements of standard-based regulations enough, virtually wasting their potential benefits and the knowledge resources they represent. That is why, inspired by systems theory, the article ends identifying two different moments in time where stakeholder know-how could be integrated into policymaking – transforming impact assessment as data generators for policymaking (via accountability data repositories) or during ex post legislative evaluations – and also one proposal referring to the "bindingness" of standards via their inclusion in regulation, in private contracts or through social and/or reputational sanctions.

REFERENCES

Adelle, C., Jordan, A., & Turnpenny, J. Proceeding in parallel or drifting apart? A systematic review of policy appraisal research and practices. *Environment and Planning C: Government and Policy*, 30(3), 401–415, (2012).

Bryson, J. J., Diamantis, M. E., & Grant, T. D. Of, for, and by the people: The legal lacuna of synthetic persons. *Artificial Intelligence and Law*, 25(3), 273–291, (2017).

Backer Catà. Economic globalization and the rise of efficient systems of global private law making: Wal-Mart as global legislator. *Connecticut Law Review*, 39(4), 1739, (2007).

Backer, L. C. Governance polycentrism or regulated self-regulation – rule systems for human rights impacts of economic activity where national, private and international regimes collide. Coalition for Peace and Ethics Working Paper No. 1/1, (2014).

Cafaggi, F. New foundation of transnational private regulation. *Journal of Law and Society*, 38(1), 20, (2011).

Delmas-Marty, M. *Le flou du droit*. Paris: Canopé, (1986).

Delmas-Marty, M. Le mou, le doux et le flou sont-ils des garde-fous? In Clam, J. & Martin, G. (eds.), *Les transformations de la régulation juridique*. Paris: LGDJ, (1998), pp. 209–219.

De Londras, F. Privatized sovereign performance: Regulating the 'Gap' between security and rights? *Journal of Law and Society* 38(1), 96–118, (2011).

Fenwick, M., Van Uytsel, S., & Wrbka, S. (eds.), *Networked governance, transnational business and the law. Heidelberg*: Springer, (2014).

Fischer-Lescano, A. & Teubner, G. Regime-collisions: The vain search for legal unity in the fragmentation of global law. *Michigan Journal of International Law*, 25(4), 999, (2004).

Fosch-Villaronga, E. Creation of a care robot impact assessment. WASET. *International Journal of Social, Behavioral, Educational, Economic, Business and Industrial Engineering. WASET*, 9(6), 1867–1871, (2015).

Fosch-Villaronga, E. ISO 13482: 2014 and its confusing categories. Building a bridge between law and robotics. In Wenger, P., Chevallereau, C., Pisla, D., Bleuler, H., & Rodić, A. (eds.), *New Trends in Medical and Service Robots*. Cham: Springer, (2016), pp. 31–44.

Fosch-Villaronga, E. & Roig, A. European regulatory framework for person carrier robots. *Computer Law & Security Review* 33(4), 502–520, (2017).

Fosch Villaronga, E. & Heldeweg, M. A. Regulering voor Experimenteren met Emergente Robot Technologie [Regulation for Experimenting with Emergent Robot Technology]. In Daskalova, V. I. & Heldeweg, M. A. (eds.), Constitutionele mogelijkheden en beperkingen voor experimenteel handelen en experimentele wetgeving. Staatsrechtconferentie 2016. Publikaties van de Staatsrechtkring – Staatsrechtconferenties nr. 20. Oisterwijk: Wolf Legal Publishers, (2017), pp. 89–107.

Fosch-Villaronga, E. & Heldeweg, M. "Regulation, I presume?" said the robot – Towards an iterative regulatory process for robot governance. Computer Law & Security Review, 34(6), 1258–1277, (2018).

Fosch-Villaronga, E. & Virk, G. S. Legal issues for mobile servant robots. In Rodić, A. & Borangiu, T. (eds.), Proceedings of the 25th Conference on Robotics Alpe-Adria-Danube Region. *Advances in Robot Design and Intelligent Control*. Cham: Springer, (2017).

Guihot, Michael, Matthew, A. F., & Suzor N.P. Nudging robots: Innovative solutions to regulate artificial intelligence. *Vanderbilt Journal of Entertainment & Technology Law* 20, 385, (2017).

Gunningham, N., Kagan, R. A., & Thornton, D. Social license and environmental protection: Why businesses go beyond compliance. *Law & Social Inquiry* 29, 307, (2004).

Howard-Grenville, J., Nash, J., & Coglianese, C. Constructing the license to operate: Internal factors and their influence on corporate environmental decisions, *Law & Policy* 30, 73, (2008).

Johnson, D. G. Technology with no human responsibility? *Journal of Business Ethics* 127(4), 707–715, (2015).

Kjaer, P. Transnational normative orders: The constitutionalism of intra- and trans-normative law. *Indiana Journal of Global Legal Studies* 20, 777, (2013).

Konok, V., Korcsok, B., Miklósi, Á., & Gácsi, M. Should we love robots? – The most liked qualities of companion dogs and how they can be implemented in social robots. *Computers in Human Behavior*, 80, 132–142, 2018.

Luhmann, N. Die Weltgesellschaft. *Archiv für Rechts und Sozialphilosophie* 57, 21, (1971).

Radaelli, C. M. & Meuwese, A. C. Better regulation in Europe: Between public management and regulatory reform. *Public Administration* 87(3), 639–654, (2009).

Renner, M. Occupy the system! Societal constitutionalism and transnational corporate accounting. *Indiana Journal of Global Legal Studies* 20, 941, (2013).

Rodić, A., Vujović, M., Stevanović, I., & Jovanović, M. Development of human-centered social robot with embedded personality for elderly care. In Wenger, P., Chevallereau, C., Pisla, D., Bleuler, H., & Rodić, A. (eds.), *New Trends in Medical and Service Robots*. Cham: Springer, (2016), pp. 233–247.

Sabel, C., Herrigel, G., & Kristensen, P. H. Regulation under uncertainty: The coevolution of industry and regulation. *Regulation & Governance* 12, 371, (2017).

Salem, M., et al. Towards safe and trustworthy social robots: Ethical challenges and practical issues. In Tapus, A., et al. (eds.), *Social Robots*. Cham: Springer International Publishing, (2015), pp. 584–593.

Snyder, D. V. Private lawmaking, *Ohio State Law Journal* 64, 371, (2003).

Tavani, H. T. Can social robots qualify for moral consideration? Reframing the question about robot rights. *Information* 9(4), 73, (2018).

Vesting, T. The autonomy of law and the formation of network standards. *German Law Journal* 5, 639, (2004).

CHAPTER 3

Standard Ontologies and HRI

Sandro Rama Fiorini, Abdelghani Chibani,

Tamás Haidegger, Joel Luis Carbonera, Craig Schlenoff,

Jacek Malec, Edson Prestes, Paulo Gonçalves,

S. Veera Ragavan, Howard Li, Hirenkumar Nakawala,

Stephen Balakirsky, Sofiane Bouznad, Noauel Ayari,

and Yacine Amirat

CONTENTS

3.1	Introduction	20
3.2	What is an Ontology and Why is it Useful	21
	3.2.1 Process of Ontology Development	22
3.3	Overview of the IEEE Effort on Robot Ontologies	23
3.4	Ontologies in IEEE 1872-2015	25
	3.4.1 Preliminaries: SUMO	25
	3.4.2 CORA: The Core Ontology for R&A	27
	3.4.3 CORAX: CORA Extended	28
	3.4.4 RPARTS: The Parts Ontology	29
	3.4.5 The POS Ontology	31
3.5	Applications of CORA to Date	33
	3.5.1 CORA as Part of a Robotic Skill Ontology	33
	3.5.2 The Cargo Delivery Scenario	35
	3.5.3 Cora as Part of a Surgical Robot Ontology	36
	3.5.4 Other Applications	38
3.6	Follow-on Efforts	38
	3.6.1 The Autonomous Robotics Study Group	38
	3.6.2 Robot Task Representation Effort	39
3.7	Conclusion and Discussion: Towards an Ontology for HRI	42
	Acknowledgment	44
	References	44

3.1 INTRODUCTION

While robots and humans might interact in a multitude of ways, communication seems to be one of the most important types. As in human–human communication, successful communication between humans and robots usually involves the sharing of symbols with a shared meaning. This is the case for traditional verbal communication, but also for the case in situations where a human communicates his or her intentions through clicks in a user interface or through commands issued to an application programming interface (API). In any case, robots have to be able to *represent* the meaning of those symbols in a computable, formal way. More importantly, humans have to be able to access and understand that representation in order to know how to communicate with the robot.

In the last 15 years, ontologies have emerged as one of the best techniques to represent information and meaning in computer systems. Since the early ages of artificial intelligence, it became clear that in order to understand humans, intelligent systems must be able to share with them a common representation of the world. There has been a multitude of approaches for doing that, where logic-based techniques came up on top. However, their high computational complexity and unfit modelling techniques limited the use of symbolic approaches in robots. New research during the 1980s and 1990s brought up the idea that intelligent systems, in order to be able to work in tandem with humans, must represent the world with logical theories modelled, taking into account the knowledge *shared* by the community in which the system is situated. These theories are what we call *ontologies*. In this context, ontologies are formal information artefacts that define the concepts of a domain as well as the relationships between these concepts. Ontologies can be used in knowledge sharing between communities of intelligent agents and humans, usually employed as a tool to provide meaning to information sharing protocols. Also, being logical theories, ontologies can be used as a knowledge source for implementing symbolic reasoning techniques.

In the case of robotics, an ontology can serve as a communication middle-layer between humans and robots. However, as groups of humans might communicate in different languages, there is nothing preventing distinct human/robot groups of employing distinct ontologies in communications. This creates communication islands akin to the information islands that prevent the integration of heterogeneous information systems. In order to help prevent such cases, the IEEE RAS Ontologies for Robotics and Automation Working Group (ORA WG) was formed with the notable objective of providing a consensus-based set of ontologies for the domain. Their aim was to link existing ISO, IEC, etc. standards, current research efforts and new regulatory frameworks to a generic Robotics and Automation Ontology [LAP+12]. The ORA WG is comprised of over 170 members, representing over 20 countries — a cross-section of industry, academia and government. The group has spent over four years to develop and publish the IEEE Standard 1872-2015 [IEE15], which specifies a set of high-level ontologies about robotics and related notions. Notably, the main component is the Core Ontology for Robotics and Automation (CORA), which formally defines the main notions of robotics and automation (R&A) as a whole. CORA and other ontologies are now being used by experts globally, both for supporting human–robot communication technologies and also for other areas of robotics. Currently, sub-groups of ORA WG are developing specific ontologies to complement IEEE 1872-2015, focusing on robot task representation and autonomous robots. We expect that the complete family of ORA ontologies will help ensure a common understanding among members of the community and facilitate more efficient integration and data transfer.

Our aim with this chapter is to give the reader a brief overview of IEEE 1872-2015 and efforts related to it. We start by discussing what ontologies are and why we need them. We then present the general structure the IEEE community groups that developed CORA and are developing new ontologies. CORA and related ontologies in IEEE 1872-2015 standard are presented next, followed by a brief overview of different works employing CORA and the current groups working on extensions to CORA. We finish with a discussion about the requirements for, and human robot interaction (HRI) ontology based on, IEEE 1872-2015.

3.2 WHAT IS AN ONTOLOGY AND WHY IS IT USEFUL

In computer science and related technology domains, an ontology is considered a formal and explicit specification of a shared conceptualization [SBF98]. The conceptualization specified by an ontology, according to this point of view, encompasses the set of concepts related to the kinds of entities that are supposed to exist in a given domain, according to a community of practitioners. Thus, the main purpose of an ontology is to capture a common conceptual understanding about a given domain. Due to this, ontologies can be used for promoting the semantic interoperability among stakeholders, since sharing a common ontology is equivalent to sharing a common view of the world. Moreover, because ontologies specify the domain conceptualization in a formal and explicit way, this ensures that the meaning of every concept is rigorously specified and can be analyzed by humans and machines. Therefore, an ontology could be used as a common basis for communication between humans and machines. Finally, ontologies can also be viewed as reusable components of knowledge, since they capture the knowledge about a domain in a task-independent way. Thus, considering that the development of knowledge models is a notoriously difficult, time-consuming and expensive process, the adoption of ontologies promotes a more rational use of the resources in a project.

An ontology includes at least a set of terms and their definitions as shared by a given community, formally specified in a machine-readable language, such as first-order logic. These terms and definitions are structured in terms of

- **classes**, which stand for concepts at all granularities

- **relations**, which establish associations between concepts

- **formal axioms**, which constrain and add consistency rules to the concepts and relations

There are different kinds of ontologies and different ways of classifying them. In [Gua98], the author proposes four main classes of ontologies:

- **Top-level ontologies**, which describe very general concepts like space, time, matter, object, event, action, etc., which are independent of a particular problem or domain

- **Domain ontologies**, which describe concepts of a specific domain

- **Task ontologies**, which describe generic tasks or activities

- **Application ontologies**, which are strictly related to a specific application and used to describe concepts of a particular domain and task

In [Obr10, PCF+13] the authors also mention a fifth kind of ontology called *core ontology*. Core ontologies can be viewed as mid-level ontologies, standing between top-level ontologies and domain ontologies. Core ontologies reuse concepts specified by top-level ontologies and specify new concepts that can be used in specific domains and tasks. They specify concepts that are general in a large domain but that are too specific for being included in a top-level ontology. In general, this kind of ontology specifies the most important concepts of a given broad domain [PCF+13].

3.2.1 Process of Ontology Development

The range of activities concerning the ontology development process, the ontology life cycle, the methods and methodologies for building ontologies and the tools and languages that support them is called *Ontology engineering*. Nowadays, there are several different methodologies that can be adopted for developing an ontology engineering process, including METHONTOLOGY [FLGPJ97], KACTUS [SWJ95], On-To-Knowledge [SSS04], DILIGENT [DSV+05], NeOn [SFGPFL12] and so on. Most of these methodologies specify sequences (or cycles) of activities that should be carried out for developing an ontology, including

- Feasibility study, which is an assessment of the practicality of a proposed project

- Knowledge acquisition, which is responsible for capturing the relevant domain knowledge from different sources

- Conceptual modelling, whose goal is to structure the captured knowledge in a semiformal ontology conceptual model

- Axiomatization, which imposes a formal structure on the modelled domain knowledge (usually adopting a representation based on First Order Logics)

- Implementation, whose purpose is to implement the ontology in a computer-processable representation format, such as OWL*

- Evaluation, which evaluates the developed ontology for ensuring its quality

---

* www.w3.orgTRowl-features

- Maintenance, whose purpose is to fix errors, and keep the quality of the ontology when it is modified, by inclusion of novel knowledge or by updating some definitions

For further details, in [SSS09] the authors provide a deep discussion about ontology engineering in general.

The fundamental objective of domain-specific ontology development is to identify, develop and document the common terms and definitions within a sub-field, so that they can serve as a common reference for the R&D community. It needs to be completed at a very sophisticated way to fulfil its goals, since only high-quality ontologies can be hoped to become cornerstones of the community effort. High quality, high profile ontologies are called Exemplary Ontologies (ontologydesignpatterns.org/wiki/Ontology:Main). The general methodology for building ontologies specifies certain modelling principles that need to be followed in order to assure that the finished tool commits to the shared knowledge. It needs to ensure the mutual agreement among stakeholders and increase the potential of reuse of knowledge, allowing smooth data integration upwards and downwards as well. When it is targeted to develop exemplary ontologies, the following attributes need to be considered [pro14]:

- the ontology must be well designed for its purpose

- shall include explicitly stated requirements

- must meet all and for the most part, only the intended requirements

- should not make unnecessary commitments or assumptions

- should be easy to extend to meet additional requirements

- it reuses prior knowledge bases as much as possible

- there is a core set of primitives that are used to build up more complex parts

- should be easy to understand and maintain

- must be well documented

3.3 OVERVIEW OF THE IEEE EFFORT ON ROBOT ONTOLOGIES

Recognizing the advantages that a standard ontology for R&A would bring to the field, the IEEE Standard Association's Robotics and Automation Society (RAS) created the Ontologies for Robotics and Automation (ORA) Working Group in 2011. The goal of the group was to develop a standard to provide an overall ontology and associated methodology for knowledge representation and reasoning in R&A, together with the representation of concepts in an initial set of application domains. It achieved this goal in 2015 with the publication of the IEEE 1872-2015 Standard Ontologies for Robotics and Automation.* The group was composed of 175 members representing 23 countries and was made up of approximately 50% educational institutions, 25% private companies and 25% government

---

* http://standards.ieee.org/findstds/standard/1872-2015.html

entities. With the release of the standard, the ORA working group completed its task and was required to disband. However, many of the working group members remain involved in this work by focusing on sub-groups, as described later in this chapter.

The IEEE 1872-2015 standard provides a unified way of representing knowledge and provides a common set of terms and definitions, allowing for unambiguous knowledge transfer among any group of humans, robots and other artificial systems. It was awarded the prestigious Emerging Technology Award by the IEEE Standards Association in December 2015. The standard was also mentioned in the "The National AI Research and Development Strategic Plan" released by President Obama in October 2016.* This strategic plan focuses on the role of AI, machine learning, automation and robotics in addressing complex national problems.

One of the main parts of IEEE 1872-2015 is the Core Ontologies for Robotics and Automation (CORA). CORA will be described in greater detail later in this chapter, but as an introduction, it aims to describe what a robot is and how it relates to other concepts. It defines four big broad entities: robot part, robot, complex robot and robotic system. The term robot may have as many definitions as authors writing about the subject. The inherent ambiguity in this term might be an issue when one needs to specify an ontology for a broad community like ours. We acknowledge this ambiguity as an intrinsic feature of the domain and, therefore, we decided to elaborate a definition based purely on necessary conditions, without specifying sufficient conditions. Thus, it is ensured that CORA covers all entities that the community actually considers as a robot, at the cost of classifying some entities as robots that may be counterintuitive to some roboticists. Also, the concepts in our ontology could be specialized according to the needs of specific sub-domains or applications of R&A.

CORA was developed to be a high-level standard in which domain-specific efforts could build from. The approach was to define concepts in CORA that were generic to all robot domains and then these domains could specialize these concepts to address their specific information requirements. When the working group that developed CORA was created, based on the interests of the working group members, we developed Figure 3.1 to show the sub-groups that we expected to emerge to specialize the concepts represented in CORA.

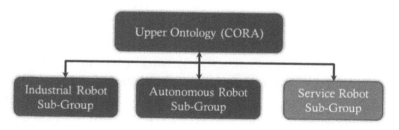

FIGURE 3.1 Initial organization of ORA groups and sub-groups. The boxes represented in dark grey show ongoing efforts, the one in light grey is currently inactive. We expect additional domain ontology sub-groups to emerge.

---

* www.whitehouse.gov/sites/default/files/whitehouse_files/microsites/ostp/NSTC/national_ai_rd_strategic_plan.pdf

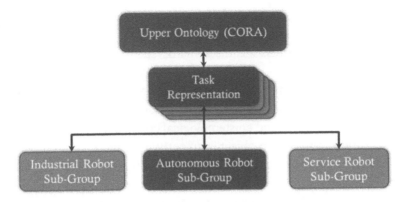

FIGURE 3.2   Present organization of ORA groups and sub-groups.

Over time, we realized that there was a level missing in the above structure. The Upper Ontology (CORA) provided very high-level concepts and the domain ontologies provided concepts that were very specific to individual domains. What was missing was a middle level that contained cross-cutting concepts that were applicable to many, if not all, robot domains. Examples of these middle-level, cross-cutting concepts could include representation of sensors and perception data, tasks and environmental objects.

The industrial robot ontology sub-group, after meeting for a few months, realized that there was a greater need for a cross-cutting representation of task information (a middle-level ontology) than for a detailed industrial robot ontology. Because of this, the group changed its name, and its scope, to focus on Robot Task Representation. More specifically, this group will develop a broad standard that provides a comprehensive ontology for robot task structure and reasoning. While initially focusing on industrial tasks, the resulting standard is expected to be applicable across most, if not all, robot domains. Hence, Figure 3.1 morphed into Figure 3.2. More details about the Robot Task Representation group are discussed later in the chapter.

3.4 ONTOLOGIES IN IEEE 1872-2015

The IEEE 1872-2015 standard is composed of a collection of ontologies covering different general aspects of R&A. These ontologies provide definitions for notions such as robot, robotic system, positioning, interaction and so on. Each ontology is specified in the language SUI/KIF, a first-order language, extending concepts and relation of Suggested Upper Merged Ontology (SUMO) top-level ontology. The ontologies are also meant to be specialized in specific domain and applications ontologies in different areas of robotics. In this section, we describe the general aspects of each ontology in IEEE 1872-2015.

3.4.1 Preliminaries: SUMO

The majority of the entities defined in the standard are specializations of the SUMO concepts and relations. SUMO is a vast top-level ontology developed as part of an IEEE-sponsored effort to create a standard top-level ontology [NP01]. While SUMO never became an actual standard, its flexibility and extensive vocabulary of terms made it one of the main top-ontologies available in the literature. It includes formal theories about processes, spatial relations, temporal relations, information objects and so on. Also, SUMO has been extended along the years to address specific domains, such as engineering and the military.

Before presenting the specifics of IEEE 1872-2015, let us consider some basic aspects of SUMO. SUMO divides all entities that exist into two big groups: physical and abstract (Figure 3.3). Physical entities exist in space-time. Abstracts do not exist in space and/or time, and include mathematical and epistemological constructs. Physical entities are separated into *objects* and *processes*. An object is an entity that has spatiotemporal parts. This concept corresponds to the notion of ordinary objects, but also include physical regions. Processes, on the other hand, are physicals that occurs in time and that are not objects. Instances of processes are physicals such as events, manufacturing processes, movements, cognitive processes and so on.

On the abstract side of the taxonomy, SUMO has concepts such as quantity, attribute, class and proposition. Quantities are akin to numeric properties one can use to characterize other entities. Attributes are lexical properties. Class and proposition concepts give SUMO the ability to represent facts about fact (e.g., metamodeling). For instance, a proposition in SUMO is an abstract entity that represents a thought. For example, the sentence "the book is on the table" expresses the proposition that there is a book situated on top of a particular table. The sentence in Portuguese "o livro está sobre a mesa" is a different sentence that expresses the same proposition. SUMO allows one to capture the materialization of a proposition as instances of Content-bearing Object, a sub-class of Object that represents one or more propositions, such as the two sentences above.

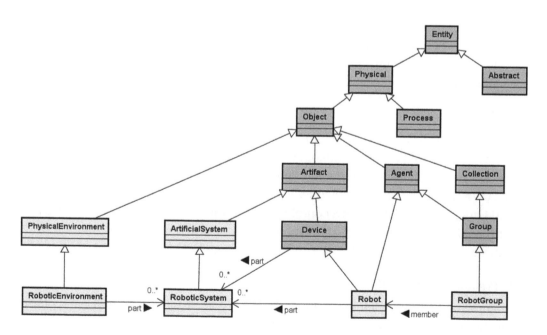

FIGURE 3.3 Taxonomic structure (arrows) of the main concepts in SUMO (light grey boxes) and CORA (dark grey boxes).

3.4.2 CORA: The Core Ontology for R&A

As discussed in Section 2, a *core ontology* is a domain ontology that aims at defining the most general concepts in a broad domain, such as medicine or geology. The core ontology for robotics and automation is the main ontology in IEEE 1872-2015. As its name implies, it aims at providing formal definitions for central notions in R&A. The focus on *notions* rather than simply on *terminology* is not an accident: CORA does not try to accommodate any possible terminology in R&A, but rather it aims at making explicit concepts and relations behind different terminologies.

CORA gravitates around three main concepts: *robot*, *robot group* and *robotic system* (Figure 3.3). As we mentioned earlier in this chapter, the term *robot* may have as many definitions as people using it. CORA acknowledges this fact by defining robot in a very general way, allowing for specific subontologies to provide the sufficient conditions for specific kinds of robots. CORA only states that *robots are agentive devices*, designed to perform purposeful actions in order to accomplish a task. According to SUMO, an instance of Device is an artefact (i.e. a *physical object product of making*), which has the intended purpose of being a tool in a class of processes. Being a device, robot inherits from SUMO the notion that devices have parts. Therefore, CORA allows one to represent complex robots with robot parts. Also, the concept Robot inherits from the Device the necessity for having a described purpose. A robot is also an *Agent*. SUMO states that agent is "*something or someone that can act on its own and produce changes in the world*". Robots perform tasks by acting on the environment or themselves. Action is strongly related to agency, in the sense that the acting defines the agent. In some cases, the actions of a robot might be subordinated to actions of other agents, such as software agents (bots) or humans.

Robots can form robot groups. A *robot group* is also an agent in the sense that its own agency emerges from its participants. The concept has been left underspecified in the standard, and can be used to describe robot teams or even complex robots formed by many independent robotic agents acting in unison.

Robotic systems are systems composed of robots (or robot groups) and other devices that facilitate the operations of robots. A good example of a robotic system is a car assembly cell at a manufacturing site. The environment is equipped with actuated structures that manipulate the car body in a way that the industrial robots within the system can act on it. Finally, an environment equipped with a robotic system is a *robotic environment*.

Apart from these three main concepts, CORA also defines the notion of *robot interface*. A robot interface is a kind of device that represents the interface of the robot with the external world. A robot has one and only one interface that aggregate all parts that the robot uses to sense, act and communicate. The robot interface can be seen as a virtual device, in the sense that it might not coincide with a particular component. Any robot interface must have at least a sensor, an actuator or a communication device (such as a networks card).

Autonomy is a core notion in R&A, yet one of the hardest to define in precise terms. CORA incorporates the idea that the degree of autonomy of a robot can only be defined in relation to the task at hand [HMA03]. Thus, CORA does not define specific *classes* of autonomous robots. It rather defines specific types of *agent* roles that a robot can have when participating in a process where it is the agent. The *agent* role is a binary predicate (which is related to, but different from the concept Agent) relating processes with the object that acts as the agent of the process. CORA defines five sub-relations of *agent*, namely, *fullyAutonomousRobot, semiAutonomousRobot, teleoperatedRobot, remoteControlledRobot* and *automatedRobot* (i.e. automaton). Each sub-relation qualifies the role of a particular robot in the process. CORA does not provide sufficient conditions for these relations but clarifies that the same robot can assume different roles in different processes.

3.4.3 CORAX: CORA Extended

Even SUMO and CORA together do not cover all aspects of R&A. CORAX is another ontology part of IEEE 1872-2015 [FCG+15] that specifies some concepts that are not present or clear in SUMO and that are too general for CORA. CORAX provides concepts such as design, environment and interaction.

Design is an important concept in engineering, especially in manufacturing. In R&A, the concept is frequently related to industrial robotics, where robots perform the job of building artefacts. Those robots have to represent the design of the artefacts they are building in order to coordinate their actions. In CORAX, a design is a kind of proposition. That is, it is an abstract concept that can be materialized in content-bearing objects, such as manuals and blueprints. Furthermore, artefacts are associated to design, so that one should expect that an artefact realizes the design. Such notions have been further extended in the architecture ontology developed by the AuR group (Section 6.1).

Furthermore, the properties of the object must be expressed in its design. For instance, the design of a phone is about an (*idealized*) phone that is materialized in the individual phones built on that design. CORAX specifies the ideal object as a separate entity called a *Design Object*, which specifies the idealized object that is the *content* of a design. The ideal phone has ideal properties, such as ideal weight and shape. These are related to real properties but have different pragmatics in modelling and reasoning. While SUMO provides two main relationships to represent properties, namely *attribute* and *measure*, CORAX specifies two analogue relationships, namely *designAttribute* and *designMeasure*. Both sets of properties, the physical and the abstract, can be used with any quantity type of attribute type already present in SUMO. In this way, we can specify that, for instance, an idealized phone (an instance of *Object Design*) has a *design shape* and a *design weight*. The properties of the design object and those of the artefact may correlate, but CORAX does not provide a theory of how that correlation occurs.

CORAX also includes the notion of *physical environment* in order to support specification of *robotic environments*. An *environment* is intuitively composed of a physical region, plus eventual objects that characterize the environment. In addition, the definition of physical environment depends on the presence of a landmark from which it is possible to define the main region of an environment. Landmarks may or may not be located within the region of interest of the environment. For instance, an office room environment depends on the physical configuration of its walls, which are located in the environment. But we can also define an arbitrary environment consisting of a cube in outer space that depends on Earth as a landmark, even if the planet itself is not part of the environment.

As CORA defines the concept Robotic System, it becomes necessary to define what is a system. CORAX specify the concept Artificial System as an artefact formed from various devices and other objects that interact with each other and with the environment in order to fulfil a purpose. This requires a basic definition of *interaction*. CORAX introduces the notion of interaction as a process in which two agents participate, where an *action* generated by one agent causes a *reaction* by the other. More specifically, an interaction process is composed of two sub-processes corresponding to action and reaction. The action sub-process initiated by *x* on *y* causes a reaction sub-process, where *y* acts upon *x* (Figure 3.4).

Finally, CORAX defines certain general classes of robot–robot and human–robot communication. Both cases are specific types of content-bearing processes (i.e. a process that carries a proposition).

3.4.4 RPARTS: The Parts Ontology

RPARTS is a sub-ontology of CORA that specifies general notions related to some kinds of robot parts. According to CORA, robots are (agentive) devices *composed of* other devices. A myriad of devices can be robot parts, and CORA cannot determine in advance what *kinds* of devices can or cannot be robot parts. Notice that this is an issue that arises at the *conceptual level*. This is a consequence of the "open-ended" nature of robots, whose designs are only constrained by human needs, human creativity and available technological resources. Therefore, a type of device that has never been considered as a potential robot part can be used as a robot part by some future designer. An ontology for R&A, as CORA is, must take this issue into account.

Furthermore, there is another issue regarding the notion of robot parts that arises at the *instance level*. None of the objects that can be classified as robot parts are *essentially* robot parts, since they can exist by themselves when they are not connected to a robot (or when they are connected to other complex devices). For instance, a power source is essentially a device, and we cannot consider a power source as a sub-class of the class of robot parts, because this would imply that all instances of power sources are always robot parts. This is not true, as a specific instance of power source can be dynamically considered as a part of different complex devices during different specific time intervals. Due to this, CORA

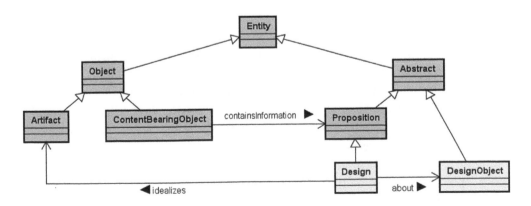

FIGURE 3.4   Entities associated with design in CORAX.

assumes that the notion of "robot part" is a *role* (in the sense previously discussed) that can be played by other devices.

In the earlier proposals of CORA [PCF+13], the notion of robot parts was considered as a *class*, whose instances are not *essentially* instances of it. Thus, instances of robot parts could cease to be robot parts, without ceasing to exist. In this sense, for example, an instance of a power source that is considered as a robot part at a given moment (when it is connected to a robot) could cease to be a robot part in another moment without ceasing to exist (as an instance of power source). Thus, *Robot part* was considered as an *anti-rigid* universal, in the sense of [Gui05]. The ontology pattern proposed in [PCF+13] was developed accordingly, inspired by [Gui05]. It represents how a specific instance of a specific kind of device (e.g., power source) could be classified as a robot part.

This pattern becomes complex when we take into account the principles advocated in [Gui05]. According to these frameworks, an anti-rigid class (e.g., robot part) cannot subsume a rigid one (e.g., power source). Considering this principle, for each rigid class *c* that can play the role of a robot part, we must create another specific anti-rigid class (a specific role) that will be subsumed by both *c* and *Robot Part*. For example, an instance of the rigid class *Wheel* only becomes a robot part when it is attached to a particular robot. Given this condition, it becomes a member of the more specific class (e.g., "*Wheel as Robot Part*"), which is subsumed by the rigid class *Wheel* and the anti-rigid class *Robot Part* (see [PCF+13] for further details).

The representation of robot parts in the final proposal of CORA was changed, mainly because the modelling pattern proposed for representing robot parts results in domain models that are overwhelmingly complex. Some classes that must be created in order to maintain the consistency of the model do not fit well into the domain conceptualization and the resulting complexity is hard to manage. Therefore, this modelling pattern could hinder the broad adoption of the ontology in the domain. Another factor leading to the revision was that it is not clear how to fit the dynamical behaviour that is expected from roles in the framework of SUMO. The modelling of roles adopted in [Gui05] relies on the notion of *possibility* (a *modal* notion). However, as pointed out in [OAH+07], the treatment of possibilities in SUMO is not clear.

Robot part is then a relationship between a given device *d* and a robot *r*, indicating that *d* is playing the role of robot part when it is connected to *r*. RPARTS defines four specific roles for robot parts.

Robot Sensing Part: responsible for sensing the surrounding environment. Formally, robot sensing parts must be measuring devices connected to the robot. A measuring device, according to SUMO, is *any device whose purpose is to measure a physical quantity*. For example, a *laser sensor* can play the role of robot sensing part when connected to a robot.

Robot Actuating Part: responsible for allowing the robot to move and act in the surrounding environment. Formally, robot actuating parts must be devices that are instruments in a process of robot motion, which is any process of movement where the robot is the agent and one of its parts is acted upon.

Robot Communicating Part: responsible for providing communication among robots and humans by allowing the robot to send (or receive) information to (or from) a robot or a human.

Robot Processing Part: responsible for processing data and information. Formally, robot processing parts must be processing devices connected to the robot. A processing device is any electric device whose purpose is to serve as an instrument in a sub-class of a computer process.

It is important to emphasize that although these different types of robot parts are modelled as relations between specific devices and robots, they are intended to behave as roles.

This modelling choice also provides interesting modularity characteristics. It keeps CORA as a minimal core of high-level concepts that provides the structure to the domain without going deep into details regarding the myriad of different devices that could play the roles specified here. In this sense, this structure of roles can be viewed as an interface (in the sense of *object-oriented programming paradigm*) that can be implemented in different ways. Naturally, this schema poses the need for sub-ontologies to define the taxonomies of devices that can play the roles specified in CORA, such as an *ontology of sensors*, *ontology of grippers* and so on.

3.4.5 The POS Ontology

Also included in the IEEE 1872-2015, the position (POS) ontology [CFP+13] specifies the main concepts and relations underlying the notions of *position*, *orientation* and *pose*. These are essential for dealing with information about the relationship between a robot and its surrounding space. In this section, we summarize the main concepts relating to positional information.

POS defines two kinds of positioning information: *quantitative* and *qualitative*. In the quantitative case, a position is represented by a *point* in a given coordinate system. In the qualitative case, a position is represented as a *region* defined as a function of a reference object. For instance, one can describe a robot as being positioned at the coordinates (x, y) in the global coordinate system, or that the robot is positioned *at the front of the box*, where *front* comprises a conical region centered on the box and pointed forwards.

POS states that a *position* can be attributed to a (physical) *object*. In this sense, when we say that "a robot x is positioned at y", this means that there is a *measure* (SUMO binary relation) that relates a given "robot x" to a *position measurement y*.

Position measurements are *physical quantities* that can be *position points* or *position regions*. A position point denotes the *quantitative* position of an object in a coordinate system. More specifically, position points are always defined in a single coordinate system. A position region is an *abstract region* in a *coordinate system* defined with reference to a series of position points.

A *coordinate system* is an *abstract* entity that is defined in relation to *a single reference object*, i.e. there is an object that is the reference for each coordinate system. For instance, the local coordinate system of a robot is referenced by the robot itself. Additionally, the reference object does not need to be at the origin of the coordinate system. This ontology does not commit to a particular kind of coordinate system. It can be stated, however, that a coordinate system defines at least one dimension in which points get their coordinate values. A fundamental aspect of coordinate systems is the notion of *transformation*, which maps position points in one coordinate system to position points in another coordinate system. Transformations can be composed, generating new transformations. In POS, an object can display multiple positions in different coordinate systems only if there is a transformation that can map between the two. In addition to that, coordinate systems are related through *hierarchies* (i.e. trees). We say that a given coordinate system c_1 is the parent of a coordinate system c_2 if there is a transformation t_1 that maps the points of c_1 to points in c_2, and there is a transformation t_2 that maps the points of c_2 to points in c_1. According to this, if two coordinate systems share a parent node in the hierarchy tree, there is a transformation between them. Usually, an agent chooses a coordinate system as the global reference frame that constitutes the *global coordinate system* (GCS) for that agent. This GCS can be *arbitrarily* chosen and does not have reference to a particular coordinate frame. *Local coordinate systems* (LCS) are defined in relation to GCS by hierarchical links. This hierarchy is arbitrary, in the sense that it can be defined by the designer or agent.

Besides the quantitative position, POS also provides concepts about qualitative positions that are defined in terms of position regions. Example of qualitative positions are "left of", "in front of", "on top of" and so on. These expressions define regions in relation to a reference object o_r in which other objects are placed. More specifically, a *position region* is composed of poses in the coordinate system generated by a *spatial operator* on the reference object. The spatial operator is a *mathematical function* that maps reference objects to regions in a coordinate system in arbitrary ways.

POS also allows for the specification of *relative positions* between objects and a given reference object. In general, this kind of information is represented through *spatial relations* that hold between objects. An example is the relation leftOf(o, o_r), which represents that the object o is positioned to the left of the object o_r. This kind of relation can be defined in POS using the notions of *relative position* and *spatial operator*. For example, the relation leftOf(o, o_r) holds when there is a qualitative position s (a position region) that was generated by the spatial operator leftOfOp over the reference object o_r, and the object o has the relative position s regarding o_r. Through this mechanism, POS provides the semantics for spatial relations like "to the left of".

The usual notion of orientation is similar to position as far as its conceptual structure is concerned. An object can have a quantitative orientation defined as a value in an orientation coordinate system, as well as a qualitative orientation defined as a region in relation to a reference object. For example, orientation is used in the phrase "the robot is oriented at 54 degrees"; the orientation value in this case is 54 in the circular, one-dimensional coordinate system of a compass. On the other hand, orientation regions capture a less intuitive notion. The expression "the robot is oriented to the north of the Earth" allows for interpretations where the robot has a range of possible orientation points around 0 degrees. Thus, we can represent "north" as a region (or interval) in the one-dimensional, circular compass coordinate system that overlaps with the general orientational extension of the object.

In POS, a position and an orientation constitute a pose. The pose of an object is the description of any position and orientation simultaneously applied to the same object. Often, a pose is defined with a position and an orientation referenced to different coordinate systems/reference objects. In addition, since objects can have many different positions and orientations, they can also have many different poses.

3.5 APPLICATIONS OF CORA TO DATE

3.5.1 CORA as Part of a Robotic Skill Ontology

Modularity of robotic ontologies and the possibility of building a specific application-related ontology from existing, well-defined building blocks is a long-looked-for property, enabling faster development of cognitive robotic systems and easier debugging. The case described below is an illustration of this approach, exploiting IEEE CORA as one of its building blocks.

The Rosetta suite of ontologies describing industrial robotic skills has been developed in a series of EU projects for almost a decade. The individual ontologies serve different purposes. The core ontology, rosetta.owl, is a continuous development aimed at creating a generic ontology for industrial robotics. It is described in [SM15] and is available on the public ontology server http://kif.cs.lth.se/ontologies/rosetta.owl.

The ontology hierarchy is depicted in Figure 3.5, where arrows denote ontology import operation.

We use either the QUDT (Quantities, Units, Dimensions and Types) or the OM ontologies and vocabularies in order to express physical units and dimensions. The core Rosetta ontology focuses mostly on robotic devices and skills, as described in [HMN+11]. According to it, every device can offer one or more skills, and every skill is offered by one or more devices. Production processes are divided into tasks (which may be considered specifications), each realized by some skill (implementation). Skills are compositional items: there are primitive skills (non-divisible) and compound ones. Skills may be executed in parallel if the hardware resources and constraints allow it. The rosetta.owl ontology is

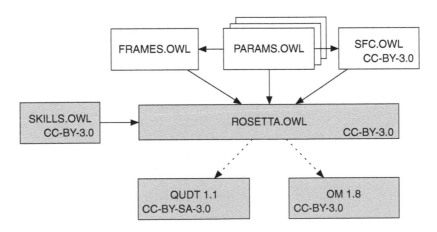

FIGURE 3.5 The Rosetta ontologies.

accompanied by topical ontologies describing behaviours (sfc.owl) as finite state machines, robotic skill parameterizations (params.owl) and feature and object frames (frames.owl). All these ontologies are available from the ontology server above.

The definition of skills has been based on the so-called production triangle: product, process, resources (PPR) [CDYM+07]. The workpieces being manufactured are maintained in the *product*-centered view. The manufacturing itself (i.e. the *process*) is described using concepts corresponding to different levels of abstraction, namely tasks, steps and actions. Finally, the *resources* are materialized in devices (capable of sensing or manufacturing). The central notion of *skill* links all three views and is one of the founding elements of the representation.

Due to the growing complexity of those ontologies and the availability of external upper ontologies like IEEE standard CORA [PCF+13], we have decided to refactor this structure into one enabling modular addition of new skills (see Figure 3.6). In this new structure, support ontologies (frames, params, sfc) have been moved to configuration.owl and coordination.owl, for separation of concerns (according to the 4C suggestion: Computation, Communication, Configuration, Coordination) and much easier maintenance. The details of this solution are found in [JMN16]. The refactored ontologies are also available from our knowledge server.

The particular advantage of using CORA in this case consists of anchoring the concept of the (industrial) robot pose in terms already defined in the position-related part of CORA. This way, any other robotic knowledge-based system also based on the common standard ontology IEEE 1872-2015 will be automatically aligned with Rosetta, at least with

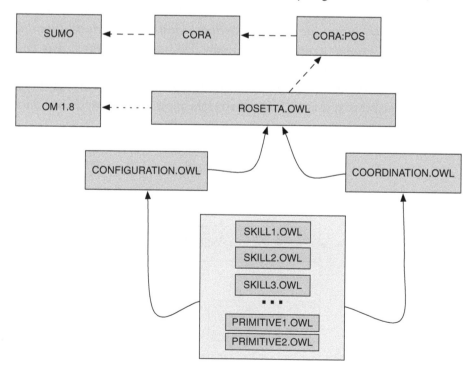

FIGURE 3.6 The refactored robotic skill ontologies.

respect to its idea of position. This should enable easier transfer of knowledge about robotic skills between different systems, possibly in an automatized manner.

3.5.2 The Cargo Delivery Scenario

CORA has been used and tested in very specific scenarios. One of them was a toy scenario where two robots with different physical and sensing capabilities communicated and coordinated to deliver cargo (a simple pen) to a human, i.e. the human solicits the cargo through a user interface and the robots coordinate themselves to pick and deliver the cargo (see Figure 3.7). To perform this task, all players should have the same communication language which must be formal and unambiguous. Otherwise, they will not be able to understand each other and, consequently, they will not attain their goal.

For this scenario, we used two robots from different manufacturers: an Aldebaran NAO H25 (aka manipulator) and a Pioneer 3DX (aka transporter). The manipulator had the cargo to be delivered to the human by request through a custom user interface. As the manipulator had its mobility limited to short distances due to its battery autonomy and speed, it could not deliver the cargo directly to the human, who could have been situated anywhere in the environment. However, it could manipulate the cargo by grabbing, lifting and/or dropping it. On the other hand, the transporter could move over long distances at higher speed than the manipulator and also could carry considerable payloads. However, it was not able to manipulate objects and had limited sensing capabilities (only range finding sensors).

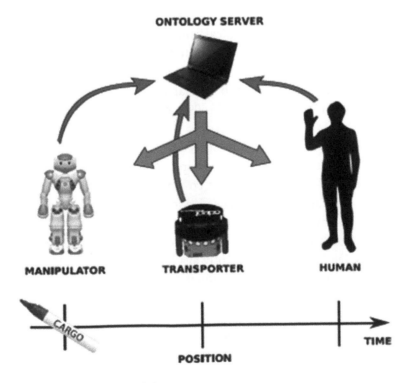

FIGURE 3.7 General organization of the system.

CORA concepts were represented using OWL and loaded into an ontology server written in Java. This server runs on a specific machine in a centralized architecture and it is responsible for managing all messages exchanged by human and robots. Thus, all server clients receive/send ontology information about themselves, which are used, for instance, to determine the relative positioning among the robots to allow the transporter to align itself and receive the cargo from the manipulator. Hence, we used the POS ontology, included in IEEE 1872-2015, to define the position and orientation of a player in a coordinate system to allow the spatial operations to determine the visibility, proximity, placement and relative orientation of a player in relation to another.

The experiment started with humans soliciting the cargo through a mobile phone application. This information was received by the manipulator and transporter, which first determined who had the cargo or had the ability to get the cargo. In this case, the manipulator had the cargo in its hands and sent this information to the system. The transporter started searching the manipulator in order to receive the cargo. When the manipulator was found, the transporter aligned itself to allow the manipulator to put the cargo on its shipment compartment. When this procedure was done, the transporter moved towards the human to complete the task. More information about this work can be found in [JRM+15].

Although this scenario is simple, it is complex enough to test our ontological framework. Ontology-based communication played a fundamental role. It endowed all players with a shared vocabulary with explicit semantics that allowed an unambiguous knowledge transfer even though using robots from different manufacturers.

3.5.3 Cora as Part of a Surgical Robot Ontology

Ontologies are widely used by the medical community to model knowledge. By using them, clinical terminology is clear and explicit to the community [GT14]. SNOMED-CT* © is nowadays the major reference in health terminology, where clinical terms are defined.

In surgeries, ontologies do exist with special focus on computer-assisted surgeries, Surgical Workflow (SWOnt ontology) [NJS+09], for assessment studies in human–computer interaction [MJD+15], and laparoscopic surgery (LapOntoSPM) [KJW+15], with application to situation interpretation, in other words, the recognition of surgical phases based on surgical activities. The latter case is of special use for HRI, when robots, surgeons, nurses and other medical staff and engineers co-work in the operating room. In fact, complete awareness of surgical procedures is needed for all agents.

Robotic ontologies with application to surgeries were recently proposed in the literature, applied to neurosurgery [PNDM+14] and orthopaedics (OROSU) [Gon13, GT15]. The latter applied CORA within the recently available IEEE 1872-2015 standard [Mad15, FCG+15]. In the following, a brief presentation of OROSU is presented focusing on a surgical procedure workflow for a proper interaction between the robot and medical staff in the operating room.

OROSU was developed with the integration of CORA [Mad15, FCG+15] and biomedical/human anatomical ontologies, sourced from *NCBO BioPortal* [NSW+09] and

* www.ihtsdo.org/snomed-ct

Open Biological and Biomedical Ontologies [SAR+07]. For tasks (surgical procedures) definition, and also as an engine to process the ontology, i.e. for reasoning, *KnowRob* [TB13] was used with success.

In the OROSU application presented in [GT15], robotic hip surgery was used to test the ontology for surgical procedure representation and reasoning. Figure 3.9 depicts an example for a complete surgical procedure definition (robotic bone tracking using an ultrasound probe) and the knowledge represented therein. This representation is suitable for a proper HRI between the medical staff and the robot, both working with the operating room ICT infrastructure. Figure 3.8 depicts an excerpt of the knowledge related to medical devices used in OROSU. For example, the sensor data is obtained using *CTimaging* or *USimaging* to gather 3D point clouds and then obtaining the 3D model of the bone.

In conclusion, the presented application is important to show the application of CORA to a complex HRI scenario. Using CORA and OROSU, robotic surgical procedures can be

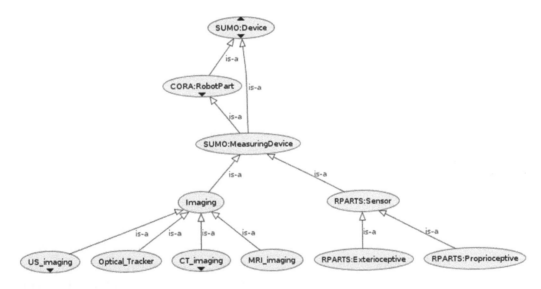

FIGURE 3.8   Some measuring devices defined in the ontology, relating SUMO, CORA and OROSU.

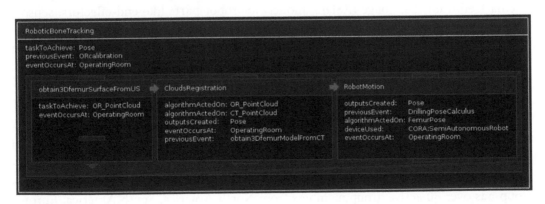

FIGURE 3.9   Example of a surgical procedure definition, relating CORA, OROSU and KNOWROB framework.

defined and used no matter what type of surgical robot (defined using CORA) is applied in different scenarios.

3.5.4 Other Applications

The ontologies in IEEE 1872-2015 have been used or cited in other contexts as well. For example, Banerjee et al. [BBK+15], have used CORAX and other ontologies as part of a stochastic integer linear program for policies for optimum high-level task partitioning between collaborative teams of human operators and mobile ground robots. They successfully demonstrated collaboration of one human–robot pair leading to shorter completion times of a kitting operation.

Using ontological representations for grounding physical layers of the various HMI technologies, Pirvu et al. [PZG16] attempted to engineer a synthetic hybrid system called ACPS (using SOA), a human centric CPS which integrates physical and human components.

In a paper on cloud robotics, [KPAG15] notes that research in robot ontologies (KnowRob and CORA) can help to address current challenges such as heterogeneity, by defining cross-platform data formats and in future helping to standardize representation of elementary concepts such as trajectories.

In his paper, Diaconescu [DW14] remarked that the Core Ontology for Web of Things (WoTCO) ontology proposed by him has many similarities at the top-level with CORA. We observe that the differences are due to CORA using SUMO and WoTCO using Unified Foundational Ontology (UFO). While detailed concepts in CORA is subsumed under R-Parts and is general, WoTCo claims to have more details of concepts specific to the Web of Things. This similarity at the top level is comforting and can be viewed as reinforcing coherence of ontological concepts at the top level.

In his paper using elements defined in CORAX, Kootbally developed a platform-independent, Industrial Robot Capability Model [Koo16] and a planning infrastructure for planning and execution of industrial robot tasks for kitting assembly. Using CORA to represent a kitting workstation, its environment and objects, Kootbally proposed a robot capability model that defined additional components and pointers to CORA and action ontology. To represent robot capabilities for manufacturing applications, using XML Schema Definition Language (XSDL), models for robot parts like end-effectors, sensors and constraints have been defined. Assembly Action Model extends the dataThing class in CORA and the Robot Capability Model outputs a process plan with the best available robot to accomplish a kitting assembly task.

3.6 FOLLOW-ON EFFORTS

3.6.1 The Autonomous Robotics Study Group

The IEEE Ontologies for Robotics and Automation Working Group (ORA) was divided into sub-groups that are in charge of studying and developing industrial robotics, service robotics and autonomous robotics ontologies. The Autonomous Robotics (AuR) Study Group has over 80 active group members from North America, South America, Europe, Asia and Africa, representing stakeholders in academia, industry and governments. The AuR Study Group's goal is to extend the core ontology for robotics and automation to represent more specific concepts and axioms commonly used in autonomous robotics. The ontology should allow one to specify the knowledge and reasoning needed to build autonomous systems that can operate in the air, on the ground and underwater.

The AuR Study Group studies various R&A domains to identify basic components including the hardware and software necessary to endow robots with autonomy. In order to develop the standard ontology for autonomous systems, the AuR Study Group has adopted the following approach:

- Development of standard vocabularies for architectural concepts in IEEE 1471/ IEC 42010

- Development of a functional ontology for robotics and automation

- Validations of developed relationships and concepts

- Use of developed vocabularies and ontology for conceptual design of sample robot application using extended 1471 concepts and extension of CORAX

For vocabulary development, the AuR Study Group has defined: "behaviour", "function", "goal" and "task". As part of the architectural concepts development, the AuR Study Group has proposed the Robot Architecture (ROA) Ontology which defines the main concepts and relations regarding robot architecture in the context of autonomous systems. Its goal is to serve as a conceptual framework so that people and robots can share information about robot architectures.

A standard ontology in autonomous robotics will provide the underlying semantics of the vocabulary used in problem-solving and communications for heterogeneous autonomous systems. The proposed standard ontology will make possible a smooth integration among these systems in order to exchange knowledge and cooperatively perform tasks. Creating a standard for knowledge representation and reasoning in autonomous robotics will have a significant impact on all robotics and automation domains, including knowledge transmission among autonomous robots and humans. As a result, the use of autonomous robots by humans will further benefit our society. To the best of the authors' knowledge, the AuR Study Group is the first group to adopt a systematic approach in developing ontologies, consisting of specific concepts and axioms that are commonly used in autonomous robots.

3.6.2 Robot Task Representation Effort

Under the original ORA working group, a sub-group was formed to examine an application ontology focused on industrial automation. This group found that with the growing demand for product variations, limited skilled manpower, increased complexity of working environments and greater requirements for robot–robot and human–robot collaboration, there is a desire to seamlessly integrate processes and systems at the task level. In this context, *task* refers to the concrete decomposition from goal to sub-goals that enables the human/robot to accomplish outcomes at a specific instance in time. In order to accomplish this, there is a need for a standard providing an explicit knowledge representation for robot tasks. Unfortunately, it was also found that no internationally recognized standard exists for describing tasks and how to integrate them. Therefore, this sub-group decided to refocus its attention on a task ontology that will represent the knowledge necessary to fully describe autonomous tasking.

Actors performing autonomous tasks need to have sufficient knowledge of their tasks to not only perform them, but to also communicate their pending activities to others, and to recognize and correct errors without the need to interrupt the process. The tasks can be either informational (i.e. storing, representing or transferring information between the actors) or physical, where the actors actually manipulate materials (e.g., the robot picks and places an object) [JJ94]. The task could also be "collaborative" (e.g., human–robot manipulation in materials handling), where autonomous robots are expected to collaborate with other robots, as well as humans.

The availability of such a standard knowledge representation will

- define the domain concepts as controlled vocabularies for robot task representation

- ensure a common understanding between different industrial groups and devices

- facilitate interoperability between robotic systems for efficient data transfer and information exchange

- increase manufacturing performance, i.e. flexibility (easier incorporation of new processes due to a common set of concepts)

The industrial sub-group of ORA morphed into the *IEEE Robot Task Representation* (RTR) Study Group, with the objective of developing a broad standard that provides a comprehensive ontology for robot task structure and reasoning across robotics domains. This work will be a supplement to the existing standard Core Ontology for Robotics and Automation (CORA) [IEE15]. This supplement will include the presentation of concepts in an initial set of application domains (e.g., in manufacturing) where robot task representation could be useful. The ontology provides a unified way to represent knowledge about robot tasks by sharing common knowledge and preserving semantic meaning. It can be utilized in manufacturing control applications, where the system needs to control multiple elements of the manufacturing process.

Our work plan for developing the standard has two aspects. The first is to develop the task ontology, extending CORA and capturing vocabularies for robot task representation by requirements analysis and surveying the literature. The final decision making on vocabularies will be achieved through consensus between different group members. The ontology will contain vocabularies for generic tasks and specialized tasks for industrial application. The second aspect is to develop a task repository, which will provide a set of instances that could be used for robotic implementation and validation of the Task Ontology.

Although the Task Ontology will be the official standard when completed, the Task Repository is necessary to help validate the standard and to provide an avenue that makes the standard more useful and applied in the industry. The Task Ontology formally defines what a task is, and specifies the properties of tasks, the properties of the hierarchy in which tasks are placed and the ways in which the performance of the capabilities required to accomplish the tasks are measured. The Task Repository enables the community to build up a shared catalogue of tasks and capabilities along with their relationships (based on elements within the Task Ontology). The purpose of the overall standard is to ensure common representations and frameworks when tasks are described, so the knowledge represented in the Task Ontology defines the structure and content of the tasks in the Task Repository.

The existence of such a repository allows for clear definitions and descriptions of tasks and the ability for a user to quickly and easily determine if a task description (and associated algorithm) exists that will accomplish their goal, even if that task may have been created for a different purpose in another domain (Figure 3.10).

To develop this ontology, we will perform the following steps:

- **Requirements Gathering**: It is important to gather the relevant information requirements from all of the target domains to ensure that the resulting knowledge representation is truly comprehensive. RTR will reach out to experts in various robotics fields, some of whom are part of the group already and to others who are outside the group, to gain a deep understanding of what is necessary to represent task information in their domains. In addition to compiling the terms and definitions, RTR will start the process of identifying cases in which the same term has different meanings in different domains, as well as the cases where the same definition is associated with different terms. The output of this process will be a glossary of terms and definition, sorted by robot domain, which will serve as the basis for subsequent steps in the work plan.

- **Surveying Similar Efforts**: There are a number of efforts that have attempted to capture aspects of task information in specific robotic domains. In this phase of the work plan, RTR will deeply analyze these efforts to see how well they capture the concepts identified in the step above and evaluate their potential use as sources of definitions for the main concepts identified. In addition, RTR will look at the way that these concepts are represented (i.e. the knowledge representation formalism that is used and the attributes and relationships that are represented) to leverage the existing representational approaches and concepts wherever possible.

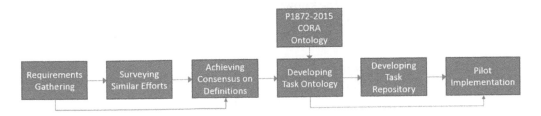

FIGURE 3.10 Robot Task Representation Study Group Work Plan.

- **Achieving Consensus on Definitions of Terms**: Coming to a consensus on terms and definitions is the most challenging, yet it is an essential part of the work. We have formed the study group so that there is representation from a wide array of robot domains. We are also closely collaborating with the autonomous robotics sub-area, which is also extending the P1872-2015 standard.

- **Developing the Task Ontology**: Building on the previous work of P1872-2015 (CORA), and using consensus definitions, RTR we will extend the CORA ontology to capture terms and definitions pertaining to robot tasks. While CORA does not specifically address robot tasks, it does define high-level concepts of robot motion that can be leveraged. In addition, SUMO defines the concept of process, which can also be built upon as appropriate. RTR will use aspects of the METHONTOLOGY ontology development methodology [FLGPJ97], which includes the development of the ontology conceptual model; the formalization of the ontology, which involves transforming the conceptual model into a formal or semi-computable model (specified in first-order logic, for example); and the implementation of the ontology, which involves transforming the previously formalized ontology into a computable model, codified in an ontology representation language, such as OWL.

- **Modelling of Shared Tasks and Capabilities in a Task Repository**: While the Task Ontology provides the structure and definitions of concepts, the Task Repository provides task instances that can be applied towards robot applications. It uses the structure of the concepts in the Task Ontology and populates the values with instances specific to individual robot types and applications. To validate the Task Ontology, RTR will create a set of task instances in the Task Repository, focusing on tasks that are generally applicable across robot domains, such as pick and place tasks or robot mobility tasks. The hope is that as the Task Ontology and associated Task Repository get used more and more, the community will populate the Task Repository with additional task instances.

- **Pilot Implementation**: Using the task instances created in the previous step, we will create two control systems for robots in different domains. These control systems will use the knowledge represented in the Task Repository to control a robot performing operations in the domain of interest. We expect one of the domains to be in the manufacturing field due to the interest and availability of these types of robots among the study group members. The second domain is still to be determined. As mentioned above, we expect the tasks to focus on pick and place and mobility operations. This process will help to validate the knowledge represented in the Task Repository as well as the structure of the Task Ontology.

3.7 CONCLUSION AND DISCUSSION: TOWARDS AN ONTOLOGY FOR HRI

In this chapter, we showed an overview of the development and content of the IEEE 1872-2015 standard and the current efforts to expand it. The main contribution of IEEE 1872-2015 is to formalize core concepts of R&A in a set of ontologies. These ontologies, and in particular CORA, are intended to be used by other researchers and practitioners as a basis not only for the development of other ontologies in R&A, but also for system and database design. We also showcased some current applications of IEEE 1872-2015 and summarized the current standardization efforts in expanding the standard to robot task representation and autonomous robots.

While IEEE 1872-2015 covers some concepts related to HRI, it still needs to be extended in order to cover the domain to an adequate level. Designing partial or completely automated mechanisms for handling human–robot interaction requires a generic and consistent model for representing, sharing and reasoning about the semantics of the perceptions, actions and interactions of both humans and robots. This model must be sufficiently expressive and abstract to cover all the complexity and heterogeneity of the technologies and systems used to capture the interactions. CORA and the remaining ontologies in IEEE 1872-2015 provide some of these notions, but lack in enough specificity to be applied directly. A CORA-based ontology for HRI could help solve this issue. A basic requirement for an HRI ontology is that it should allow for consistent description of the spatial and temporal context of robot and user, integrating robot perception and human interpretation of the interaction situation, as well as instructions and queries. The HRI ontology should allow one to model the semantics of static entities, such as the description of the space and its constituents, but also the dynamic entities that describe the events, situations, circumstances and changes of the interactions. The ontology should be placed at the middle level of Figure 3.2, beside the task ontology, serving as a basis for the implementation of application-specific models in HRI systems.

HRI ontology requires a suitable representation language that could allow for models to be easily translated into formal models for AI planning or to the semantic web. The language must allow for the formal description of interactions between humans, robots and the other objects of the real world according to a human-like narrative approach. That means that the language should allow for the definition of conceptual n-ary relations between static and dynamic entities. For example, representing an interaction such as "the-man-gives-the-cup-to-the-robot" requires at least a quaternary predicate relating the man, the cup, the robot and the act of giving. The HRI ontology must allow one to represent complex dynamic entities according to a narrative approach inspired by the human way of reporting stories and events. To allow for that, HRI ontology must provide conceptual constructs corresponding to *verbs* describing the interactions of a robotic domain such as moving, sensing, grasping, behaving, changing state and so on. The NKRL language [ACA13, Zar13] could be a good candidate to specify dynamic and static entities of the CORA HRI ontology

The problem of connecting perceptions with the corresponding concepts describing static and dynamic entities in the HRI ontology requires the modelling of physical symbol grounding procedures. For example, from the perspective of an embodied robot that interacts with humans and objects in the environment, the grounding of its symbolic system needs to consider the complexity of its sensorimotor readings. In the context of multi-robot and Internet of Things environments, the problem becomes more complex as symbols are not only grounded, but commonly shared. Most of the state-of-the-art attempts have dealt with the grounding of static entities and new grounding techniques are needed for grounding dynamic entities. Therefore, the HRI ontology must propose a grounding methodology that will deal with the grounding of perceptions and situated verbal and non-verbal communication or dialogues between humans and robots. Symbolic grounding is called perceptual anchoring when specifically referring to the building of links between the robot's low-level processes (i.e. odometers, camera, radar, ultrasound) and the high-level semantic representations. Due to the complexity of grounding, it should be better to limit the perceptual anchoring to the concepts and rules that systematically creates and maintains in time the correspondences between symbols and sensor and actuation data that refers to the same physical object and the same human.

The driving force for using HRI ontology should be the use of constraint-based techniques to model and reason about the dependencies between the symbolic information returned by the perception systems, temporal objects and the dynamic entities describing interactions between humans and robots. For that, the ontology should include constructs to represent time relations, such as Allen's Interval Algebra. Uncertainty must be taken into account at the ontology level in order to allow a sound and tractable coupling of dynamic temporal objects and dynamic entities and avoid ambiguous reasoning. Thus, HRI ontology must include uncertainty measures with logical statements to describe simultaneous and nested dynamic entities. Considering the heterogeneity, redundancy and conflicts between perception and actuation systems, the use of belief theory at the symbolic level, for instance, would help to assign confidence values to assertions about dynamic entities and rules processed by reasoning engines.

ACKNOWLEDGMENT

T. Haidegger's research is supported by the Hungarian State and the European Union under the EFOP-3.6.1-16-2016-00010 project. T. Haidegger is a Bolyai Fellow of the Hungarian Academy of Sciences, and he is supported through the New National Excellence Program of the Ministry of Human Capacities.

REFERENCES

[ACA13] N. Ayari, A. Chibani and Y. Amirat. Semantic management of human-robot interaction in ambient intelligence environments using n-ary ontologies. In *2013 IEEE International Conference on Robotics and Automation*, pp. 1172–1179, Institute of Electrical and Electronics Engineers (IEEE), Karlsruhe, Germany, May 2013.

[BBK+15] A.G. Banerjee, A. Barnes, K.N. Kaipa, J. Liu, S. Shriyam, N. Shah and S.K. Gupta. An ontology to enable optimized task partitioning in human-robot collaboration for warehouse kitting operations. In *Proceedings of the SPIE*, volume 9494, 94940H, 2015.

[CDYM+07] A.F. Cutting-Decelle, R.I.M. Young, J.J. Michel, R. Grangel, J. Le Cardinal, and J.P. Bourey. ISO 15531 MANDATE: A product-process-resource based approach for managing modularity in production management. *Concurrent Engineering*, 15(2): 217–235, 2007.

[CFP+13] Joel Carbonera, Sandro Fiorini, Edson Prestes, Vitor A.M. Jorge, Mara Abel, Raj Madhavan, Angela Locoro, P.J.S. Gonçalves, Tamás Haidegger, Marcos E. Barreto, and Craig Schlenoff. Defining positioning in a core ontology for robotics. In *Proceedings of IEEE/RSJ International Conference on Intelligent Robots and Systems (IROS)*, pp. 1867–1872, Tokyo, Japan, November 2013.

[DSV+05] Denny Vrandecic, Sofia Pinto, Christoph Tempich, and York Sure. The DILIGENT knowledge processes. *Journal of Knowledge Management*, 9(5): 85–96, 2005.

[DW14] I.M. Diaconescu and G. Wagner. Towards a general framework for modeling, simulating and building sensor/actuator systems and robots for the web of things. In *Proceedings of the CEUR-WS*, volume 1319, pp. 30–41, 2014.

[FCG+15] Sandro Rama Fiorini, Joel Luis Carbonera, Paulo Gonçalves, Vitor AM Jorge, Vítor Fortes Rey, Tamás Haidegger, Mara Abel, Signe A. Redfield, Stephen Balakirsky, Veera Ragavan, et al. Extensions to the core ontology for robotics and automation. *Robotics and Computer-Integrated Manufacturing*, 33: 3–11, 2015.

[FLGPJ97] Mariano Fernández-López, Asunción Gómez-Pérez and Natalia Juristo. METHONTOLOGY: From ontological art towards ontological engineering. Workshop on Ontological Engineering. Stanford, CA, 1997.

[Gon13] Paulo J.S. Gonçalves. Towards an ontology for orthopaedic surgery, application to hip resurfacing. In *Proceedings of the Hamlyn Symposium on Medical Robotics*, pp. 61–62, London, UK, June 2013.

[GT14] Paulo J.S. Gonçalves and Pedro M.B. Torres. A survey on biomedical knowledge representation for robotic orthopaedic surgery. *Robot Intelligence Technology and Applications*, 2: 259–268, 2014.

[GT15] Paulo J.S. Gonçalves and Pedro M.B. Torres. Knowledge representation applied to robotic orthopedic surgery. *Robotics and Computer-Integrated Manufacturing*, 33: 90–99, 2015.

[Gua98] Nicola Guarino. Formal ontology and information systems. In *Proceedings of FOIS*, volume 98, pp. 81–97, Trento, Italy, 1998.

[Gui05] Giancarlo Guizzardi. *Ontological Foundations for Structural Conceptual Models*. Phd thesis, CTIT, Centre for Telematics and Information Technology, Enschede, the Netherlands, 2005.

[HMA03] Hui-Min Huang, Elena Messina and James Albus. Toward a generic model for autonomy levels for unmanned systems (ALFUS). In *Proceedings of Performance Metrics for Intelligent Systems*, Gaithersburg, MD, 2003.

[HMN+11] Mathias Haage, Jacek Malec, Anders Nilsson, Klas Nilsson, and Slawomir Nowaczyk. Declarative knowledge-based reconfiguration of automation systems using a blackboard architecture. In *Proceedings of the 11th Scandinavian Conference on Artificial Intelligence*, pp. 163–172, Trondheim, Norway, 2011.

[IEE15] IEEE. IEEE Standard Ontologies for Robotics and Automation. *IEEE Std. 1872-2015*, 2015.

[JJ94] S. Joshi and S. Jeffrey. *Computer Control of Flexible Manufacturing Systems – Research and Development Edition*. Dordrecht, Springer Netherlands, 1994.

[JMN16] Ludwig Jacobsson, Jacek Malec and Klas Nilsson. Modularization of skill ontologies for industrial robots. In *Proceedings of International Symposium on Robotics*, Munich, Germany, June 2016.

[JRM+15] Vitor A.M. Jorge, Vitor F. Rey, Renan Maffei, Sandro Rama Fiorini, Joel Luis Carbonera, Flora Branchi, João P. Meireles, Guilherme S. Franco, Flávia Farina, Tatiana S. da Silva, Mariana Kolberg, Mara Abel and Edson Prestes. Exploring the {IEEE} ontology for robotics and automation for heterogeneous agent interaction. *Robotics and Computer-Integrated Manufacturing*, 33: 12–20, 2015.

[KJW+15] Darko Katić, Chantal Julliard, Anna-Laura Wekerle, Hannes Kenngott, Beat-Peter Müller-Stich, Rüdiger Dillmann, Stefanie Speidel, Pierre Jannin and Bernard Gibaud. Lapontospm: An ontology for laparoscopic surgeries and its application to surgical phase recognition. *International Journal of Computer Assisted Radiology and Surgery*, 11(4): 1–8, 2015.

[Koo16] Z. Kootbally. Industrial robot capability models for agile manufacturing. *Industrial Robot*, 43(5): 481–494, 2016.

[KPAG15] B. Kehoe, S. Patil, P. Abbeel and K. Goldberg. A survey of research on cloud robotics and automation. *IEEE Transactions on Automation Science and Engineering*, 12(2): 398–409, 2015.

[LAP+12] S. Lemaignan, R. Alami, A.K. Pandey, M. Warnier and J. Guitton. Bridges between the methodological and practical work of the robotics and cognitive systems communities-from sensors to concepts, chapter towards grounding human-robot interaction. *Intelligent Systems Reference Library*, Berlin Heidelberg, Springer, 2012.

[Mad15] Raj Madhavan. The first-ever IEEE RAS standard published. *IEEE Robotics & Automation Magazine*, 22(2): 21, 2015.

[MJD+15] Andrej Machno, Pierre Jannin, Olivier Dameron, Werner Korb, Gerik Scheuermann and Jürgen Meixensberger. Ontology for assessment studies of human–computer-interaction in surgery. *Artificial Intelligence in Medicine*, 63(2): 73–84, 2015.

[NJS+09] T. Neumuth, P. Jannin, G. Strauß, J. Meixensberger, and O. Burgert. Validation of knowledge acquisition for surgical process models. *Journal of the American Medical Informatics Association*, 16: 72–80, 2009.

[NP01] Ian Niles and Adam Pease. Towards a standard upper ontology. In *Proceedings of the International Conference on Formal Ontology in Information Systems – Volume 2001*, FOIS'01, pp. 2–9, New York, NY, USA, ACM, 2001.

[NSW+09] N.F. Noy, N.H. Shah, P.L. Whetzel, B. Dai, M. Dorf, N. Griffith, C. Jonquet, D.L. Rubin, M.-A. Storey, C.G. Schute, et al. Bioportal: Ontologies and integrated data resources at the click of a mouse. *Nucleic Acids Research*, 37(s2): 170–173, 2009.

[OAH+07] Daniel Oberle, Anupriya Ankolekar, Pascal Hitzler, Philipp Cimiano, Michael Sintek, Malte Kiesel, Babak Mougouie, Stephan Baumann, Shankar Vembu, Massimo Romanelli, et al. DOLCE ergo SUMO: On foundational and domain models in the SmartWeb integrated ontology (SWIntO). *Web Semantics: Science, Services and Agents on the World Wide Web*, 5(3): 156–174, September 2007.

[Obr10] Leo Obrst. Ontological architectures. In R. Poli, M. Healy and A. Kameas, (eds.), *Theory and Applications of Ontology: Computer Applications*, pp. 27–66. Dordrecht, Springer, 2010.

[PCF+13] Edson Prestes, Joel Luis Carbonera, Sandro Rama Fiorini, Vitor A.M. Jorge, Mara Abel, Raj Madhavan, Angela Locoro, Paulo Goncalves, Marcos E. Barreto, Maki Habib, et al. Towards a core ontology for robotics and automation. *Robotics and Autonomous Systems*, 61(11): 1193–1204, 2013.

[PNDM+14] R. Perrone, F. Nessi, E. De Momi, F. Boriero, M. Capiluppi, P. Fiorini and G. Ferrigno. Ontology-based modular architecture for surgical autonomous robots. In *The Hamlyn Symposium on Medical Robotics*, p. 85, London, UK, 2014.

[pro14] NeOn project. Ontology design patterns (ODP), 2014.

[PZG16] B.-C. Pirvu, C.-B. Zamfirescu and D. Gorecky. Engineering insights from an anthropocentric cyber-physical system: A case study for an assembly station. *Mechatronics*, 34: 147–159, 2016.

[SAR+07] B. Smith, M. Ashburner, C. Rosse, J. Bard, W. Bug, W. Ceusters, L.J. Goldberg, K. Eilbeck, A. Ireland, C.J. Mungall, et al. The OBO Foundry: Coordinated evolution of ontologies to support biomedical data integration. *National Biotechnology*, 37: 1251–1255, 2007.

[SBF98] Rudi Studer, V. Richard Benjamins and Dieter Fensel. Knowledge engineering: Principles and methods. *Data & Knowledge Engineering*, 25(1): 161–197, 1998.

[SFGPFL12] Mari Carmen Suárez-Figueroa, Asuncion Gomez-Perez and Mariano Fernandez-Lopez. The neon methodology for ontology engineering. In M.C. Suárez-Figueroa, A. Gómez-Pérez, E. Motta and A. Gangemi (eds.), *Ontology Engineering in a Networked World*, pp. 9–34, Berlin Heidelberg, Springer, 2012.

[SM15] Maj Stenmark and Jacek Malec. Knowledge-based instruction of manipulation tasks for industrial robotics. *Robotics and Computer-Integrated Manufacturing*, 33: 56–67, 2015.

[SSS04] York Sure, Steffen Staab, and Rudi Studer. On-to-knowledge methodology (OTKM). In Steffen Staab, and Rudi Studer (eds.), *Handbook on Ontologies*, pp. 117–132, Berlin Heidelberg, Springer, 2004.

[SSS09] York Sure, Steffen Staab and Rudi Studer. Ontology engineering methodology. In Steffen Staab and Rudi Studer (eds.), *Handbook on Ontologies*, pp. 135–152, Berlin Heidelberg, Springer, 2009.

[SWJ95] Guus Schreiber, Bob Wielinga and Wouter Jansweijer. The KACTUS view on the 'O' word. In *IJCAI Workshop on Basic Ontological Issues in Knowledge Sharing*, pp. 159–168, Citeseer, 1995.

[TB13] Moritz Tenorth and Michael Beetz. Knowrob: A knowledge processing infrastructure for cognition-enabled robots. *The International Journal of Robotics Research*, 32(5): 566–590, 2013.

[Zar13] Gian Piero Zarri. Advanced computational reasoning based on the {NKRL} conceptual model. *Expert Systems with Applications*, 40(8): 2872–2888, 2013.

CHAPTER 4

Robot Modularity for Service Robots

Hong Seong Park and Gurvinder Singh Virk

CONTENTS

4.1 General Requirements of Robot Modularity   52
4.2 Module Safety   55
4.3 Hardware Module   62
4.4 Software Module   65
4.5 Summary   69
References   70

CURRENTLY, MODULARITY IS BECOMING an important issue in the field of robotics because it can reduce initial and maintenance costs for robots and quickly spread their application. Modularity refers to the process of separating and assembling the modules (or components) of a system. In this chapter, "module" refers to an independent unit that can be easily separated, exchanged, and reused with slight or no modification. Many commercial robots have been developed and manufactured through modularity, but the coverage of modularity has been limited to one robot, one type of robot, or one company's robot; hence, the cost of robots cannot be reduced further.

The reorganization of the personal computer market in the 1980s from the CP/M market to the DOS market was also due to modularity and the release of (infrastructure) interfaces for modularity. In addition, the reusability of software through an interface standard made the software (SW) market much larger, and the standardization of communication protocols has stimulated the communication market and related markets. Because individual robot technologies have reached a certain level at present, modularity of robot technologies and related standardization techniques are needed in order to reduce robot costs and disseminate their application.

Modules can be can be classified into hardware (HW) modules and SW modules. There are two types of HW modules: a pure HW module and a module combining HW and SW. Of course, it can be argued that the latter case is a composite module combining HW and SW. Regardless of whether the module is a composite module, a generalization is that a module is a HW module if it can be touched and has some physical attribute; otherwise, it is a SW module. It can be more easily understood that, generally, a tangible module is a HW module and otherwise is a SW module. Therefore, it is more appropriate to consider a HW module if the reuse or exchange unit is of the HW type and a SW module if the unit is of the SW type. Modularity of a robot is important because it lowers the price of a robot via re-use and makes maintenance easy, but it is also important in assuring the safety of a robot when the robot is made by combining modules. It is necessary to check issues related to the safety of the modules used in a robot in order to ensure overall robot safety.

Let us define a module and a composite module (these definitions are being developed in the ISO committee ISO TC299/WG6 Modularity for service robots). Modules can be generally divided into basic modules and composite modules. A module, a basic module, and a composite module are redefined based on [1] as follows:

- Module: a component with special characteristics such as to facilitate design, interoperability, easy reconfiguration, integration, etc.

- Component: a part or element of something more complex; note that, in this section, the word "part" is used instead of the word "component" for clarity.

- Basic module: a type of module that cannot be further subdivided into modules.

- Composite module: a module made up of multiple modules.

A module is developed using components (or parts) while meeting the requirements (reusability, interoperability, and composability) described in Chapter 2. The process of building a robot and a composite module is explained using basic modules and shown by example in Figure 4.1. First, basic modules are developed; these are used to build composite modules or full robot systems.

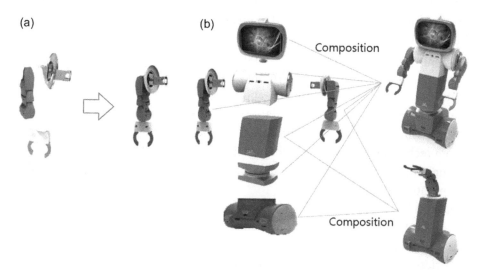

FIGURE 4.1   Modules and robots composed of modules and components [2]. (a) Components (or parts) of a basic module; (b) Basic modules and components of a composite module and a robot.

For example, consider a motor-based smart actuator as a module of a robot. This module contains both HW and SW parts, and is generally regarded as a HW module because it is tangible in its final product form. In addition the module can be used for various types of robots such as service robots, medical robots, and industrial robots. Additionally, if the robot is well-designed mechanically using smart actuators, it can be replaced by new modules with the same types of actuators or reused in modules used in the other robots in case the smart actuator fails. Considering the operating environment of the three kinds of robots suggested as examples using smart actuator modules, it can be seen that the safety levels of the robots (e.g., SIL in IEC and PL in ISO) can be applied differently depending on the robots' environments. Although the three kinds of robots are presented as examples of the use of the smart actuator module, the safety level of the smart actuator (Safety Integrity Levels [SIL] defined in IEC 61505 and Performance Levels [PL] defined in ISO 13849) is applied differently depending on the environment in which these robots are used.

According to the required safety levels of the robots, the safety levels of the smart actuators used in the robots can be different. For example, smart actuators can have different safety levels where they are used in robots that clean in a people-free environment, robots that clean in an environment with humans present, and surgical robots which operate as medical equipment. Of course, it is better to use rated actuators, but unfortunately these actuators are more expensive. Developers and manufacturers of smart actuators have generally developed and produced them for their expected applications, but users can use these to develop other types of robots for unexpected applications. Users must check the safety level of the module of interest and verify its suitability for the safety level of the robot used in the intended application. In other words, it is necessary to know the safety level of the smart actuator to determine the safety level of the robot used in the target application.

Developers and manufacturers of modules must provide information about the safety level of the module. We consider what safety-related information the module may provide via some examples. As mentioned before, the types of modules are classified as a HW module and a SW module. The former is divided into the mechanical module and electrical/electronic (EE) module. In fact, a smart actuator, as shown in Figure 4.2, is a hardware module consisting of hardware parts and software parts, including a motor, encoder, driver, mechanical parts, joints, hardware communication parts, OS, communication SW, sensing SW, actuating SW, control SW, monitoring SW, etc. The safety level of the module can be calculated through a combination of these parts, which means that the safety level can vary depending on the parts' properties (e.g., mean time between failures (MTTF), SIL or PL, and safety functions) and the combination of parts used in the modules. Therefore, developers and manufacturers of parts or modules must indicate the level of safety provided and/or information to calculate the safety level of the module. For example, a mechanical joint part illustrated in Figure 4.2 comes with safety-related information such as joint strength and operating time in a humid environment. Electrical/electronic parts such as the motor, driver, and encoder indicate MTTF, interface signals, and safety-related signals such as error and stop signals, if provided.

In this chapter, requirements for robot modularity are suggested and module safety, the hardware module, and the software module are discussed in detail.

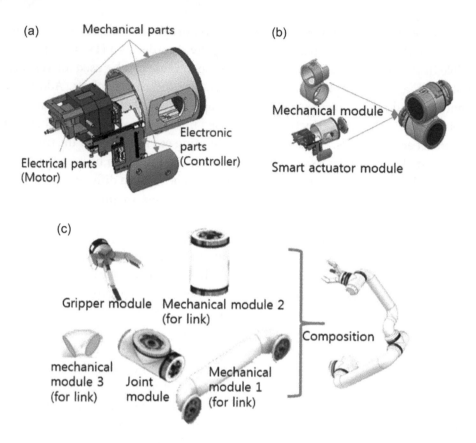

FIGURE 4.2   A smart actuator and its components: the mechanical module, joint module, and manipulator module [3]. (a) Concept diagram of a smart actuator; (b) Joint module (composite module); (c) Manipulator module (composite).

4.1 GENERAL REQUIREMENTS OF ROBOT MODULARITY

For robot modularity, ISO TC299 WG6 has presented ten principles [1], but only the four most important requirements are presented in this chapter: (1) reusability, (2) composability, (3) interoperability, and (4) safety. These requirements apply to both the HW module and the SW module.

Reusability is the ability to be used repeatedly or in different applications with minimal/without changes. That is, a module with reusability can be used as part of a new module with minimal/without changes. In order to achieve this, it is necessary to define the following interfaces according to the characteristics of the module; interfaces between software modules, interfaces between electrical modules, and interfaces for connectivity linkages between mechanical modules.

From the software viewpoint, subroutines and functions are the simplest examples of reusability. In addition, the communication protocol is another example. If the face recognition software developed for one robot is reused in other types of robots and robots of other manufactures with minimal/without changes, then the software is said to be reusable. From the hardware viewpoint, modular power supplies are good examples of reusability. In addition, other types of examples are signaling and connectors for communication such as ethernet, CAN, RS232, and USB, where the former three are for electrical interfaces and the last is for mechanical interfaces. From the point of view of composite modules, a manipulator with two smart actuators also has mechanical parts to fix it to a rigid body such as the ground or a robot body. In order to reuse the manipulator, the mechanical interface/specification for linkage to the rigid body is standardized so that the manipulator can be fixed to the body. Of course, a standardized or open communication protocol should be used to control the manipulator.

Composability is the ability to assemble modules (hardware and/or software modules) logically and physically using various combinations into new types of module which can perform the bespoke functionalities of the user. Note that composability can be considered part of system integration: the process of integrating modules to build larger modules and complete a system.

In order to make a manipulator, some smart actuator modules are selected and some mechanical parts for links and joints are attached properly to each actuator module. Then each module is linked to other modules to build the manipulator. At the same time, some software modules are combined together to control the manipulator for the intended target functions. Examples include kinematics modules, inverse kinematics modules, coordination modules with synchronization, and control modules for smart actuators, an example of which is shown in Figure 4.3a. Figure 4.3b shows that the mobile platform can consist of a navigation module and a wheel-control module, which are types of composite modules. Some examples of composition and system integration are illustrated in Figures 4.1 through 4.3.

Interoperability is the ability of a module whose interfaces are described and open to link to and function together with other modules and to provide its functions to the other modules or exchange and make use of data without any modification. Of course, modules with interoperability can be substituted and used as modules performing the same (or similar) functions of other robots. If a module of the robot can be reused in other type of robots or in other manufacturers' robots, the module is said to be interoperable.

For interoperability of a mechanical robot module including a smart actuator, the module must easily link to other mechanical robot modules manually or by use of simple tools such as screwdrivers. In addition, the mechanical module can be removed and must be able to be substituted by other interoperable modules with ease. To achieve this purpose, some interfaces are described explicitly and openly, examples of which are the specification of mechanical linkages, specification of connectors, and the electrical signaling or communication protocols used in the module. Connectors can be classified into electrical, pneumatic, and hydraulic types. Electrical connectors can be divided into power and signaling modes. A module is said to be interoperable if it is physically linked (or (linked mechanically and connected via connectors) to other modules, can exchange data with other module without any problems, and performs to the (physical and logical) functions of the module without any errors.

Safety is the state of being protected from harm or other non-desirable things or being free from danger, risk, threat of harm, injury, or loss to personnel and/or property which

(a)

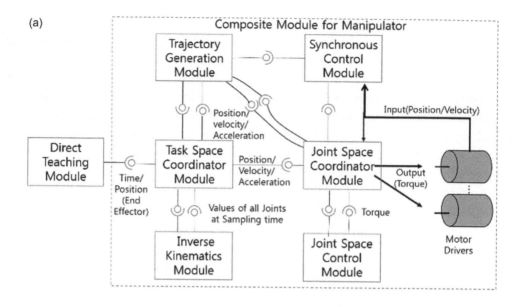

(b)

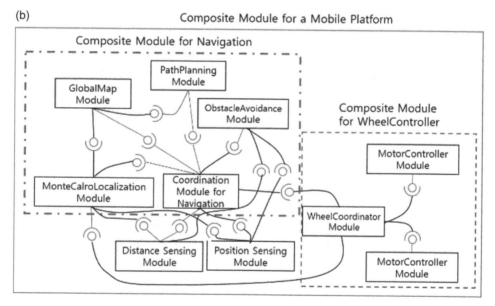

FIGURE 4.3   Two examples of composition of SW modules. (a) Composite module for a manipulator; (b) Composite module for a mobile platform.

can occur intentionally or by accident. Safety can be classified into inherent safety or needing complementary (or protective) safety measures. The former is safety provided by the module itself and the latter is safety provided by additional devices. Module safety and robot system safety mean the states in which a robot module and a robot system operate suitably according to the user's intent (e.g., acceptable risk) even when a fault occurs. Consider the example of not being hurt by a mechanical part. An example of inherent safety is rounding the corners of the mechanical part; examples of complementary safety is attaching soft, plastic-like protectors at the corners or attaching a safety guide that helps to connect a mechanical joint to a mechanical link safely. Another example of the former type of safety is detecting faults caused by known errors in electronic parts and preventing them from developing into hazardous situations.

Note that robot system safety is assessed by risk assessment and risk reduction as presented in ISO 12100 and IEC 60204-1 for general safety; ISO 13849-1 and IEC 62061 for functional safety; and specific safety requirements IEC 61508-1, -2, and -3 for functional safety of electrical/electronic/programmable electronic safety-related systems; IEC 61800-5-1, -2, and -3 for adjustable-speed electrical power drive systems; safety requirements ISO 10218-1, -2, and ISO TS 10566 for service robots in industrial applications; and ISO 13482 for personal care robot applications.

Module safety requirements can be divided into different levels according to the parts that constitute the module. For example, pure mechanical modules do not detect faults, and sensor modules cannot detect faults by themselves. The former can protect from harm using a complementary guide or cushion, and the latter can detect sensor faults using an additional function detecting faults in reading sensor values. In other words, module safety can be classified into the following levels according to the provided functions or roles (it is assumed that faults are known):

- Level 1: The module itself and other modules do not detect faults.

- Level 2: The module itself does not detect faults, but other modules can detect them.

- Level 3: The module itself detects some faults, but other modules can detect all faults.

- Level 4: The module itself detects some faults and controls some detected faults using the its own safety function, but other modules can detect all faults.

- Level 5: The module (or system) itself detects and controls detected faults using its own safety function and can detect some unknown faults using (complementary) safety functions.

For module safety, a risk assessment and risk reduction process for the robot system needs to be performed at all the levels if the robot system requires safety. When the specification, shape, or code of the modules is changed or the configuration of the modules is changed in composite modules, the risk assessment and risk reduction process must be performed anew. Note that a fault is a potential defect inherent in a module and an error is a deviation from the normal operation of a module, while failure occurs due to errors. In this book, "security" means information security. If the information or data in a module of a robot is modified by hacking, then the module cannot operate as intended, and the operator or the robot can enter a risk situation. Therefore, security can also be included within safety.

4.2 MODULE SAFETY

Module safety must be defined carefully because its definition is related to specific applications. A robot can be made by combining modules, and the safety level of the robot is determined depending on the application of the robot where the safety level is shown in

Table 4.1. Hence, the following engineering approach is needed: (1) determine the safety level for the robot used in the application; (2) survey and collect modules suitable for the determined safety level, and if the proper modules do not exist, then modules should be developed; (3) design and compose modules to suit the safety level desired; (4) add complementary safety measures if necessary.

If the robot is a finished product, the safety levels of its assembled modules should be calculated to determine the safety level of the robot. If the robot does not satisfy the desired safety level, then it must not be used in the target application; in that case, redesign of the robot is required.

However, the following problem arises in developing a module: in a few cases, it is possible to develop modules to be used in a specific robot when developing a module, but in most cases they are developed without specifying a particular application. For example, in the case of an ultrasonic sensor module capable of measuring distance, it may be used in modules such as manipulators or mobile platforms or it may be applied to robots such as entertainment robots or guide robots or industrial robots. The safety level of a robot or module differs depending on its application. It can therefore be very difficult to determine the relevant safety level for a module. If the module developer does not provide information to allow the safety level to be checked, the developers of composite modules (or robots) based on the module must verify the module in order to determine the safety level of the composite modules (or robots) being designed. This can be a burden on developers of composite modules (or robots), increasing the price of the module (or robot). Therefore, module developers need to provide a substantial amount of information to check the safety level of modules derived from their products such as composite modules and robots. Many standards are currently being provided for the safety of robots.

Following the overall design procedure for a robot or module to determine safety objectives is known as a verification and validation (V&V) procedure [7]. The design of electrical/electronic modules is a subset of the overall design procedure of a robot or module. The module provides safety functions in the relevant safety level to achieve the required risk reduction. Module design is part of the risk reduction strategy of the robot when providing safety functions as the inherent safety part of the design or as a control of interlocking guards or protective devices. Therefore, module design is very important. Note that it is not necessary to consider the safety function for modules (or parts) unrelated to safety, but the safety function of a non-safety-related module should be considered if the module has

TABLE 4.1 Safety Levels for a Robot [4,5,6]

PL	Average Probability of a Dangerous Failure Per Hour (PFHD) 1/h	SIL (IEC 61508-1) High/Continuous Mode of Operation
a	$\geq 10^{-5}$ to $< 10^{-4}$	No correspondence
b	$\geq 3 \times 10^{-6}$ to $< 10^{-5}$	1
c	$\geq 10^{-6}$ to $< 3 \times 10^{-4}$	1
d	$\geq 10^{-7}$ to $< 10^{-6}$	2
e	$\geq 10^{-8}$ to $< 10^{-7}$	3

some impacts on the safety of a composite module. For each safety function, the characteristics and the required safety level should be specified, documented, and verified.

As mentioned earlier, a module can be classified as HW, SW, or both. For each case, the safety verification method may be similar in an overall sense, but slightly different in detailed areas. For example, IEC 61508 presents functional safety of electrical/electronic/programmable electronic systems, which are related to electrical/electronic modules and/or software modules. ISO 10218 provides safety requirements for industrial robots, which consider hazards from mechanical parts and electrical/electronic parts. ISO 12100 suggests general principles for design safety of machinery.

The V&V procedure for safety of a robot system is shown in Figure 4.4, which can apply to a robot from a system viewpoint. Note that the V&V process is related to electrical/electronic parts and software parts, but mechanical parts are not mentioned in the process. ISO 12100, ISO 10218, ISO 13482, and ISO 13849 provide safety requirements related to mechanical and environmental aspects. ISO 13849 covers safety-related parts of control systems similar to those of IEC 61508.

Next we focus on the safety of electrical/electronic HW modules, where modules may include software parts. Failures that can occur in these modules can be classified into two types as follows:

- Safe failures: failures that do not affect the safety function of the system.

- Dangerous failures: failures resulting in dangerous situations in the application with great effects on risk to human life under certain situations.

These two types of failures can be either detected or undetected. A dangerous and detectable failure can bring the robot system into a safe sate using several means that can

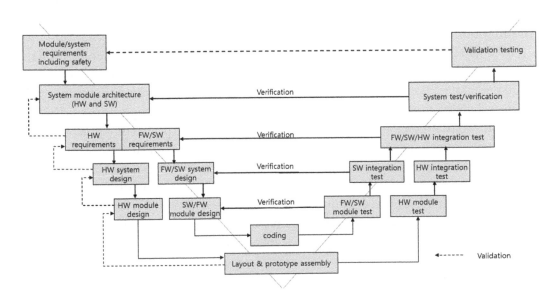

FIGURE 4.4 System lifecycle for V&V for safety.

be used to assure the safety of the system and humans involved. However, a dangerous and undetectable failure can cause the system to enter a critical state, causing the system to shut down unstably or making humans unsafe.

To determine the PL/SIL, it is very important to know the structure of a robot and the HW and SW of the modules used in the robot. The failure probabilities of the modules and the robot are obtained using this structure. Of course, the failure probability for the HW parts used in the module (e.g., CPU, sensors, memory ICs, resistors, capacitors, etc.) must be provided by the part manufacturers. Otherwise, the developer should calculate these probabilities through testing. This process is repeated for modules, composite modules, and robots.

If the developer of a module can provide a dangerous failure probability for a particular application, it helps in developing a composite module or a robot. Of course, if the application is unspecified, then it is impossible to check whether the failure can lead to a hazardous situation or not. In this case, it is also very useful to provide the failure probability (or MTTF) of the module alone. In other words, if the (dangerous) failure probability is provided for a HW module, developers can easily calculate the (dangerous) failure probability of other composite modules or robots that include it. In addition, related documents may be provided to validate the module. To avoid this, a certification system may be required. If the HW module is a power supplier or a programmable power drive system, the dangerous failure probability of the module should be provided because the HW module can bring humans into a risk state. In the case of a sensor that measures distance, it may affect human safety depending on the application, so it is sufficient to be provided with only the failure probability (or MTTF) of the module rather than its dangerous failure probability.

In particular, the SW part performs the V&V procedure specified in ISO/IEC standards, which reduces the possibility that detectable errors are not processed. A software module is made up of a number of functions, some of which detect errors and, if necessary, handle errors in a safe manner or inform other modules of the type of error. Those software functions should also be designed to handle all detectable errors and to handle possible errors that cannot be detected.

If SW and HW parts are used in a module at the same time, there is a possibility that the failure probability may be higher. Therefore, it is necessary to design SW parts to reduce the failure probability. For HW and/or SW modules, it is necessary to provide the (dangerous) failure probability to calculate the safety level of robots (or other composite modules) that uses them and to provide a way to reduce the dangerous failure probability if necessary.

Items related to module safety are summarized from key international standards related to safety of robots or machinery. ISO 12100 specifies "Safety of machinery - General principles for design - Risk assessment and risk reduction." The following is a summary of ISO 12100 in terms of a robot and its modules, and explains which items the module provides for its safety [8]:

The risk reduction process for a robot is the process of eliminating hazards or of separately or simultaneously reducing each of the following two elements:

- Severity of harm from the hazard under consideration.

- Probability of occurrence of that harm.

The risk reduction process should be applied in the following three steps.

Step 1: Design for Inherent Safety

Design to eliminate hazards or reduce their associated risks by a suitable choice of design features of the robot/module itself and/or interaction between the robot/module and the related (or exposed) person.

Step 2: Design for Additional Safeguarding and/or Complementary Protection

In most cases where the intended use and reasonably foreseeable misuse are considered, it may not be possible to eliminate a hazard or reduce its associated risk sufficiently or completely, even though we use the design method with inherent safety in step 1. Hence, the additional safeguarding and complementary protective methods are designed and used to reduce risks.

Step 3: Design for Information for Use

There may remain some risks associated with the robot despite the design processes in steps 1 and 2, so those risks are identified in the information for use.

Step 1 is the most important in the risk reduction process. This is because protective measures based on the characteristics of robots or parts themselves can be effective. However, it is known from experience that well-designed complementary safeguards may fail, and information for use may not be suitable in some situations. An inherently safe design approach can be achieved by taking into account the design characteristics of the robot/module itself and/or the interaction between the person and the robot/module.

In cases where step 1 cannot reasonably remove hazards or reduce risk sufficiently, step 2 is used, and persons can be protected against hazards by using complementary protective measures associated with additional equipment (e.g., safeguards, emergency stop equipment, etc.).

The following considerations are considered in step 1, taking into account the properties of the modules (or parts) of the robot (or module) and/or characteristics of the robot (or module):

- Geometrical factors such as the travelling and working area, the forms and relative locations of the mechanical parts (for example, avoiding crushing and shearing hazards, sharp edges and corners, and protruding parts).

- Physical aspects such as limiting the actuation force and the mass and/or velocity used to avoid mechanical hazards and related risks.

- General technical knowledge of robot design used to cover mechanical stresses such as stress limits and static and dynamic balancing, materials and their properties such as hardness, toxicity, and flammability, and emission values for noise and vibration.

- Guarantee of stability for safe use In specified conditions of use whose factors are the geometry of the base, weight distribution, dynamic forces due to moving parts, vibration, and oscillations of the center of gravity.

- Pneumatic and hydraulic hazards in using the considered type of robot.

- Electrical hazards during disconnection and switching of electrical circuits.

- Guidance on electromagnetic compatibility.

- Safety functions implemented by programmable electronic control systems validated to ensure that specified performance targets such as SIL have been obtained. Validation includes testing and analysis to show that all parts interact correctly to perform the safety function and that unintended functions do not occur. This process is performed in terms of HW and SW aspects. HW such as sensors, actuators and controllers are designed and installed to meet both the functional and performance requirements of the safety function(s) to be performed by means of structural constraints, selection and/or design of modules with a known and proper probability of (dangerous) random hardware failure, and incorporation of techniques used within HW, through which systematic failures can be avoided and systematic faults controlled. SW such as operating SW and application SW is designed to satisfy the performance specifications for the safety functions. Application SW should not be reprogrammable by the user. Otherwise, access to SW dealing with safety functions should be restricted by passwords for the authorized persons.

- Provision of diagnostic systems to aid in fault finding.

- Minimizing the probability of failure of safety functions, examples of which are the use of the following parts/modules: reliable parts/modules, parts/modules with known failures, and duplicate (or redundant) modules.

The following is a summary of ISO 13849 in terms of the module, especially for a control system/module, and explains which items the module provides for its safety [4]. ISO 13849 specifies the safety of the machinery-safety-related part of a control system (SRP/CS), where SRP/CS is part of a control system that responds to safety-related input signals and generates safety-related output signals. It can be seen that all modules that have input/output (I/O) and require its safety are types of SRP/CS, an example of which is shown in Figure 4.5. In other words, an HW module with I/O is equivalent to the control system in ISO 13849, where "HW module" means only an electrical/electronic module without software parts and does not include mechanical parts.

Determining the safety functions of a robot is part of the risk assessment and reduction process. In addition, the safety functions of the control system (or HW module) are included in the safety functions of a robot. The safety function of a module can be implemented by one or more SRP/CSs and several safety functions can share one or more SRP/CSs. For example,

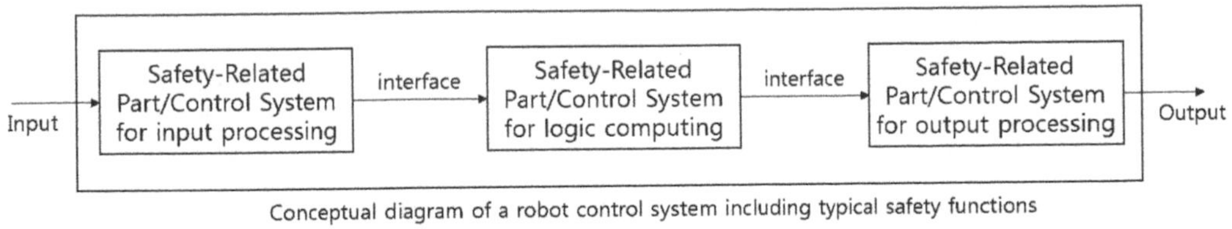

Conceptual diagram of a robot control system including typical safety functions

FIGURE 4.5   Example of a HW module composed of SRP/CSs (safety-related parts of control systems) [4].

safety functions can be separated into a motor control part, a computing part, and a power control part. Of course, one SRP/CS can implement safety functions and standard control functions for the module.

Figure 4.5 shows the combination of SRP/CSs for input, computing for control logic, and output. In addition, interconnecting methods such as parallel bus and serial lines are used for data exchange between two modules in Figure 4.5 as listed below. In Figure 4.5, the input module, the output module, and the computing module can also be examples of the SRP/CS module and the HW module in Figure 4.5 is a type of composite module.

The ability of safety-related parts to perform a safety function depends on the safety level. The safety level should be estimated for the combination of SRP/CSs and/or SRP/CS performing each safety function. The safety level of the SRP/CS is determined by estimating the following items [4]:

- Mean time to dangerous failure (MTTFD) value for a single part.

- Diagnostic coverage.

- Common cause of failure.

- Structure.

- Behavior of the safety function under fault condition(s).

- Safety-related software.

- Systematic failure.

- Ability to perform a safety function under expected environmental conditions

These items can be divided into two groups as follows.

1. Quantifiable items such as MTTFD value for single components, DC, CCF, and structure

2. Qualitative items such as behavior of the safety function under fault conditions, safety-related software, systematic failure, and environmental conditions, which affect the behavior of the SRP/CS

As an example, IEC 61800-5-x provides safety requirements for adjustable-speed electrical power drive systems including the power conversion, drive control, and motor [6,7,9]. As shown in the title of the standard of IEC 61800-5-x, safety requirements of the module can be suggested even if its application to a robot (e.g., as a manipulator for a service robot or industrial robot, mobile platform, cleaning robot, etc.) is not clear. This standard lists safety functions provided by the module. Each safety function may require a safe interface to communicate with other functions or composite modules or robots. Design of the interface is very important because the integrity of the interface affects the determination of the safety level of the associated safety function. The standard suggests that safety and integrity specifications should be made with a safety requirement specification.

4.3 HARDWARE MODULE

The hardware module should meet the requirements suggested in Section 1. That is, the hardware module basically provides reusability, composability, and interoperability, and safety may be provided depending on the application of the module. In other words, it is not necessary to provide safety when the module is used in applications that do not require safety. If the module is used in applications requiring safety, hardware modules with appropriate safety levels to match the safety level of the robot application should be selected or designed and developed. If the selected (or developed) module cannot meet the required safety level of the robot, then a redundancy structure or complementary method should be used to meet the targeted safety level. This section describes the requirements of the HW module for reusability, composability, and interoperability as the safety aspect was explained in Section 2.

As already mentioned, the HW module can be classified into the following:

- A purely mechanical module.

- A purely electrical/electronic module.

- A module consisting of mechanical parts and electrical/electronic parts.

Robots are composed of a combination of these modules from the hardware view point.

In a robot, mechanical parts constitute the skeleton or the frame, and the electrical/electronic parts operate with the mechanical parts to achieve the desired behavior. For safety, the stability of the mechanical parts and faults in the electrical/electronic parts are very important. In addition, various types of robots (for example, industrial robots, service robots, etc.) can be built depending on the configuration of the mechanical module. The electrical/electronic module, which is the actuating or sensing device, can be attached to the mechanical module to which other mechanical modules can be linked. This step continues until the robot is made. In other words, this process is called system integration. In order to make this process easier, there is a need for reusability, composability, and interoperability between modules. Interfaces of HW modules can be classified as follows:

1. Interfaces between mechanical modules and/or mechanical parts of the HW modules.

2. Interfaces between mechanical modules (or parts) and electrical/electronic modules.

3. Interfaces between electrical/electronic modules.

Interface type a) includes interfaces between mechanical modules, interfaces between a mechanical module and mechanical parts containing an electrical/electronic interface (hereafter called a mechanical part of a HW module), and interfaces between mechanical parts of HW modules. An examples of interface type (a) is shown in Figure 4.6. Interface type (b) is the interface of a mechanical module for attaching electrical/electronic modules to the mechanical module. This example may be applicable when attaching a sensing electrical module on the mobile platform. An example of interface type (b) is shown in Figure 4.7. Interface type (c) is an interface used to connect electrical/electronic modules, and its examples are interfaces such as ethernet and RS 422. An example of interface type (c) is shown in Figure 4.7. Of course, the electrical interface includes a connector as a mechanical part. Interface type (c) is applied in cases where the connections between these

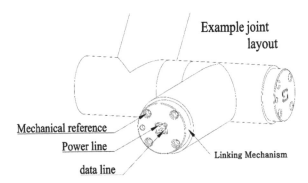

FIGURE 4.6   Mechanical interface with electrical interfaces for a joint module [1].

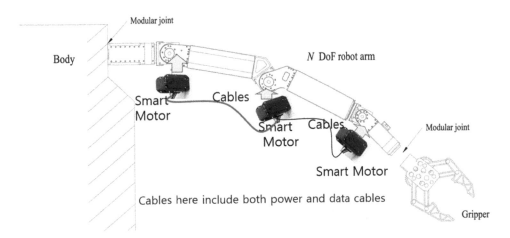

FIGURE 4.7   Mechanical interface and electrical interfaces using external cables.

connectors are cables. If this connector is attached to a mechanical part and used to connect to another module, it corresponds to interface type (b).

The interface design considerations include safety, power, data exchange, mechanical issues, etc. Methods of data exchange are divided into analog and digital signals, and digital signaling methods are recommended in order to conform to international standards.

In particular, as an interface part can have great influence on safety, it must be carefully designed. For example, in the case of interface type (a), a safety guide may be needed to prevent a person from being hurt when linking the mechanical module. In the case of interface types (b) and (c), if the mechanical module (or part) moves freely or with some limits, the electrical/electronic module or connector should be fixed so that they do not slip off.

It is very important to design the interface well to ensure reusability, interoperability, and composability of these modules. There is a need for a way to safely connect and disconnect the connectors for power and data while performing the physical operation of mechanically attaching and detaching the robot module. If these requirements are not met properly, the module can be exposed to safety risks which can result in malfunction, failure, or unsafe behavior.

The following issues are considered to ensure proper linking and function between mechanical parts/modules [1].

- Consider mechanical aspects such as module alignment, module positioning, and module locking with the desired stiffness in static and planned dynamic motions.

- Electrical (data) signals and power connections must not be damaged during the mechanical positioning and locking process.

- It is easy to attach and detach the mechanical interfaces.

- Mechanical parts used as interfaces should have rigidity to ensure the minimum number of cycles for attaching/detaching the mechanical interfaces. Of course, the same criteria should be used for electrical connectors attached to mechanical parts.

- Module interfaces must have sufficient stiffness to deliver static and dynamic forces within the appropriate safety margin between the modules.

- Modules should be able to be installed with minimal tools or without tools.

Examples of HW modules are shown in Figures 4.2, 4.6 and 4.7. These figures illustrate HW modules consisting of basic mechanical modules or composite modules with mechanical modules and electrical/electronic modules. Consider the following three examples for electrical/electronic modules:

1. A laser sensor board consisting of a PCB, CPU, laser sensor, communication chip, and memory, some ICs, some capacitors/resistors, and some SW such as a light OS, management of the sensor, communication protocol, etc.

2. A fusion sensor board consisting of a PCB, CPU, three types of sensors (a laser sensor IC, supersonic sensor IC, and vision sensor IC), communication chip, memory, some ICs, some capacitors/resistors, and some SW such as a light OS, management of the sensors, communication protocol, etc.

3. Another fusion sensor consists of a management board, a laser sensor board, a supersonic board, and a vision board where the management board consists of a CPU, memory, and a communication chip along with SWs. The fusion board collects sensor values from three types of sensor boards, receives commands from a controller, and sends the collected and/or fusion data to the controller.

In case (1), a laser sensor board can be considered as a module. However, because the PCB, CPU, laser sensor, communication chip, and OS are parts of the laser sensor board, they cannot become modules. In case (2), the fusion sensor module can be considered as a basic module because the board consists of parts such as a CPU, ICs, etc., which cannot be further subdivided into modules. That is, the fusion sensor module can be seen as a kind of basic module which provides fusion of sensor data. For case (3), the fusion sensor module is a kind of composite module consisting of a laser sensor module, supersonic module, and vision module where each board is a type of module.

4.4 SOFTWARE MODULE

Software typically has some forms such as functions, subroutines, components, and modules which are executed in a processing unit such as a CPU. A function or subroutine is a procedure (or a sequence of instructions) that performs a given task, but a module or component can be considered as a set of one or more functions or subroutines. A software module is a module that is executed in a processing unit such as a CPU and should basically guarantee the reusability, composability, and interoperability mentioned above. In terms of safety, unlike for the HW module, the failure probability cannot be obtained; however, when faults occur, it is possible for the SW module to identify and isolate the faults more precisely in order to minimize their impact.

In particular, a software module should explicitly provide its requirements for safety (for example, responses to known errors and unknown errors, etc.) and its functional requirements. The software module should be made according to the V&V procedure, which involves checking those requirements. For implementation of inherent safety, it is important to quickly identify and handle faults that occur in the SW module and/or the HW module.

The execution characteristics of the software module in the robot can be classified into the following three types:

- Periodic.

- Sporadic (real-time and asynchronous).

- Non-real-time.

The periodic and sporadic modules are real-time modules. A real-time module can be classified as either soft real-time or hard real-time. The former is a module for which the validity of a result degrades after its deadline but which can be continuously executed. The latter is a module which should be executed correctly within the deadline and causes a failure after deadline. In general, periodic modules are related to motor controls and sporadic modules are modules for event handling. A non-real-time module may be console SW that interacts with the user.

The software module should be designed to satisfy the following guidelines [1]:

1. Support exchange of data and services with other modules.

2. Support real-time services if necessary.

3. Have unique identifiers and obtain values of necessary properties for proper operation and interoperability.

4. Support modular-level safety depending on fault types likely to occur in the software module.

5. Support software platform-independence.

Item (5) means that the software module can be executed via interfaces implemented by a variety of programming languages under different operating systems with different document file formats or databases.

Operating systems or middleware are required to properly manage SW modules made according to these guidelines. SW modules should be executed on middleware in order to provide reusability, composability, and interoperability. Middleware should be able to manage these SW modules according to their characteristics so that users or developers can easily utilize them.

In order for the software module to provide reusability, composability, and interoperability, the interface must be well-defined, as mentioned in the HW module. The interface of the software module can be classified into the following three types:

• An interface for exchange of data between SW modules.

• An interface between SW and HW modules (a device driver is called).

• An interface between SW modules and an operating system or middleware.

In particular, interfaces for exchange of data between SW modules can be divided into the following types:

• Between modules within the same processing unit.

• Between modules in different processing units in the same robot.

• Between modules in the robot and modules in other robots.

• Between the robot and the modules on the server.

The following ways exist to exchange data between modules through interfaces: shared memory, server/client, publish/subscribe, and remote procedure call. In addition, there are ethernet, fieldbus (EhterCAT, CAN, Profibus, etc.), RS422/485, wireless communication (WiFi, Bluetooth, 3G/4G, etc.), etc. in terms of physical means.

The software framework for modularization can consist of software modules, middleware, operating systems, and hardware abstraction modules for hardware-dependent drivers. Hardware-dependent drivers are driver software that hardware device manufacturers provide to access their hardware. The structure of the software framework for modularity is shown in Figure 4.8.

A software module executing in a software framework consists of two parts as follows: an execution part and an attribute part to support the proper execution. The attribute part consists of attribute values of the software module and/or the related hardware modules. Examples of software attributes are the version number, type of OS being used, service type provided, and type of execution such as periodic, sporadic, and non-real-time execution. Examples of hardware attributes are the origin of the robot, the pose of the hardware sensor module with respect to the origin of the robot, the operating range of hardware actuating/sensing modules, and so on.

As mentioned earlier, SW modules can also be divided into basic and composite SW modules. Examples of the former could be sensing SW modules that read a sensor's values from basic HW sensor modules such as ultrasonic sensors, infrared sensors, or touch sensors, and send the value to other SW modules. A composite software module could

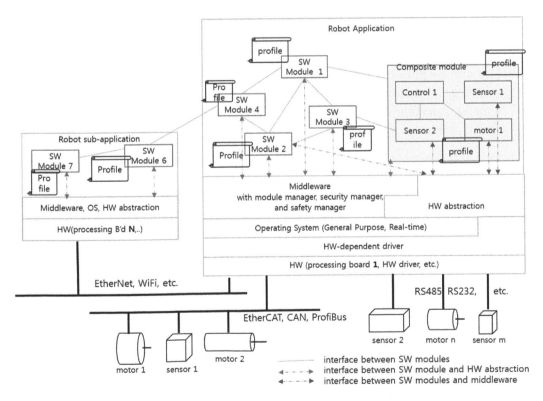

FIGURE 4.8   Architecture of software framework for service robot modularity.

comprise two or more basic software modules, and its examples include manipulation, mobility, navigation, and sensor fusion software modules. Note that a composite SW module can be implemented in a basic SW module.

The attribute values provided for proper execution are stored into the attribute profile and listed as follows [1,10]:

1. Information for the software module: manufacturer's name, module ID, version number, module type, manufacturer's address, and copyright, if relevant.

2. Execution environment: OS type, execution type (periodic, sporadic, or non-real-time), and execution period, if the execution type is periodic.

3. API types provided by modules for negotiation among software modules.

4. Information for data exchange (e.g., communication protocol and the name/ID of the hardware device, driver if necessary).

5. Values necessary to initialize the module.

6. Information for safety and security.

7. Granularity of the module (basic or composite). Note that, for a composite module, a list of basic or composite software modules used in the module is provided for checking their dependency.

8. Communication type such as ethernet, EtherCAT, CAN, RS485, or USB.

9. Pose and location of the hardware modules with respect to the origin of the robot.

10. Size and weight of hardware modules and their range of (joint) motions/measurements (e.g., measurement ranges and distances of laser scanners, size and weight of a manipulator, number of axes, range of joint motion, linkage method of each joint, size of mobile base, etc.).

11. Origin of the robot and the forward direction with respect to the origin, if necessary.

The software module needs the hardware properties to access and control the hardware modules used in the module to achieve the desired function of the module, which can be listed in (8)–(11).

Note that items (8)–(11) are not necessary for software modules not using hardware modules.

Figure 4.8 shows a software-module-based architecture that includes modules with an attribute profile, middleware controlling the modules, and so on. In addition, Figure 4.8 illustrates the relationship between the software module and the hardware module and between the software module on one processing board and that on another processing board. Software modules that can access hardware devices have two options. The first is to use the hardware-dependent driver directly and the second is to use the hardware abstraction model through which the hardware-dependent driver is linked. There is a difference between the two methods when the module accesses other hardware modules of the same type. For example, consider a SW module that measures distance using an ultrasonic sensor and an infrared sensor. For the former case, whenever the hardware module is changed, the software module should be changed to use the corresponding device driver. However, for the latter case, the software module does not need to be changed, even though the hardware module may be changed. This is because a hardware abstraction layer is used. In this layer, the abstracted API is mapped to the real hardware device driver. The disadvantage of this approach is that the execution time is slightly longer than that of the former method; however, the difference may be almost negligible.

An example of the operation of the middleware is as follows: the middleware manages mainly the execution and configuration of software modules, and can consist of a module manager, security manager, safety manager, etc. The module manager checks and uploads/downloads the files associated with the module (e.g., an execution file and an attribute file). The security manager monitors and controls what an unauthorized user can access and the sensitive data is received. The safety manager monitors the status of the software modules, predicts whether the software modules will operate safely, and controls the execution of the modules so that the robot can operate safely. The middleware must be tightly coupled with the normal OS or real-time OS in order for the modules to run within soft or hard real-time constraints.

4.5 SUMMARY

Various issues related to robot modularity have been studied to date. Modules should basically provide reusability, interoperability, and composability and provide safety-related information according to the type of the module. Module safety can be clarified by specifying the application, but in the case of a basic module, the safety level cannot be clearly set because its application is not specified. However, since a basic module can be included in a composite module for a specific application, at least the failure probability of the basic module should be provided in order for developers of the composite module to easily combine the basic modules. In addition, if the module provides a safety function, it is necessary to describe it.

Standardization of interfaces is very important for reusability, interoperability, and composability of a module. The standardization of these interfaces can lead to many kinds of standards because there are many kinds of modules. Therefore, it is necessary to make standards by grouping as many similar kinds of interfaces as possible. It is important to make a standard that is common to all modules of the same type. In other words, it is necessary to make a standard that contains the necessary minimal interface for all modules of the same type.

In order to use a SW module dynamically, it is important for users to easily operate robot SW modules periodically, sporadically, and in non-real-time and to facilitate data exchange between SW modules. Middleware performing these functions is important.

It is expected that the interfaces of the robot modules will be standardized, and that various robots can then be made by purchasing the modules at a low price.

REFERENCES

1. ISO, ISO/NP 22166 -1 Modularity for service robots – Part 1 – General requirements.
2. ISO, ISO 13849 Safety of machinery — Safety-related parts of control systems — Part 1: General principles for design.
3. ISO, ISO 10218-2 Robots and robotic devices — Safety requirements for industrial robots — Part 2: Robot systems and integration.
4. ISO, ISO 12100 Safety of machinery — General principles for design — Risk assessment and risk reduction.
5. IEC, IEC 61508-1, Functional safety of electrical/electronic/programmable electronic safety-related systems – Part 1: General requirements.
6. IEC, IEC 61508-2, Functional safety of electrical/electronic/programmable electronic safety-related systems – Part 2: Requirements for electrical/electronic/programmable electronic safety-related systems.
7. IEC, IEC 61508-3, Functional safety of electrical/electronic/programmable electronic safety-related systems – Part 3: Software requirements.
8. OPRoS, www.ropros.org.
9. M-TECH, http://m-tech.co.kr.
10. J.-J. Kim, S. Hong, W. Lee, S. Kang, et al., ModMan: Self-reconfigurable modular manipulation system for expansion of robot applicability, the 19th International Conference on Climbing and Walking Robots and Support Technologies for Mobile Machines (CLAWAR 2016), London, September 2016.

CHAPTER 5

Human–Robot Shared Workspace in Aerospace Factories

Gilbert Tang and Phil Webb

CONTENTS

5.1	Introduction	71
5.2	Drivers for Human-Robot Collaboration in Aerospace Manufacturing	72
5.3	Challenges in Human–Robot Collaboration in Aerospace Manufacturing	73
	5.3.1 Limitations of Robots	73
	5.3.2 Safety of HRI	74
	5.3.3 Working Environment	74
	5.3.4 Human Factors	75
	5.3.5 Human–Robot Interface	75
5.4	Recognising and Defining Different Types of Collaborative Activities	75
5.5	Industrial Case Studies	76
	5.5.1 Case Study: GKN Aerospace's Fokker Business	76
	5.5.2 Case Study: Airbus A350 XWB Wing Skin Drilling and Tacking	77
	5.5.3 Case Study: Boeing 777 Fuselage Automated Upright Build	77
	5.5.4 Case Study: Airbus's Futurassy Project	78
5.6	Concluding Remarks	78
	References	79

5.1 INTRODUCTION

The application of robotics technology in aerospace manufacturing is relatively new and the rate of technology adoption has remained slow compared with other manufacturing sectors. However, increasing global demand for aerospace products of high and consistent quality at higher production rates and a widening skill gap within the workforce have encouraged the deployment of flexible automation solutions and collaborative systems [1]. The introduction of industrial collaborative robots combined with updated robot safety standards in recent years have broadened the potential of robotic applications in complex environments and make their deployment possible in conjunction with manual processes. Collaborative robots can operate in manual working environments without additional safeguards, but they are still limited in performance and capabilities. However, it is also important to consider the type of process and end-effector as these may pose a greater risk than the manipulator alone. On the other hand, conventional industrial robot systems have the capabilities required for completing a much broader range of manufacturing tasks, but they require safeguarding to exclude operators from their working envelope. Before the introduction of contactless safety monitoring technology, robots were traditionally caged and totally separated from people. The cages not only prevent any kind of collaboration between robots and humans, but they also require substantial floor space which is highly restricted for most small and medium enterprises (SMEs). With the introduction of safety monitoring technology, it is possible to prevent human workers from colliding with a moving robot without any hard safeguards, but such setups tend to require complex risk assessments prior to implementation onto the factory floor. The updated industrial robot safety standards ISO 10218-2 indicates that it is acceptable to use off-the-shelf safety monitoring systems for human detection, but there must be a safe separating distance between the moving robot and people. Furthermore, the ISO/TS 15066 was introduced recently to supplement the requirements and guidance on collaborative industrial robot operation given in the aforementioned standards.

In collaborative systems, human operators and robots can work together as a team and it is logical to consider the human operators as an integral part of the system. In this case, human operators and robots must interact and communicate effectively and efficiently in order to maximise the productivity of the system. Therefore, the design process of collaborative systems should consider aspects beyond technology such as human factors, human–robot interface, human–robot interaction (HRI) and safety.

This chapter discusses drivers and challenges in implementing industrial collaborative systems in aerospace manufacturing and four industrial cases are described.

5.2 DRIVERS FOR HUMAN–ROBOT COLLABORATION IN AEROSPACE MANUFACTURING

Aerospace manufacturing involves various discrete stages where subassemblies of increasing size and complexity are progressively combined to produce the final product. Starting from the basic level, raw materials are machined and fabricated into parts and then assembled into simple subsystems. They are subsequently combined into larger more complex subsystems and into higher-level assemblies that form the wings, fuselage, tailplane and the final aircraft. The key processes involved in the assembly of these parts are drilling, countersinking, fastening and riveting. These processes can be labour intensive and time consuming, and they are associated with many ergonomic issues such as musculoskeletal injuries. Current automation of these processes uses very large 'monument' machines that are very costly and relatively inflexible. Furthermore, the introduction of ever more stringent health and safety legislation along with an increasing fear of litigation resulting from industrial injuries is making the continuation of conventional assembly methods using manual handling and processes such as hand drilling and riveting undesirable. Hand riveting, in particular, is linked to vibration-induced conditions of the hands and arms and is becoming more and more strictly regulated. Moreover, most of the economies that form the traditional centre of the aerospace manufacturing industry have an ageing labour force and a general shortage of the highly skilled labour required by the industry. It is widely agreed that automation is one of the best possible solutions to these issues. However, the use of custom-made machine and fixed automation are economically prohibited in many cases due to high change over cost and substantial initial investment. On the other hand, robots are highly reconfigurable, adaptable and flexible enough for changes in the design of products as well as changes in the processes.

The primary reasons for slow technology adoption are the limitations of robots. For instance, their working envelope relative to the size of the parts and their relative positional inaccuracy and lack of stiffness but they have increased usage in aerospace applications as their capabilities improve [2]. Another challenge for using robots in aerospace manufacturing is the deployment of robot systems in manual environments that was impossible before the introduction of collaborative technology. Furthermore, many aerospace manufacturing processes require production workers to work within confined spaces with limited access or to work on complex geometries that require the dexterity and flexibility of humans. In this case, human and robot work teams could address some of these shortfalls by combining their strengths and resulting in a production system that is flexible, efficient and effective. Robots could assist in carrying out tedious and monotonous tasks with human workers performing intellectually demanding tasks.

5.3 CHALLENGES IN HUMAN–ROBOT COLLABORATION IN AEROSPACE MANUFACTURING

There are a number of unique challenges associated with humans and robots cooperating in aerospace manufacturing processes and these factors have influenced the progress of technology adoption in various ways.

5.3.1 Limitations of Robots

The robots used in aerospace applications are generally conventional industrial systems of anthropomorphic design with six degrees of freedom and typical payload capabilities of over 200 kg. The high payload capability is often required not for the loads that they are required to carry but the process forces encountered, for example, reaction forces from drilling or countersinking. This is an area where collaborative robots are currently deficient with a maximum payload of 35 kg available on the market and their force-torque limited safety function could be sensitive to forces and vibration-induced from work processes, but collaborative robots are improving at a fast pace with increased performance and capabilities. It is possible to use conventional industrial robots in a collaborative cell when integrated with a safety-rated monitoring system [6], but the robot and the human operator must be separated by a safe distance as described in the robot safety standards

ISO 10218-2. The calculation of the minimum safe distance depends heavily on the robot speed, and it is often necessary to significantly restrict the speed of the robot to achieve a usable safe separation distance.

Current high payload robots and collaborative robots have repeatability better than ±0.08 mm, whereas a decade ago, articulated robots could not meet the normal quoted manufacturing tolerance of 0.1 mm for aerospace applications [2]. Similar to conventional robot systems, the accuracy of collaborative robot systems can be enhanced by using metrology or vision guided systems for guidance and calibration. To address limitations in robot reach, robot arms can be mobilised via linear track systems or mobile platforms to expand the working envelope for the relatively large aerospace parts and flexibility for sharing resources [3].

5.3.2 Safety of HRI

Safety is a particularly important consideration when using robots in aerospace manufacturing, not only due to the high-performance heavy-duty robots used in these applications but also the layout of the shared open workspace. Collaborative robots could be used in some processes at subassembly levels where only a small payload is required, but in many cases, the hazards lie in the task itself, for example, pinch point from drill bit and sealant nozzle, ejection of swarf [4]. In this case, protective equipment such as safety monitoring 3D cameras and safety laser scanners could be used for both conventional and collaborative robots to monitor the robot work space in real-time [5,6]. These systems are programmable for adapting into different workstation layouts and safety profiles, the layout of the shared workspace could be segregated into zones with different levels of risk. For example, it can reduce the speed of the robot when workers are detected in a warning zone or to trigger a protective stop when they reached the danger zone; the human operator can resume robot operation from a protective stop once they have confirmed that the workspace is safe for continuing the work. The setup of safety monitoring for any large-scale manufacturing cells must consider all possible blind spots when positioning safety sensors because large parts could hide human operators away from the view of a sensor which could bypass the safety check during recovery. A multi-sensor configuration could ensure that a workspace is fully monitored at all times.

5.3.3 Working Environment

Many aircraft being manufactured today were designed between 15 and 30 years ago, before automation was considered feasible, so their product and factory designs are not optimal for robot operations. There are often multiple processes being carried out simultaneously in the same workstation due to the relatively large size of the parts to optimise the workflow. While it is a significant challenge to retrofit a robot system into these existing workstations to automate some of the procedures, it is also an opportunity to utilise and demonstrate the full advantage of collaborative technology to have a shared workspace between human workers and robots. However, the implementation of the new process must be carried out swiftly to minimise disruption to production.

5.3.4 Human Factors

Human operators are an essential part of a collaborative production system and therefore the well-being of these human operators can directly affect the overall performance of the system. Trust has been identified as a key element for the productivity of human–robot collaboration and research has been carried out to develop evaluation methods to quantify the different levels of trust in HRI and factors that influence trust in industrial robots [7]. The level of trust must be optimised to minimise human error and to avoid other human factors issues. For example, overtrust could lead to a drop in situational awareness which could result in poor reactions in the event of unexpected incidents, and too little trust will increase the cognitive workload of the human operators. The human factors of a collaborative system could be affected by variables which include separation distance between humans and robots, size, speed, trajectory and the level of autonomy. Research is being carried out to draw links between these different system parameters for a better understanding on how to improve useability in industrial collaborative systems [8].

5.3.5 Human–Robot Interface

A successful human–robot team exhibits three characteristics: interpredictability, common ground and directability. A human operator should have awareness of the robot's state and its immediate future state in order to react appropriately to the robot's action, which will avoid costly interruption of the process. The robot and its operator should be working towards a common goal and the human operator should be able to change its course when necessary. Therefore, the design of the human–robot interfaces has a great effect on how well a system will perform. It is particularly difficult in aerospace manufacturing as robots and human operators could be separated by greater distance compared with other industries, and while humans and robots are working together in a dynamic shared workspace they could be working on different tasks. A contactless user interface will enable human operators to give commands to robots anywhere within the workspace; this type of communication could be achieved using natural user interfaces such as gesture control, voice control and multi-modal systems [9,10]. Furthermore, a human–robot interface should be designed using a user-centred methodology to address key human factor issues that include cognitive and physical workload, awareness and trust; user interface and collaborative system should be evaluated through iterative development processes with the goal to maximise useability.

5.4 RECOGNISING AND DEFINING DIFFERENT TYPES OF COLLABORATIVE ACTIVITIES

Any activities or processes that involve humans and robots working in a shared workspace vary in their level of interaction and proximity; these scenarios are classified into coexistence, cooperation and collaboration. **Coexistence** describes situations where the human operator and robot do not interact during the process in any way and do not share a common goal. In human–robot **cooperation**, the human and robot complete their individual stages of the process within the same workspace but at different times. For example, in aircraft assembly, an industrial robot can manipulate and position a part and a human operator subsequently secures the part to the aero-structure. **Collaboration** involves a much higher level of interaction where the human and robot work towards a common goal – working together in proximity and at the same time. A collaborative system may consist of a robot assistant helping the human partner in a coordinated and synchronous manner, for example, a robot holding a component for the human operator to work on and to change position and orientation of the part when required and without the human having to vacate the working area.

The individual activities in collaborative processes can be classified into three categories: interaction, interruption and intervention. **Interactions** are routine activities which involve the operator and the robot working together inside a collaborative workspace in proximity to each other. A crucial aspect of interaction is the presence of two-way communications between the partners throughout the process. Examples of interaction are hand-guided assembly and robot-assisted assembly. **Intervention** describes a situation where either the robot or the human operator has to stop work temporarily as their next task depends on the other party completing their task. Examples of these activities include refill and removal of materials, manual inspection, maintenance and manual rework. The operator can carry out the work within the collaborative workspace or through an interface window. **Interruption** describes unexpected events that cause disruption to both automated and manual processes due to external influences such as an Estop, intrusion of unauthorised personnel, stopping to enable an unrelated process to proceed in the same physical area or other unforeseen occurrences (e.g., breakdown). The human operator, in this case, is responsible for remediation such as a programme restart to resume normal activity.

5.5 INDUSTRIAL CASE STUDIES

In this section, four industrial use-cases of human–robot collaboration and use of collaborative robots in aerospace manufacturing are described.

5.5.1 Case Study: GKN Aerospace's Fokker Business

GKN Aerospace launched an idea to introduce collaborative robots in their production plants in mid-2016. Amongst sub-companies involved in this initiative were Fokker Aerostructures and Fokker Landing Gear [11].

Fokker Aerostructures proposed to use a KUKA LBR iiwa 14 kg payload collaborative robot for drilling on the A350 Outboard Flap assembly line. The robot has to perform drilling using an automated drill unit (ADU) by inserting the ADU into various predrilled holes on a drilling template with overall hole clearance of 0.1 mm. The collaborative robot will be used in a shared workspace with humans, so it was considered to operate the collaborative robot in collaborative mode with speed restricted to 250 mm/s and force/torque limitations applied, but the low speed has no significant effect on productivity since the drilling positions are very close together. For the final solution, the collaborative robot will be mounted on either a gantry system or mobile platform.

Fokker Landing Gear selected the sealant application for automation after evaluating several manual activities. In the landing gear system, bushings are installed to protect components for wear at rotary surfaces. The sealant application involves applying a bead of sealant at the transition between bush and component to prevent corrosion. The manual process was physically demanding and tedious due to the number of bushings, which led to an unstable quality of sealant bead. Furthermore, aerospace sealant consists of elements which pose health and safety risks with prolonged exposure. To automate this process, a Universal Robot UR10 was used with a sealant dispensing end-effector. A human operator has to insert a sealant cartridge with mixed sealant into a holder on the end-effector. The sealant dispensing is controlled by pressure applied to a piston at the back of the cartridge and the flow of sealant is regulated by a volume driven system. The robot speed is limited to a safe application level while matching the flow of sealant being dispensed through a metallic nozzle. A force sensor was installed to detect any pressure applied on the dispensing nozzle to stop the collaborative robot and prevent possible injury caused by the sharp component. The human operator is responsible for a final visual inspection before the subassembly is released for further processing.

Both presented cases expect to provide economic advantage from reduced man hours and ergonomic benefits by minimising unhealthy work processes.

5.5.2 Case Study: Airbus A350 XWB Wing Skin Drilling and Tacking

An example of HRI in these applications is the drilling and tacking of A350 XWB wing skins at the Airbus factory in Broughton, North Wales, UK. The primary assembly cells are where carbon fibre composite wing boxes are assembled in a purpose-built jig. The horizontally oriented wing boxes are drilled and tacked in two separate levels, upper and lower work stations.

A gantry type robot is used for the drilling and slave fastener insertion of the upper wing skin and a bespoke cell transferable robotic drilling machine is used to carry out the same operations on the bottom wing skin. During the drilling operations, production workers must observe the operation to ensure that it is going smoothly. In the event of the robot reaching a point of uncertainty or error, the worker will interact with the robot by checking and confirming that it is appropriate to carry on. The workers also intervene with the robot for interval tasks such as refilling lubricant and emptying the swarf bin. To ensure the safety of the production workers, the robots and gantries are integrated with laser safety sensors to monitor the surroundings and tactile sensors for post-collision protective stop. As an additional precaution, robot operators have to hold a dead man's switch to activate the robots [12].

5.5.3 Case Study: Boeing 777 Fuselage Automated Upright Build

The Fuselage Automated Upright Build (FAUB) process is another example of integrated robotic drilling and riveting applications. FAUB is used on the production line that assembles the forward and aft fuselage sections of the Boeing 777 jetliner. Two of the drivers for this robot deployment are to reduce repetitive stress injuries on the production workers and improving quality to reduce costly rework [13]. This process involves cooperation between human operators and robots where the floor beams, frames and panels are loaded and assembled manually prior to the automated process. Mobile robot systems move into their working positions once components are in place and synchronous robots combine the fuselage panels by working in pairs from both sides of the fuselage to complete the process simultaneously. The robot on the exterior side of the fuselage is equipped with a multi-purpose end-effector for drilling the hole, inserting the fastener and hammering it, while the robot on the interior stabilises the structure for creating the rivet [14,15].

Robot operators monitor the process from workstations outside of the robots' working envelope to ensure any requirements for intervention are attended to immediately.

5.5.4 Case Study: Airbus's Futurassy Project

Aircraft manufacturers are seeking ways of automating repetitive tasks using robots to free up their highly skilled production workers for higher value tasks that utilise human strengths. The main challenge is to properly integrate the robots into the human workspace to maintain a safe and productive shared working environment. Airbus has experimented with humanoid robots in their Puerto Real plant in Cádiz, Spain, to automate their assembly processes. The aim was to introduce a harmonised robotic solution that is transferable to other Airbus sites. The collaborative robot used in the research project was HIRO, a twin-arm upper body humanoid platform made by Kawada Industries. The plan was to integrate the robot at the A380 rudder spar assembly station to share riveting tasks with their human counterpart [16].

5.6 CONCLUDING REMARKS

The development of robotic and safety technologies has broadened the applications of industrial robots in aerospace manufacturing where the working environment is predominately manual.

Collaborative robots have the advantage of being able to be deployed onto the shop floor without the requirement of hard safeguards which would enable aerospace suppliers and manufacturers to automate some of their processes with a relatively low cost and complexity when compared with conventional systems. This kind of system allows for close integration between humans and robots where separating distance is low and interaction is frequent.

For final stage assembly processes where large components are involved, high performance robots integrated with safety monitoring systems are used. However, the level of HRI is restricted to cooperation where humans and robots work on subsequent stages without direct interaction. In this case, the robot operator who monitors the robots for anomalies could be performing other manual tasks simultaneously, and often with the presence of other production workers in coexistence.

With the continued improvement of interactive and robotic technologies, the integration between humans and robots in an aerospace manufacturing environment is advancing towards a proximity level where humans and robots will work together in a truly collaborative fashion.

REFERENCES

1. Webb, P. (2010). Automated Aerospace Manufacture and Assembly. In R. Blockley & W. Shyy (eds.), Encyclopedia of Aerospace Engineering. Chichester: Wiley

2. Summers, M. (2005). Robot capability test and development of industrial robot positioning system for the aerospace industry (No. 2005-01-3336). SAE Technical Paper.

3. Jackson, T. (2017). High-accuracy articulated mobile robots (No. 2017-01-2095). SAE Technical Paper.

4. Vogel, C., & Saenz, J. (2016). Optical workspace monitoring system for safeguarding tools on the mobile manipulator VALERI. In ISR 2016: 47st International Symposium on Robotics; Proceedings of, Munich, Germany (pp. 1–6). VDE.

5. Fritzsche, M., Saenz, J., & Penzlin, F. (2016). A large scale tactile sensor for safe mobile robot manipulation. In The Eleventh ACM/IEEE International Conference on Human Robot Interaction (pp. 427–428). Christchurch, New Zealand: IEEE Press.

6. Walton, M., Webb, P., & Poad, M. (2011). Applying a concept for robot-human cooperation to aerospace equipping processes (No. 2011-01-2655). SAE Technical Paper.

7. Charalambous, G., Fletcher, S., & Webb, P. (2016). The development of a scale to evaluate trust in industrial human-robot collaboration. *International Journal of Social Robotics*, 8(2), 193–209.

8. Charalambous, G. (2014). The development of a human factors tool for the successful implementation of industrial human-robot collaboration. PhD thesis, Cranfield University, Cranfield, United Kingdom.

9. Tang, G., Asif, S., & Webb, P. (2015). The integration of contactless static pose recognition and dynamic hand motion tracking control system for industrial human and robot collaboration. *Industrial Robot: An International Journal*, 42(5), 416–428.

10. Brown, C. C., MacNair Smith, H., Miller, J., & Page, T. (2005, March). The design and development of a robotic assembly system for consumer products assisted by voice control. Society of Manufacturing Engineers (SME), Dearborn, MI. Technical Paper TP05PUB32, 1–8.

11. Muijs, L., & Snijders, M. (2017). Collaborative robot applications at GKN aerospace's fokker business (No. 2017-01-2091). SAE Technical Paper.

12. Wingbox Assembly Lines (2017), https://electroimpact.com/wingbox.aspx.

13. Mechanic and Machine: Boeing's Advanced Manufacturing Improves 777 Assembly (2017), www.boeing.com/features/2017/02/faub-777-assembly-02-17.page.

14. Aerospace Manufacturing on Board with Robots (2016), www.robotics.org/content-detail.cfm/Industrial-Robotics-Industry-Insights/Aerospace-Manufacturing-on-Board-with-Robots/content_id/5960.

15. Thank These Riveting Robots for Planes that Don't Fall Apart (2017), www.wired.com/2017/03/boeing-faub-assembly-robot-777/.

16. Airbus Plant in Spain Spearheads the FUTURASSY Project (2014), www.airbus.com/newsroom/press-releases/en/2014/02/airbus-invests-in-robotics-as-part-of-its-commitment-to-innovation.html.

CHAPTER 6

Workspace Sharing in Mobile Manipulation

José Saenz

CONTENTS

6.1   What are Mobile Manipulators?   81
6.2   Simple Versus True Mobile Manipulation   82
6.3   Motivation for Mobile Manipulators   82
6.4   Starting Point: Risk Analysis   83
    6.4.1   Pick and Place Task   84
    6.4.2   Third-Hand Applications Featuring Hand-Guiding   84
    6.4.3   Processes Involving Contact (Manipulator and/or Tool in Contact with a Part)   84
    6.4.4   Process Without Contact with Parts   85
    6.4.5   Process Without HRC   85
6.5   Risk Analysis: Focus on Simple Mobile Manipulation   85
    6.5.1   Simple Mobile Manipulation: Only Platform Motion   85
    6.5.2   Simple Mobile Manipulation: Only Manipulator Motion   86
6.6   Safety Sensors   86
6.7   Special Challenges in Mobile Mobility   87
    6.7.1   Integration of Two Separate Systems   87
    6.7.2   Forces and Speeds Due to Combined Motions   87
    6.7.3   Unplanned Restart/Error Recovery   87
6.8   Conclusion   87
References   88

6.1 WHAT ARE MOBILE MANIPULATORS?

Mobile manipulators are defined as a combination of a mobile robotic platform or autonomously guided vehicle (AGV) together with a robotic manipulator (in particular, an articulated robotic arm). For the purposes of this chapter, we will focus on autonomously guided platforms, as opposed to passively mobile platforms such as the KUKA FlexFellow[1] or the Bosch APAS.[2] Example systems that are covered under this definition include the research platforms LiSA, PR2,[3] VALERI,[4] Care-o-Bot, ANNIE, and CARLoS, as well as systems that have recently or will soon become commercially available, including KUKA KMR, fetch, Tiago, and Magazino (Figures 6.1 and 6.2).

6.2 SIMPLE VERSUS TRUE MOBILE MANIPULATION

In the literature,[5] there has also been a distinction between simple mobile manipulation and true mobile manipulation.[6] In the case of simple mobile manipulation, the system is operated as two separate entities; either the platform moves or the manipulator moves, and the simultaneous movement of both sub-systems is not allowed. In the case of true mobile manipulation, the platform and manipulator are treated as a single kinematic chain, resulting in a system with a high degree of redundancy and higher overall complexity, but with more options in terms of fulfilling specific tasks that need to be completed in one move. This choice has large implications, both for the task to be carried out, but specifically for how to safeguard the mobile manipulator.

6.3 MOTIVATION FOR MOBILE MANIPULATORS

Given their large operational workspaces on the shop floor, there is a strong motivation from industrial end-users for mobile manipulators to be collaborative in nature and to be able to work side by side with humans. This frees up floor space and offers maximum

FIGURE 6.1 Examples of mobile manipulators from research, from left to right: VALERI mobile manipulator, ©Fraunhofer IFF; LiSA mobile laboratory assistant, ©Fraunhofer IFF; CARLoS mobile manipulator, ©AIMEN; ANNIE mobile manipulator, ©Fraunhofer IFF.

FIGURE 6.2 Examples of commercially available mobile manipulators, from left to right: KUKA KMR mobile manipulator, ©KUKA AG; Fetch mobile manipulator with Freight Base, ©fetch robotics; TORU Cube ©Magazino GmbH.

flexibility in terms of where the mobile manipulators can work. These advantages, however, place a great number of requirements on mobile manipulators including

- Accurate localization on the shop floor.

- Accurate referencing of the robot relative to parts, especially when the parts are not in fixtures or the fixtures are not in a fixed pose relative to the room or other points of reference.

- Ensuring human safety when robots work in a collaborative workspace without separating fences.

In general, the challenges regarding localization can be viewed within the context of the paradigm change, from deterministic, program based robotics where all parts are in fixtures with exact locations and the robot can move blindly, to a more cognitive, sensor-based paradigm where the environment and parts need to be sensed and the robot needs to react to eventual changes.[7,8] A simplified safety analysis for a mobile manipulator may try to separate the platform motion from the manipulator motion (simple mobile manipulation) and then use standard safeguarding techniques for each mode. As we will see in this section, the combination of mobility and manipulation capabilities leads to emergent properties in safety that are novel. This chapter will focus on safety challenges due to the combination of mobility with manipulation capabilities.

6.4 STARTING POINT: RISK ANALYSIS

The recently published standards ISO 10218-1[9] and -2,[10] as well as ISO TS 15066,[11] provide a useful starting point for discussing the safety of mobile manipulators. One of the main concepts for considering the safety of a specific system is the risk analysis. In short, there is not a specific robotic component (e.g., robot, sensor, tool, etc.) that is inherently safe. A risk analysis, which considers the entire system, the form of collaboration, and the application, is necessary for every robotic installation. It therefore follows that in order to discuss and understand the safety challenges of mobile manipulators, it is necessary to consider them in the full context of a robotic application. Typical industrial applications for mobile manipulators include

- Pick and place

- Third-hand applications featuring hand-guiding

- Processes involving contact (manipulator and/or tool in contact with a part)

  - Drilling, riveting ([12])

  - Assembly ([13])

- Process without contact with parts

  - Inspection (VALERI, Mainbot[14])

- Process without HRC (due to chemical exposure and/or other types of non-ergonomic aspects)

  - Painting

  - Welding (CARLoS Project)

6.4.1 Pick and Place Task

The name pick and place describes this general type of task well. In such cases, the robot has to pick up a specific object or carrier with multiple parts and transport them to a separate location. This can be kits, for example, which are assembled in one location and delivered to the assembly line at another location. This, however, can also include tasks where the robot is stationary for the entire pick and place actions, but then moves to different stations at different locations to carry out other tasks. This includes a wide range of warehouse and logistics tasks.

Normally, this task does not require any work on the same part by a human, so co-existence[15] is the most typical type of collaboration. However, in cases where humans need to be in the same area as the robot to carry out parallel tasks or where contact between humans and robots can occur (again most likely due to space constraints), the type of collaboration could be classified as sequential collaboration or even true collaboration. Currently, there are no known cases in industry featuring parallel collaboration, where a human works on the same part that the robot is picking, while it is being picked. In research, such a use-case was demonstrated by Fraunhofer IFF,[16] but this has only been a research demonstration up until now.

This type of task typically only requires simple mobile manipulation. There is no clear necessity to be able to move the platform and the manipulator at the same time to pick or place an object.

6.4.2 Third-Hand Applications Featuring Hand-Guiding

Applications featuring mobile manipulators as a third hand have been described for assisting during the manual assembly of components. In known cases, the application features extremely sensitive and expensive components that are manually mounted onto systems with a small lot size. Given the sensitivity of the parts and their high variability, the combination of a human operator with a robot to carry the load and hold it in a stable position while being fastened was seen as a suitable and economical means to utilize the mobile manipulator. This task can be classified as collaboration and is safeguarded through hand-guiding. This task currently only requires simple mobile manipulation.

6.4.3 Processes Involving Contact (Manipulator and/or Tool in Contact with a Part)

A large number of processes require contact between the robot and the part in order to complete the task. A few examples include drilling, riveting, and/or applying sealant. These processes are different from pick and place tasks, as they feature additional hazards due to the tooling for performing the process. These types of processes are typically safeguarded by safety-rated monitored stop or speed and separation monitoring, due to the risks from contact with, for example, rotating tools, and the types of collaboration involved include co-existence, sequential collaboration, and in limited cases, parallel collaboration. Specific tasks such as drilling or riveting can be better executed by a system featuring simple mobile manipulation. Other tasks such as applying sealant along a long groove can also require true mobile manipulation.

6.4.4 Process Without Contact with Parts

Inspection is a typical example of a process that does not require contact with parts. For such tasks, the robot can perhaps move close to a part, but it typically is working with tools that do not have a high hazard potential. These types of tasks do not usually require the presence of humans during normal operation, and the type of collaboration is typically co-existence. Should other tasks nearby require the presence of humans in the same working area, it is possible to have sequential cooperation, parallel cooperation, or even collaboration. Since no contact forces between the tool and the robot are expected, it is even possible to use the sensitivity in the joints of a robot to detect possible collisions with humans reliably. As such, it is possible to safeguard such processes through safety-rated monitored stops, speed and separation monitoring, and power and force limiting.

6.4.5 Process Without HRC

This final group of processes is here to remind the reader that while mobile robots may be collaborative in general, there are nevertheless certain processes for which it is not necessary to have humans in the same workspace. An example of such tasks includes when the robot is carrying a particularly dangerous tool, like for welding or a laser cutter, or where other hazardous emissions (sound, particles, etc.) are released due to the process. These applications only feature co-existence and are typically safeguarded by a safety-rated monitored stop.

6.5 RISK ANALYSIS: FOCUS ON SIMPLE MOBILE MANIPULATION

Looking beyond the processes carried out by the mobile manipulator, there is also the possibility (particularly for simple mobile manipulation) of looking at the risks arising due to platform motion and separating them from the risks due to manipulator motion.

6.5.1 Simple Mobile Manipulation: Only Platform Motion

For platform motion, the standard DIN EN 1525[17] specifies maximum allowable contact forces when bumpers or other types of sensors detect contact between the mobile platform and a person are used.[18] The final contact force after braking should not exceed 750 N for a testing body with a diameter of 200 mm and a height of 600 mm. Furthermore, for a testing body with diameter 70 mm and height of 400 mm, the initial contact force must not exceed 250 N and the final force acting on the body, after braking is finished, may not be larger than 400 N. These limit values are in contradiction to the biomechanical limits currently specified by the ISO TS 15066, which states a maximum permissible force of 130 N and a maximum permissible pressure of 220 N/cm^2 for the middle of the shin for quasi-static contact, and double those values for the case of transient contact. In any case, when contact between the platform and a human is allowed, tests need to be carried out with the complete system to determine the maximum allowable speed which results in forces and pressures below those specified in the standards.

Alternative standard safeguarding modes include a safety-rated monitored stop or speed and separation monitoring. In this case, separation distances as defined in the ISO 13855[19] should be applied.

A further consideration that places restrictions on the environment, and possibly the application, is the requirement from DIN EN 1525 that a minimum safety distance of 0.5 m in width and 2.1 m high must be available on both sides of the platform. If the platform drives with a continuous speed along a stationary part, and there is less than 0.1 m distance between all parts of the platform and the stationary part, then it is sufficient if there is a minimum safety distance on 0.5 m in width and 2.1 m in height only one side of the platform. This can be a particularly large challenge when inserting mobile manipulators into existing workspaces, which were not initially designed to allow the minimum safety distance. Even when working at the minimum distance, the robot will need to be safeguarded in that instance according to power and force limiting, which can greatly reduce the maximum allowable speed when moving through the tight space.

6.5.2 Simple Mobile Manipulation: Only Manipulator Motion

The manipulator motion can be safeguarded in a number of ways. The simplest case is to continue with the safeguarding modes: safety-rated monitored stop or speed and separation monitoring. In this case, manipulator motion will be stopped when a human approaches the robot at distances determined by ISO 13855 and or ISO TS 15066. This strategy simplifies the hardware requirements since any robot tool and parts to be manipulated are safeguarded as well. This is not the case should power and force limiting be chosen as the safeguarding mode. Considering that a large portion of currently used mobile manipulators feature a lightweight robot arm as the manipulator, and further considering that many lightweight robot arms feature internal measures to allow for power and force limiting, it is principally possible to switch to this safeguarding mode during pure manipulator motion. Nevertheless, as previously stated, it is also important to consider the tool used, the parts manipulated, and the process during this decision.

6.6 SAFETY SENSORS

Given the risks involved for typical applications, the type of collaboration necessary for a given application, and the safeguarding mode to be used, it is then possible to choose a suitable safety sensor (either a single type or a combination of different types). Typical, commercially available safety sensors for mobile manipulators include

- Laser scanner
- Ultrasonic proximity detectors
- Bumper (or some kind of tactile sensor)
- Torque sensing in joints of manipulator

In research there have also been instances of the increased use of tactile sensors,[20] wearable-based sensors[21] (for person localization), and camera-based safety sensors,[22] either stationary in specific workspaces where collaboration can take place or on the mobile manipulator. Ambient, stationary sensors have been one approach to increase speed, but have not been seen outside of research.

6.7 SPECIAL CHALLENGES IN MOBILE MOBILITY

In the following, we would like to briefly highlight specific safety challenges that are particular to mobile manipulators. These challenges have been described in more detail by Marvel and Bostelman[23] and are the focus of ongoing work to harmonize standards (e.g., reduce contradictions between ISO/TS 15066 and EN 1525) and develop validation[24] methods, in particular the R15.08[25] from the American National Standards Institute (ANSI).

6.7.1 Integration of Two Separate Systems

Typically, a mobile manipulator consists of an existing AGV upon which a manipulator is mounted. Thus, it is an integrated system featuring two separate control systems and safety loops, which do not necessarily allow for the exchange of safety-critical information.

6.7.2 Forces and Speeds Due to Combined Motions

Again, assuming that the mobile manipulator is an integrated combination of two separate systems, issues such as the dynamic stability of the platform while the manipulator is supporting a heavy load, or combined velocities that are higher than a single controller allows, can be quite a challenge.

6.7.3 Unplanned Restart/Error Recovery

A particular challenge for safety in mobile manipulation is defining correct behaviour due to an unplanned restart or from error recovery. The system needs to be sure that a manipulator and/or platform motion can be safely executed without risk of collision with the environment. This places high requirements on the environmental sensing, as well as the overall localization of the system. Platforms which can be manually moved by an operator are especially at risk of collision during a restart.

6.8 CONCLUSION

Due to their flexibility, mobile manipulators have a large potential for use in a wide variety of domains, from industrial manufacturing and warehouse logistics to healthcare and domestic applications in the home. Thanks to recent advances in robotics, first mobile manipulators are now commercially available and their widespread uptake is expected.

In order to discuss the topic of safety and mobile manipulators, we described typical applications according to the type of collaboration involved, the process being carried out, and any specific safety hazards. While each application is different and requires its own in-depth risk analysis, we hoped to provide a starting point for understanding safety issues concerning mobile manipulators. We provided a brief overview of existing safety sensors used to safeguard mobile manipulators. Finally, we identified several current open questions, challenges, and disagreements in existing standards. One issue not covered in this chapter is the current contradiction between the need for more flexible robotic systems, even including robot programs created by AI systems, and current requirements for safety and validation. This, however, is a general robotics issue not exclusive to mobile manipulation. Nevertheless, as mobile manipulation is one of the main drivers behind the paradigm switch from deterministic, program-based robotics to a cognitive, sensor-based paradigm, this author expects that mobile manipulators will feature heavily in these new developments.

REFERENCES

1. KUKA AG (Ed.). (n.d.). KUKA flexFELLOW. Retrieved April 11, 2018, from www.kuka.com/en-de/products/mobility/mobile-robots/kuka-flexfellow.
2. Robert Bosch GmbH (Ed.). (n.d.). APAS assistant mobile. Retrieved April 11, 2018, from www.bosch-apas.com/en/apas/produkte/assistant/beispiel__apas_assistant_auf_mobiler_platform/apas_assistant_17.html.
3. J. Bohren et al., "Towards autonomous robotic butlers: Lessons learned with the PR2," *2011 IEEE International Conference on Robotics and Automation*, Shanghai, 2011, pp. 5568–5575.
4. K. Zhou et al., "Mobile manipulator is coming to aerospace manufacturing industry," *2014 IEEE International Symposium on Robotic and Sensors Environments (ROSE) Proceedings*, Timisoara, 2014, pp. 94–99.
5. O. Khatib, "Mobile manipulation: The robotic assistant," *Robotics and Autonomous Systems* 26, 1999, pp. 175–183.
6. L. Petersson and H. Christensen, "A framework for mobile manipulation," *1999 IEEE International Symposium on Robotics Systems IROS*, Coimbra, 1999, pp. 359–368.
7. Z. Pan, J. Polden, N. Larkin, S. V. Duin, and J. Norrish, "Recent progress on programming methods for industrial robots," *ISR 2010 (41st International Symposium on Robotics) and ROBOTIK 2010 (6th German Conference on Robotics)*, Munich, Germany, 2010, pp. 1–8.
8. A. Perzylo, N. Somani, S. Profanter, I. Kessler, M. Rickert, and A. Knoll, "Intuitive instruction of industrial robots: Semantic process descriptions for small lot production," *2016 IEEE/RSJ International Conference on Intelligent Robots and Systems (IROS)*, Daejeon, 2016, pp. 2293–2300.
9. ISO 10218-1:2011: Robots and robotic devices -- Safety requirements for industrial robots -- Part 1: Robots.
10. ISO 10218-2:2011: Robots and robotic devices -- Safety requirements for industrial robots -- Part 2: Robot systems and integration.
11. ISO/TS 15066:2016: Robots and robotic devices -- Collaborative robots.
12. KUKA AG (Ed.). (n.d.). Aerospace systems engineering. Retrieved April 11, 2018, from www.kuka.com/en-my/products/production-systems/aerospace-systems-engineering/material-transport-solutions/mobile-robotic-platform
13. The Boeing Company (Ed.). (2017, February 23). 787-10 Rollout. Retrieved April 11, 2018, from www.boeing.com/features/2017/02/faub-777-assembly-02-17.page
14. I. Maurtua, L. Susperregi, A. Fernández, C. Tubío, C. Perez, Rodríguez, T. Felsch, and M. Ghrissi, "MAINBOT - Mobile Robots for Inspection and Maintenance in Extensive Industrial Plants", Energy Procedia, 49, 2014, pp. 1810–1819. https://doi.org/10.1016/j.egypro.2014.03.192
15. R. Behrens, J. Saenz, C. Vogel, and N. Elkmann, "Upcoming technologies and fundamentals for safeguarding all forms of human-robot collaboration," *8th International Conference Safety of Industrial Automated Systems (SIAS 2015)*, Königswinter, Germany, pp. 18–23.
16. "ANNIE: Demonstration of Mobile Robot Skills - Human Assistance." Edited by Fraunhofer IFF, YouTube, 29 Oct. 2015, https://youtu.be/U8o_j1rVgNU

17. DIN EN 1525:1997-12: Safety of industrial trucks – Driverless trucks and their systems; German Version EN 1525:1997.

18. The EN 1525 has not been harmonized with to the new Machinery Directive and should be replaced by the upcoming EN ISO 3691-4. Nevertheless, until it is finalized, the EN1525 should be applied.

19. ISO 13855:2010: Safety of machinery – Positioning of safeguards with respect to the approach speeds of parts of the human body.

20. J. Saenz and M. Fritzsche, "Tactile sensors for safety and interaction with the mobile manipulator VALERI," *47th International Symposium on Robotics – ISR 2016*, Munich, Germany, pp. 1–7.

21. SafeLog - Safe human-robot interaction in logistic applications for highly flexible warehouses. (n.d.). Retrieved April 11, 2018, from http://safelog-project.eu/

22. C. Reardon, H. Tan, B. Kannan, and L. DeRose, "Towards safe robot-human collaboration systems using human pose detection," *2015 IEEE International Conference on Technologies for Practical Robot Applications (TePRA)*, Woburn, MA, 2015, pp. 1–6.

23. J. Marvel and R. Bostelman, "Towards mobile manipulator safety standards," *Proceedings of the IEEE International Symposium on RObotic and Sensors Environments (ROSE)*, Washington D.C., 2013, pp. 31–36.

24. T. Jacobs, U. Reiser, M. Haegele, and A. Verl, "Development of validation methods for the safety of mobile service robots with manipulator," *ROBOTIK 2012; 7th German Conference on Robotics*, Munich, Germany, 2012, pp. 1–5.

25. ANSI R15.08:TBD: Industrial Mobile Robot Safety (in process).

CHAPTER 7

On Rehabilitation Robotics Safety, Benchmarking, and Standards

Safety of Robots in the Field of Neurorehabilitation—Context and Developments

Jan F. Veneman

CONTENTS

7.1   Introduction   91
7.2   Safety, Product Certification, and Standards   92
7.3   Rehabilitation Robots   93
7.4   General Background on Safety for Medical Devices   94
    7.4.1   Product Standards   96
    7.4.2   Process Standards   97
    7.4.3   Installation and Environmental Standards   97
    7.4.4   In-Process Standards   98
    7.4.5   Scope of Safety Standards   98
    7.4.6   Medical Electrical Equipment   98
7.5   Development of a New Standard for RACA Robots   100
7.6   Conclusion   102
References   102

7.1 INTRODUCTION

"Rehabilitation robots" involve the use of robots as tools in physical therapy, for example, for the purpose of neurorehabilitation, which is to improve manipulation functionality of the arm and hand, or to improve walking in subjects that have suffered a cerebrovascular accident (CVA or stroke). This is a relatively new field of collaborative or interactive robots that has found a growing application in modern healthcare (Krebs et al. 1998, 2000).

For several decades, the efforts in research and development of such robots have steadily increased, and at this moment in time (early 2019), there are several such robots available as products on the market, and many innovations in this field are still to be expected. With the use of robots as tools for therapists in tasks that traditionally were performed manually or using low-tech tools by these therapists, the safety of such devices both for therapists, care-workers, and, most of all, patients has become an important topic. The topic of safety includes both the factual safety related to the use of the devices, as well as the formal approach to their product safety, as is assured through processes of product certification.

This chapter will introduce the topic of product safety, product certification, and related safety standards for the field of rehabilitation robots. It includes a short introduction to the safety regulation of medical devices and the role of standards in regulation. It will give special attention to how the safety of rehabilitation robots is going to be considered in the specifically targeted safety standards that are currently in development.

7.2 SAFETY, PRODUCT CERTIFICATION, AND STANDARDS

In Europe, products are allowed on the market when their safety is ascertained through formal procedures of safety certification, generally known as CE marking (main steps in the process are indicated in Figure 7.1). Conformity assessment is the activity of assuring that the specific requirements as defined by regulation(s) or directive(s) that apply for the type of product are actually met.

For medical devices, the requirements for the European market are provided in the Medical Device Regulations. For medical devices that are not in vitro diagnostic, Regulation (EU) 2017/745 applies, which in 2017 started replacing the prior Medical Device Directive (Council Directive 93/42/EEC on Medical Devices, short: MDD, 1993).

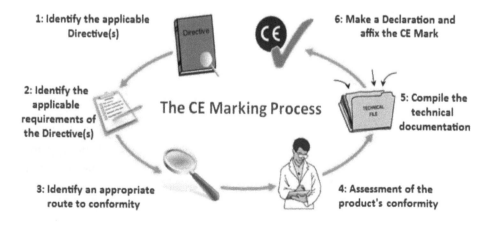

FIGURE 7.1 The process of CE marking.

This new regulation entered into force on 25 May 2017 but will only fully apply after a transition period of three years following its entry into force in the spring of 2022. The European Commission intends the MD Regulation, as compared with the MDD, to establish a modernized and more robust EU legislative framework to ensure better protection of public health and patient safety. The main goal of these new regulations is to ensure: (1) a consistently high level of health and safety protection for EU citizens using these products; (2) the free and fair trade of products throughout the EU; and (3) that EU legislation is adapted to the significant technological and scientific progress occurring in this sector over the last 20 years.

The regulation demands manufacturers to demonstrate product safety according to product type and this is typically performed by following international safety standards. These standards provide secured, normative methods to implement and demonstrate the safety of specific products. Safety standards, as for example published by ISO and IEC and their related national or regional institutes (e.g., CEN and CENELEC for EU), are often not obligatory to follow, but are still generally used as they are legally considered to be the established state-of-the-art regarding safety, and following them demonstrates that the manufacturer has implemented a sufficient level of safety in case liability issues arise.

7.3 REHABILITATION ROBOTS

Rehabilitation robots are robotic devices that are applied in the field of "Physical Medicine and Rehabilitation" (PM&R), also known as "physiatry," "physiotherapy," "Rehabilitation Medicine," or "Physical and Rehabilitation Medicine" (PRM), depending on context and region. The robots used in this field are devices that directly interact mechanically with the user (patient) and can move the users' limbs or support their body posture. They are called "robots" because of their use of robotic technology, such as actuators, sensors, and motion controllers, as well as advanced or learning motion programs. The term "rehabilitation robot" in this chapter is not used for assistive devices that help the user to carry out activities of daily living without direct interaction to body movements and is only used for devices that train a patient in order to improve specific movement functions (or in some cases to slow down degeneration of function or to avoid secondary complaints related to movement impairments). In other contexts, the word may be used differently and, for example, includes assistive devices such as electronic wheelchairs, feeding robots, or socially interactive robots. Examples of rehabilitation robots as intended here are, for example, exoskeleton-type devices that are connected to the patient's arm or leg and interact with the limbs in order to activate and train movement functions in the patient (Díaz et al. 2011; Prange et al. 2006). These devices can replace and support the physical efforts of a physical therapist by providing robotic support to the movements of the limbs, or may also provide specific assistance, such as bodyweight support, in order to make task execution for the patient or the therapist easier or safer.

FIGURE 7.2 Left – the " Lokomat®Pro V6" (Jezernik et al 2003, photo courtesy of of Hocoma AG, Switzerland) is an example of a rehabilitation robot intended to train walking in subjects that suffered from a stroke or other neurological damage. It combines a bodyweight support structure with exoskeleton-like elements that can support and measure hip, knee, and pelvis motion, in order to perform gait training on a treadmill, while receiving motivational and informative feedback. Right – the "Arm Assist" (Perry et al. 2013) is an example of a rehabilitation robot to train arm and hand functionality in the same patient groups. It is a tabletop mobile frame that can measure and support arm and hand movements. It also measures how much the patient leans on the device. All this information is used in game-based rehabilitation exercises.

7.4 GENERAL BACKGROUND ON SAFETY FOR MEDICAL DEVICES*

"Medical devices" are defined in different ways in different countries following national regulations and associated safety regulations differ per country. An international organization, the International Medical Device Regulators Forum (IMDRF), formerly known as the Global Harmonization Task Force (GHTF), is targeting national legislative bodies, and is becoming increasingly important concerning the unification of definitions and regulations of "medical devices." The IMDRF (www.imdrf.org/) defines a "medical device" as follows:

> Medical device means any instrument, apparatus, implement, machine, appliance, implant, in vitro reagent or calibrator, software, material, or other similar or related article:
>
> (a) Intended by the manufacturer to be used, alone or in combination, for human beings, for one or more of the specific purpose(s):
>
> • Diagnosis, prevention, monitoring, treatment, or alleviation of disease
>
> • Diagnosis, monitoring, treatment, alleviation of, or compensation for an injury

---

* This section was strongly based on the information provided in, and partly cited from, Zimmermann, B. (2016). Standards and safety aspects for medical devices in the field of neurorehabilitation. In Reinkensmeyer, D. V. & Dietz, V. (eds.) (2016). *Neurorehabilitation Technology* (pp. 249–281). Springer, Cham.

- Investigation, replacement, modification, or support of the anatomy or of a physiological process

- Supporting or sustaining life

- Control of conception

- Disinfection of medical devices

- Providing information for medical or diagnostic purposes by means of in vitro examination of specimens derived from the human body

(b) Which does not achieve its primary intended action in or on the human body by pharmacological, immunological, or metabolic means but which may be assisted in its intended function by such means.

Note 1: The definition of a device for in vitro examination includes, for example, reagents, calibrators, sample collection and storage devices, control materials, and related instruments or apparatus. The information provided by such an in vitro diagnostic device may be for diagnostic, monitoring, or compatibility purposes. In some jurisdictions, some in vitro diagnostic devices, including reagents and the like, may be covered by separate regulations.

Note 2: Products which may be considered medical devices in some jurisdictions but for which there is not yet a harmonized approach are

- Aids for disabled/handicapped people

- Devices for the treatment/diagnosis of diseases and injuries in animals

- Accessories for medical devices (see Note 3)

- Disinfection substances

- Devices incorporating animal and human tissue

which all may meet the requirements of the above definition but are subject to different controls.

Note 3: Accessories, intended specifically by manufacturers, to be used together with a "parent" medical device to enable that medical device in achieving its intended purpose, should be subject to the same IMDRF procedures as applied to the medical device itself. For example, an accessory will be classified as though it is a medical device in its own right. This may result in having a different classification for the accessory than for the "parent" device.

Note 4: Components to medical devices are generally controlled by the manufacturer's quality management system and the conformity assessment procedures for the device. In some jurisdictions, components are included in the definition of a "medical device."

Requirements related to the safety of medical devices are regulated in national laws and regulations and are to be fulfilled prior to putting them as products on the market.

Compliance must be verified and often placement of a medical product on the market has to be formally approved. The scope and form of the procedures are subject to a certain spectrum. Basically, all rules follow the purpose of patient safety by demanding a risk-benefit analysis as well as of sufficiently protecting both user and third parties in general. Regulatory systems (such as the European Medical Device Directive and the Medical Device Regulation that now replaces it) classify "medical devices" in several product classes on the basis of their risk potential; and consequently apply different requirements for the different product classes (see, for example, Annex VIII of the Medical Device Regulation).

The manufacturer of the medical device plays an important role by specifying, among other things, the intended use of the medical device, which is a core component of a risk-benefit analysis. One should be aware that like "medical device," the term "manufacturer" is not defined in a coherent sense worldwide. It is important to understand that the manufacturer is not only responsible for the design and manufacturing process, but also medical device registration and all the aspects of product life cycle and quality management processes that are included in the responsibilities of the manufacturer.

Robots, a special category of devices, have been used in manufacturing for a long time, but for some time, have been introduced in the "service sector," including the medical field. Both industrial and medical application sectors have their own standards and safety mechanisms that do not necessarily mutually agree. The big difference between both the industrial and general service domain robots on one side and medical devices using robotic technologies on the other side is the involvement of patients. Only medical devices treat patients with all their limitations, and therefore require a fundamentally different approach to product safety. Even though many medical devices have a "degree of autonomy" and according to definitions could be called a robot, the word is not currently commonly used in the medical field. However, in the research field, words like "rehabilitation robot" and "surgical robot" have become very common.

Besides these official directives and regulations, it should be mentioned that there are a lot of other documents available to help and guide manufactures of medical devices, but also the national regulators in the field of medical device technology.

The applicable standards are often indicated indirectly during medical device registration procedures as evidence of standards fulfillment requirements. In particular, the product standards contain details for safety aspects, which can either be of a general or highly device-specific nature. An overview of different classes of standards that may be relevant for a medical device is provided in the following.

7.4.1 Product Standards

Product standards are related to a specific product or group of products. They include:

- Standards that state safety or performance parameters and include reference test methods that can be used to demonstrate conformity to those parameters, (e.g., IEC 60601-1 and the associated supplementary standards and special specifications for medical electrical devices).

IEC 60601-1 Medical Electrical Equipment; Part 1: "General requirements for basic safety and essential performance" is the key standard for all medical devices which are a medical electrical equipment or system. In the IEC 60601-1 series, other specific "collateral" standards are included which have a specific focus like usability engineering and apply for all medical electrical equipment or systems for which this focus is relevant. Details are shown in 13.2.2 "Standards for Medical Electrical Devices for Neurorehabilitation."

In some cases, international standard organizations write additional technical reports for specific standards to give the user of the standards more background information and guidance on how to use the specific standard. IEC publishes their technical reports regarding the IEC 60601 series in the IEC 60601-4-x format.

- Disclosure and test method standards where adherence to declared pass/fail criteria is necessary to demonstrate safety and performance of medical devices.

7.4.2 Process Standards

A number of standards fall into this category, including

- Quality system standards that establish a framework for the manufacturer to be able to design, develop, and produce medical devices that consistently meet specifications (e.g., standards for "good manufacturing practices (GMP)." Quality management standards like ISO 13485:2016 cover the whole life cycle of a medical device; this includes the design and development phase, production, purchasing of parts, storage; transporting; servicing; document management and other aspects. Where a registration procedure for medical devices is required, normally the conformity to (national) Quality Management System standards (ISO 13485) is part of the process.

- Standards for processes used for the design, development, or production of safe and effective medical devices (e.g., sterilization, biological evaluation, clinical investigation, sterility, biocompatibility, or risk management and usability engineering).

7.4.3 Installation and Environmental Standards

The standards for installation are generally appropriate for medical devices which must be installed before operation. These can include

- Construction and installation standards

- System standards, addressing the proper precautions and procedures for interconnection of multiple devices into a single system (medical electrical system)

- Commissioning standards, addresses the proper testing and inspection procedures applying to permanently installed equipment and systems prior to initial use

- Environmental standards, addresses precautions and testing to ensure that a medical device does not negatively affect its environment and the environment does not degrade or otherwise impair the performance of a medical device (e.g., electromagnetic compatibility standards)

7.4.4 In-Process Standards

These can include

- Routine in-service testing standards to ensure that the safety of medical devices is maintained over the useful life of the medical device

- Quality assurance and calibration standards to ensure the continued proper function and accuracy of medical devices, where relevant to safety

7.4.5 Scope of Safety Standards

Each standard contains a short statement on its scope. This scope ensures that each standard is restricted to specific well-defined aspects and makes reference to other related standards of wider application for all other relevant aspects. The underlying standard hierarchy is built on *basic safety standards*, including fundamental concepts, principles, and requirements with regard to general safety aspects, applicable to all kinds or a wide range of products, processes, and services (basic safety standards are sometimes also referred to as horizontal standards; note that ISO uses the term "horizontal" in the same way as IEC uses the term "collateral"); *group safety standards*, including safety aspects, applicable to several, or a family of similar products, processes, or services dealt with by two or more technical committees or subcommittees, making reference, as far as possible, to basic safety standards; and *product safety standards*, including all necessary safety aspects of a specific or a family of product(s), process(es), or service(s) within the scope of a single technical committee or subcommittee, making reference, as far as possible, to basic safety standards and group safety standards (product safety standards are sometimes referred to as "vertical" standards in ISO or "particular" in IEC).

7.4.6 Medical Electrical Equipment

Electrically operated medical devices will have to consider the IEC 60601 standards series as product standard, which is supplemented by the ISO 80601 standards.

The IEC 60601 standards series defines safety requirements and essential performances for medical electrical devices and medical electrical systems. IEC 60601-1 is the general base standard, defining the basis for the basic safety and the essential performance characteristics of any medical electrical device and medical electrical system. For the user of this standard, it is important to know which version is accepted and in which country. The last published version is IEC 60601-1 Edition 3 with amendment 1 from 2012-08 (IEC 60601-1:2005+A1:2012). A small number of countries accept only the previous editions, while other countries have a longer transitory period for the new one. Additional to this situation, the user of standards should be aware of national deviations which occur quite often.

The base standard is accompanied by a series of further requirements of a general nature (coded as IEC 60601-1-x, referred to as collateral standards) as well as by specific requirements for certain specific types of medical devices (coded as IEC 60601-2-x and ISO 80601-2-x, referred to as particular standards).

Standards from the IEC 60601-2-x series can relate directly to certain medical devices in neurorehabilitation and should be carefully evaluated. A standard that could be (in part) applicable is, for example

- IEC 60601-2-10:2012 AMD1:2016 CSV Consolidated Version; Medical Electrical Equipment – Part 2–10: Particular requirements for the basic safety and essential performance of nerve and muscle stimulators

Currently (early 2019), IEC and ISO are finalizing development of particular standards for different types of "medical robots." The foreseen ISO 80601-2-78 can become applicable for medical devices in the area of neurorehabilitation. The expected content of this new standard will be detailed below. The foreseen ISO 80601-2-77 may become applicable for medical devices for surgery.

All standards from the IEC 60601 family are dealing with basic safety and essential performance. Therefore, it is important to understand the meaning of these terms defined in IEC 60101-1 (3):

- Basic safety is defined as "freedom from unacceptable risk directly caused by physical hazards when medical electrical equipment is used under normal conditions and single fault condition."

- Essential performance is defined as "performance of a clinical function, other than that related to basic safety, where loss or degradation beyond the limits specified by the manufacturer results in an unacceptable risk." NOTE essential performance is most easily understood by considering whether its absence or degradation would result in an unacceptable RISK.

Medical electrical equipment or a medical electrical system that does not function properly could result in unacceptable risk for patients, operators, or others. In order to achieve its intended use, medical electrical equipment or the medical electrical system needs to perform within certain limits. These limits are usually specified by the manufacturer and for specific devices also in collateral or particular standards of the IEC 60601 series.

Examples of defined essential performances of specific medical devices are

- Correct administration of a drug by a syringe pump where inaccuracy/incorrect administration would cause an unacceptable risk to the patient

- The ability of an electrocardiograph/monitor to recover from the effects of the discharge of a defibrillator where the failure to recover could lead to an incorrect response by the medical staff that would present an unacceptable risk to the patient

- Correct operation of an alarm system in an intensive care or operating room monitoring system where an incorrect/missing alarm signal could lead to an incorrect response by the medical staff that would present an unacceptable risk to the patient

- Correct output of diagnostic information from medical electrical equipment that is likely to be relied upon to determine treatment, where incorrect information could lead to an inappropriate treatment that would present an unacceptable risk to the patient

7.5 DEVELOPMENT OF A NEW STANDARD FOR RACA ROBOTS

As indicated previously, at this moment, a specific standard for rehabilitation robots is in development in a joint effort between ISO Technical Committee TC 299 (Robotics) and IEC/SC 62D (Electromedical Equipment) (Jacobs et al. 2017). This standard is currently under vote (early 2019) and is numbered ISO/IEC 80601-2-78.* The number 80601 indicates that it is part of the IEC 60601 series of standards, with the 8 indicating the collaboration with ISO. The -2 indicates that it is a "particular"-type of standard, valid for a specific class of medical devices, and -78 is the numbering in the range of 60601 particulars.

ISO and IEC standards are confidential documents that have to be purchased. In this section, some directions proposed in this standard will be explained; obviously, the information given here at this point of time does not have any formal value. It is only meant to indicate the direction the new standard is taking.

The scope of this standard indicates that the standard is targeted very specifically to a type of medical devices defined by their clinical purpose. It is currently formulated in the DIS as "This International Standard applies to the general requirements for BASIC SAFETY and ESSENTIAL PERFORMANCE of MEDICAL ROBOTS that physically interact with a PATIENT to support or perform REHABILITATION, ASSESSMENT, COMPENSATION or ALLEVIATION related to the PATIENT'S MOVEMENT FUNCTIONS following an IMPAIRMENT."

All the capitalized words are formally defined terms that are being used in the strict sense of their definition. An important point is that the standard does not only focus on rehabilitation robots as described above but on "medical robots to support or perform rehabilitation, assessment, compensation or alleviation." The standard has drafted the term RACA robots for these devices. RACA robots are further defined as

- REHABILITATION, ASSESSMENT, COMPENSATION AND ALLEVIATION ROBOT (RACA ROBOT): MEDICAL ROBOT intended to perform REHABILITATION, ASSESSMENT, COMPENSATION, or ALLEVIATION comprising an ACTUATED APPLIED PART

---

* See www.iso.org/standard/68474.html.

The novel and characteristic element of such devices, the ACTUATED APPLIED PART is further defined as

- APPLIED PART that is intended to provide actively controlled physical interactions with the PATIENT that are related to the PATIENT's MOVEMENT FUNCTIONS that are needed to perform a CLINICAL FUNCTION of a RACA ROBOT

Note 1: "Actively controlled" as used above is intended to mean controlled by the RACA ROBOT, including shared control with the PATIENT or OPERATOR.

Note 2: Actively controlled physical interactions include position control, force control, impedance control, admittance control, or any other controls that regulate the interaction between a RACA ROBOT and the PATIENT.

Note 3: Each ACTUATED APPLIED PART is part of an actuation system according to clause 9.8.1 of IEC 60601-1.

These definitions clarify why the standard combines different types of robot, and not only robots used for rehabilitation, as the characteristic of all these devices is that they perform "actively controlled physical interactions" to a patient, a unique and novel feature that is not found in other types of medical devices. Whether performing actively controlled physical interactions is done for training a patient (rehabilitation), for assessing a patient (assessment), for supporting a patient (compensation), or related to secondary complaints (alleviation; e.g., pain and circulation problems) does not fundamentally change the approach to device safety that is required, at least when these interactions are targeted at the movement functions of the patient.

Most of the differences in safety approaches, compared with the general 60601-1 standard, are related to this aspect of mechanical power exchange between RACA robot and patient. Because of the purpose of RACA robots, their structure is very different from other medical devices; think, for example, of exoskeleton devices that are connected in parallel with the human limb structures to create natural movement in the leg or in the arm. Especially if such exoskeletons are wearable devices, they are very different from other known portable or body-worn medical equipment, and hence their safety approach related to stability and possible load on the patients will need special and type-specific consideration.

The standard, among others, provides examples on how to determine the total load to be considered when evaluating the device safety related to the strength of different components such as the supportive structure and the actuators of the device that is intended to move or support specific parts of the patient's body.

Another aspect of rehabilitation robots, different from any other type of medical device, and that therefore is considered in this particular safety standard, is the so-called "shared control" that may be implemented and implies that the motions that are made inside the device are a result of both the patient and the robot's actions. This specific concept is important when analyzing possible "unintended motion" that can occur in the device and which is a concept used in the general safety standard.

In this fashion, for the largest part, the particular standards aim to clarify how already available concepts can or should be interpreted or used in the context of RACA robots.

This will help both manufacturers and regulators establish a homogenous approach to the safety of RACA robots, which facilitates both market introduction and the product safety of this type of device.

7.6 CONCLUSION

This chapter has introduced what types of devices are considered rehabilitation robots and how the regulatory and standardization domains consider the safety aspects of these robots, defining them in the near future as RACA robots: robotic devices for the purpose of rehabilitation, assessment, compensation, and alleviation. Some specifics expected in the associated IEC 806010-2-78 standard compared with the general IEC 60601-1 were outlined.

REFERENCES

Díaz, I., Gil, J. J., & Sánchez, E. (2011). Lower-limb robotic rehabilitation: Literature review and challenges. Journal of Robotics, 2011, 759764.

Jacobs, T., Veneman, J. F., Virk, G. S., & Haidegger, T. (2017). The flourishing landscape of robot standardization [industrial activities]. IEEE Robotics & Automation Magazine, 25(1), 8–15.

Jezernik, S., Colombo, G., Keller, T., Frueh, H., & Morari, M. (2003). Robotic orthosis lokomat: A rehabilitation and research tool. Neuromodulation: Technology at the Neural Interface, 6(2), 108–115.

Krebs, H. I., Hogan, N., Aisen, M. L., & Volpe, B. T. (1998). Robot-aided neurorehabilitation. IEEE Transactions on Rehabilitation Engineering, 6(1), 75–87.

Krebs, H. I., Volpe, B. T., Aisen, M. L., & Hogan, N. (2000). Increasing productivity and quality of care: Robot-aided neuro-rehabilitation. Journal of Rehabilitation Research and Development, 37(6), 639.

Perry, J. C., Rodriguez-de-Pablo, C., Cavallaro, F.I., Belloso, A., & Keller, T. (2013). Assessment and training in home-based telerehabilitation of arm mobility impairment. Journal of Accessibility and Design for All (CC) JACCES, 3(2), 117–135.

Prange, G. B., Jannink, M. J., Groothuis-Oudshoorn, C. G., Hermens, H. J., & Ijzerman, M. J. (2006). Systematic review of the effect of robot-aided therapy on recovery of the hemiparetic arm after stroke. Journal of Rehabilitation Research and Development, 43(2), 171.

CHAPTER 8

A Practical Appraisal of ISO 13482 as a Reference for an Orphan Robot Category

Paolo Barattini

CONTENTS

8.1	Introduction	104
8.2	Using the ISO 13482	105
8.3	The Hazards Identification, Risk Evaluation and Safety Assessment	106
8.4	Definition of the System Boundaries	109
8.5	Definition of the Ground Rules and Assumptions	109
	8.5.1 Background Assumptions	109
	8.5.2 Assumed Environmental Conditions	109
	8.5.3 Operating Profiles	110
	8.5.4 Product Misuse or Abuse by the User	110
	8.5.5 The Definition of Failure Modes to Be Used in the Robotised Scrubber's FMECA	110
	8.5.6 Definition of Information Basis	111
	8.5.7 Definition of the Criticality and Ranking approach	111
	8.5.8 Definition of Failure Effects	112
	8.5.9 Definitions for the Capability of Failure Detection	112
	8.5.10 Diagrams	112
	8.5.11 Definition of the Necessary Performance Level of Safety-Related Functions	112
	8.5.12 Hazard Analysis and Risk Assessment Specific Activities	112
	8.5.13 Synthesis of Hazards Identification and Risk Assessment	114
	8.5.13.1 Details About "Orange" Level Hazards	114
8.6	Tracking the Completion of Recommended Actions and Ensure Risk Reduction to an Acceptable Level	119
8.7	Rendition, Practical Commentary and Conclusions	119

8.1 INTRODUCTION

In this chapter, we present our work related to the risk and safety assessment of a floor washing robot intended for professional use in view of a future certification. The professional robotised scrubber prototype can possibly be classified under the category of "service robot" and not that of industrial robot. This work was done in the frame of the European project FLOBOT, supported by the European Commission through the Horizon 2020 Programme (H2020-ICT-2014-1, Grant agreement no: 645376). The author of the present chapter at that time worked for the company Ridgeback s.a.s., Turin, Italy, that took care within the project of standards, safety, risk assessment and path to certification.

The robotised scrubber is 150 cm long, 70 cm wide, with a height of 70 cm and weight of 300 kg. It runs on batteries and it cruises at a maximal speed of 5 km/h. It does not have any manipulator or other external effector apart from the rotating brush in contact with the floor, which is safely covered by the robot body.

The definition of an industrial robot as per ISO 8373:2012 indicates an automatically controlled, multi-purpose manipulator programmable in three or more axes, which can be either fixed in place or mobile, for use in industrial automation applications. Our robot is not capable of manipulation. Essentially, it is a robotised version of the professional grade floor washing machines that in the local jargon are called ride-on scrubbers. These devices brush the floor with water and detergents and vacuum-dry it. Currently, there is no specific international standard, neither ISO nor IEEC, dedicated to this specific type of robot. This is regrettable since there are now at least three companies that are offering robotised scrubbers and one French company offering a robotised sweeper. Additionally, the professional cleaning market is a growing sector and a huge potential market for this kind of robot.

The IEC 60335-1 and -2 is a standard by the International Electrotechnical Commission that takes care of the safety of electrical appliances. Within its scope are both devices for household and similar purposes, and devices that are not intended for normal household use but that, because of their condition or setting for use, can be dangerous to the public. This typically refers to those appliances that are used in professional activities by non-specialised workers in shops, in light industry and on farms. The standard quotes a few examples such as catering equipment, cleaning appliances for commercial use and appliances for hairdressers. It contains very detailed requirements such that the parts in contact with the cleaning liquids must be resistant to the solutions used in that machine or the requirement to use fuses or other technical solutions in order to prevent electric overload. This is discussed in more detail in Section 8.2 of the standard IEC 60335, which is devoted to particular requirements for vacuum cleaners and water-suction cleaning appliances. It also includes some tests for specific aspects. Nevertheless, it is not useful as a reference for risk assessment and safety of robotised devices. This standard covers, among others, professional grade scrubbers and sweepers but it does not include any kind of autonomous robotic device or robotised machine.

ISO 13482: 2014 concerns personal care robots. These are defined as any device that is intended to improve the quality of life of users. User kind is not specified so that the applicability of the norm is at a wide range. The norm actually says that the definition of personal care robots is irrespective of the user's age or capability. This can be interpreted, turning the negative expression into a positive sentence, as saying that any kind of user goes. It considers three types of devices: mobile servant robots, physical assistant robots and person carrier robots. These kinds of robots have physical dimensions, the fact that they are earth bound and that they have a limited motion speed in common. It is self-evident that the norm refers to those robots that, at the time of publication, were on the market or on the verge of becoming market products. The physical dimension of the three considered categories usually is quite extensive. Additionally, the norm specifies which kind of robots are not covered. The standard does not cover devices travelling above 20 km/h of speed.

This standard does not provide a definition of the quality of life that the robot supposedly should improve. So it allows a wider interpretation, apart from the one implied by the three kinds of robots quoted in the standard itself. Possibly this is because the definition of what quality of life is can be quite difficult.

In other words, there are many different definitions of the quality of life that evolved over time. Also, this means that there are many different ways of measuring the quality of life. Or vice-versa because of the different choices on how to measure the quality of life and the sundry different "quality of life" definitions. Possibly, the experts that drew up the ISO 13482 did not want to become entangled in the controversial matter of referring to one out of too many definitions that can have also different ideological backgrounds. Our personal feeling is that the generic use of the term quality of life refers essentially to the health dimension and to the physical capability of the user.

ISO 13482 nevertheless after the initial reference to the quality of life never mentions it again, since the standard is not concerned with the practical results of the activity of the robot but simply with safety. Whether the use by the worker of a robotised scrubber instead of a ride-on or walk-behind device improves her quality of life is still debatable.

Because of the dimensions and speeds covered by ISO 13482, it is the best reference standard for our robotic scrubber safety.

Regarding the category service robot that may cover our scrubber, there are few standards under development under the wings of the chapter ISO/TC 299. Possibly, these in the future could be applied to scrubber robots. They are: ISO/CD 22166- Robotics – Part 1: Modularity for Service Robots – Part 1: General Requirements; ISO/CD TR 23482-1 [Robotics – Application of ISO 13482 – Part 1: Safety-Related Test Methods; ISO/DTR 23482-2 Robotics – Application of ISO 13482 – Part 2: Application Guide.

8.2 USING THE ISO 13482

There are many standards in robotics. It also appears that little by little, as the number and types of robots on the market grows with the application to sundry domains including agriculture, logistics, maintenance and repair of infrastructures, surface and underwater robots and flying robots, the number of standards is bound to inflate.

Actually, there are two lines of thought regarding this matter. Some experts deem necessary the creation of highly specific standards, while other authors rather deem that it is redundant to create too many standards, so that they repeat the same requirements for safety-related functions that are present in robots with similar features but in different application areas. For example, a wheeled robot has the same requirements with regards to safe motion and travelling whether it is a scrubber or a delivery robot, both working in interiors.

Still, the latter approach is not formalised. So far, we can use the ISO 13482 for our scrubber robot only as a useful reference, i.e. an educated guideline to travelling robots intended for interiors with speed and mass within the standard specifications but we cannot claim that in such a way the robot scrubber was developed in conformity to the EU Machinery Directive, at least formally, in principle.

ISO 13482 is a harmonised standard. This means that it is officially acknowledged and conforming to this standard ensures conformity to the EU Machinery Directive.

Also, it is quite deep and specialised because it is a Type-C Standard, i.e. it deals with detailed safety requirements for a particular machine or group of machines.

In fact, we used both the Machinery Directive and the standard as a reference. We went through the exercise of checking if the standard captures all the relevant requirements for our robot. We made our list of requirements starting from our consortium knowledge, always referring to the machinery directive, and then we compared it with the ISO 13482 requirements.

We compared our analysis using as a reference the Machine Directive to the ISO 13482 listed hazards to ensure that no hazard related to part, component, process and function of a robotised scrubber (robotised scrubber prototype) goes undetected or is excluded from the risk assessment since the Machine Directive is the overarching umbrella while ISO 13482 refers to some specific categories and embodiments of robots.

The standard is structured in eight chapters. The first three chapters present what the standard is about, external references to other relevant technical standards and definitions that help with the wording used as specific robotics jargon.

The following chapters are those of immediate use and include risk assessment, safety requirements and protective measures, safety-related control system requirements, verification and validation and information for use.

At the end of the standard, five annexes are appended. One annex is a non-exhaustive list of hazards for personal care robots. This is a compact format for information presented extensively elsewhere in the previous chapters.

We considered and tested this list as a complementary checklist to our hazard identification activities. The other four annexes present examples that are a useful reference for quite specific and relevant typical issues such as safety zones around the robot

8.3 THE HAZARDS IDENTIFICATION, RISK EVALUATION AND SAFETY ASSESSMENT

We started our work during the inception and design phase. Multiple partners were involved: a professional cleaning devices company was in charge of mechanical engineering and integration; one robotics company was in charge of navigation and localisation software and of software integration; one university was in charge of a software module for the identification and tracking of humans through the RGB images; one university was in charge of a software model for dirt and small objects identification on the floor; and our company, Ridgeback s.a.s., was in charge of some software apps and of the risk and safety assessment.

ISO 13482 prescribes the hazards identification activities and the risk assessment activities. The approaches and methods are not specified because there are multiple established approaches and methods, each one having pros and cons.

So the first step was to decide conjointly with the partners which methods for risk and safety assessment to use.

The natural choice was the failure mode, effects and criticality analysis (FMECA) approach because the robotics company (in charge of integration) had personnel that had previous experience and who were used to the FMECA. The other partners agreed promptly.

The FMECA procedure typically consists of the following logical steps:

- Define the system
- Define ground rules and assumptions in order to help drive the design
- Construct system block diagrams
- Identify failure modes (piece part level or functional)
- Analyse failure effects/causes
- Classify the failure effects by severity
- Perform criticality calculations
- Rank failure mode criticality
- Determine critical items
- Identify the means of failure detection, isolation and compensation
- Perform maintainability analysis
- Document the analysis, summarise uncorrectable design areas
- Identify special controls necessary to reduce failure risk
- Feed results back into the design process
- Make recommendations
- Follow-up on corrective action implementation/effectiveness

FMECA can be done at two different levels or better at both levels. One level is the functional module level, the other is at the single piece/component level. At each level, it is considered what effects a failure of the module or component can entail, i.e. the possible harm caused by a failure that is quantified (a risk). Usually, the hardware parts and components come with some information provided by the producer about their failure rate. So this makes it easier to estimate the probability of failure.

We performed the FMECA at piece level for the hardware components. Where possible, a quantitative approach was used. The technical experience and engineering wisdom of the partners were used in a qualitative approach when quantitative information was not available.

The software was considered at the module level, but no extensive quantitative information was available apart from development documentation and unit tests at lab level.

For the basic definition of hazards and risks, because the robotics scrubber is intended for the work environment and professional use, we referred to Occupational Safety and Health Administration (OSHA) definitions.

Briefly, according to OSHA Guidelines:

- A hazard is anything that can cause harm (e.g., chemicals, electricity, working with ladders.

- Risk is the chance of harm being done with an indication of how serious the harm could be.

- Harm is a negative safety and health consequence (e.g., injury or ill health).

Another common definition of hazard in relation to health and safety in work environments is: "A Hazard is a potential source of harm or adverse health effect on a person or persons".

The layperson quite often does not distinguish between Hazard and Risk but uses them as synonyms, which they are not.

For example, imagine a supermarket fresh fish bench. At delivery time, because of the melting ice of the fish delivery boxes, there will be a water spill on the floor. The water spill on the floor is a slipping hazard to the workers. If a movable fence or another barrier is used to restrict access to the spill area, then the risk has been controlled and possibly reduced to a minimum while the hazard persists.

Also, for the definition of risk in a work environment, we have a more structured version that is: "risk is the likelihood that a person may be harmed or suffers adverse health effects if exposed to a hazard".

The level of risk is defined in relation to the harm that follows by the exposure to a hazard.

A hazard can cause harm through a single one-time exposure or it can be effective through multiple exposures or continuous low-level exposure.

To counteract the identified and quantified risks, control measures are needed.

Control measures typically are: hazard elimination; substitution/upgrade of an element that is the main source of risk so to lessen the overall risk (in robotics, a simple example is the substitution of a robot body's sharp corners part with newly designed parts with smooth profiles; hazard isolation (in robotics, this is typically achieved through fencing the areas in which the robot works); training, instruction, safe work practices; and use of personal protective equipment.

It must also be remembered that the acceptability of the risk can also depend on the intended use and application of the robot.

The scrubber robot has three main modes of operation: autonomous mode; mapping mode (driven manually to map the environment before the use); and manual mode (driven by a tablet application with a virtual joystick).

In addition, there are multiple categories of individuals related to hazards and risks: the worker of the facility management company (cleaning service provider); the worker of the end-user facility; other third parties workers present on the premise (for example, external maintenance personnel); clients; and by-passers.

8.4 DEFINITION OF THE SYSTEM BOUNDARIES

In this step, the "system" to be analysed was defined as the robotised scrubber mobile platform. The tablet application was included within the boundaries of the system, being the mission programming and supervision interface as well as the control for the manual modes (joystick and mapping modes).

The system was partitioned into an indentured hierarchy such as systems, subsystems or equipment, units or subassemblies and piece parts. Functional descriptions have been created for the systems and allocated to the subsystems, covering the autonomous mode, mapping mode and joystick mode – the main operational modes. Mission phases have been defined in the frame of the definition of the requirements for the tablet app menu for mission planning.

8.5 DEFINITION OF THE GROUND RULES AND ASSUMPTIONS
8.5.1 Background Assumptions

- The product will be manufactured and assembled within engineering specifications.

- Incoming parts and materials meet design intent.

- Software modules will undergo debugging at module level and module validation at lab level with test data from the scenario validation environment or a similar one.

8.5.2 Assumed Environmental Conditions

It is assumed that the operation of the robotised scrubber system will be in interiors, on smooth floor surfaces, with a range of temperatures from 4 to 35°C, with no major electric magnetic fields interferences and working for the so-called "regular cleaning" that means everyday cleaning with a certain specified pressure of the brush, in opposition to deeper cleaning performed with other means, no rugged floors, no carpets, no inclinations exceeding the posted capacity of the robot and use of a local stable wi-fi network extended over the entire area of work. No harsh environmental conditions in relation to moisture, powders and sands are assumed.

8.5.3 Operating Profiles

The operating profiles considered are those identified during the design phase and activated through the tablet mobile app according to the different level of access granted to the users according to their privileges.

- Autonomous mode

- Joystick mode (manual mode: a tablet application with a virtual joystick interface is used to drive the robot)

- Mapping mode (manual mode used to create the map, the robot is controlled by a table application)

8.5.4 Product Misuse or Abuse by the User

The intended users are the professional cleaning operators of the facility management companies that will receive training for the use of the robot. We assume that no intentional abuse of the product will be intentionally done.

Since the speed of operation is limited in all the modes, and the cleaning operations are only active in autonomous mode, under this point of view, only a few areas may be subject to abuse, i.e. situations in which the human role is wider, which is essentially the mapping mode, and the use of the joystick mode for local transfer. In such a case, the abuse may consist of intentionally/accidentally driving along objects or against obstacles.

Other possible conditions outside of specifications are the use of the robotised scrubber to transport weights or as a surface on which to lay objects as though it were a table or a work bench. Additionally, pushing the robotised scrubber or sitting on it are to be considered product misuses. All of these may lead to dirt obstructing sensors, damage to sensors or other mechanical damage.

8.5.5 The Definition of Failure Modes to Be Used in the Robotised Scrubber's FMECA

In the robotised scrubber's FMECA, for hardware components, software components and functions, we adopted the following failure definitions:

- Untimely operation

- Failure to operate when required

- Loss of output

- Intermittent output

- Erroneous output (given the current condition)

- Invalid output (for any condition)

- Unintended output

Additionally, we added the failure (having impact on safety) to meet, in relation to specific items and issues of the robotised scrubber, the constraints and limits defined by the design or by standards:

- Exceeding posted design limits
- Exceeding standard limits
- Emission of harmful substances

8.5.6 Definition of Information Basis

Information basis includes

- Commercial parts information provided by the producers
- Certified components declared failure rate by the producers
- Design documentation
- Functional specifications provided by the technical and engineering team of the consortium
- The professional cleaning machine's internal company statistics on failure rate and failure mode of the hardware used in this prototype, hardware that has already been used in their similar models and commercial preventive maintenance plans based on failure rates
- Engineering experience and wisdom of the technical partners

8.5.7 Definition of the Criticality and Ranking approach

It was agreed with the partners to adopt the occurrence, severity, detectability, definitions and levels already used by the robotics company for the FMECA based on their previous experience and application to their other models of autonomous robots.

The scale for severity ranges from 1 to 10.

The scale for frequency of occurrence ranges from 1 to 10.

The scale for non-detectability ranges from 1 to 10. The lowest value (1) corresponds to higher probability of detection.

Failure mode criticality assessment may be qualitative or quantitative. For qualitative assessment, a mishap probability number is assigned to each item (component/function).

Use of severity rankings, risk priority numbers (RPNs) and FMECA results allow the prioritisation of issues for corrective or mitigating actions.

The FMECA team forwards the results and recommended actions to the project coordinator that will take care of consulting the technical partners and organise panel discussions. and follow-up for execution where deemed necessary or implementable within project resources limits and time constraints.

8.5.8 Definition of Failure Effects

Failure effects are determined and entered for each row of the FMECA matrix, considering the criteria identified in the ground rules. Effects are separately described for the local, next higher and end (system) levels. System level effects may include

- System failure

- Degraded operation

- System status failure (system status check fails)

- No immediate effect

The failure effect categories used at various hierarchical levels are tailored using engineering judgment.

8.5.9 Definitions for the Capability of Failure Detection

For each component and failure mode, the ability of the system to detect and report the failure in question is analysed. The following categories are used to define the possible feedback and conditions of the failure detection:

- Normal: the system correctly indicates a safe condition to the supervisor/operator/crew

- Abnormal: the system correctly indicates a malfunction requiring crew action

- Incorrect: the system erroneously indicates a safe condition in the event of malfunction or alerts the crew to a malfunction that does not exist (false alarm)

8.5.10 Diagrams

The main components of the robotised scrubber are depicted in block diagrams (Figure 8.1).

8.5.11 Definition of the Necessary Performance Level of Safety-Related Functions

According to the ISO 13842:2014(E), paragraph 6.1.2.1, definition of robot categories, the robotised scrubber can be considered as corresponding to the "Type 1.2" robot category, because it is small, slow and without a manipulator, but it cannot be classified as lightweight. The standard asks for the required performance level for safety functions for the different subcategories of robots. In relation to the robotised scrubber, it is necessary to consider the categories in Table 8.1.

8.5.12 Hazard Analysis and Risk Assessment Specific Activities

The following activities were performed:

- Brainstorming sessions evaluating safety issues and hazards based on the current system configuration and functions. It used a "what if approach" as well as a "worst case" mishaps identification.

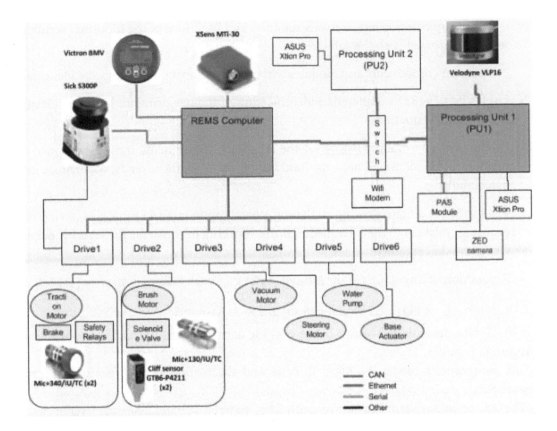

FIGURE 8.1   Robotised scrubber physical architecture.

This is not part of the FMECA method. Nevertheless, it is needed because the FMECA is mostly an engineering approach. Externalities such as human performance and behaviour variability, and accidental situations, are not predefined and are not easily identified by the FMECA.

- Contacts and discussion with the consortium technical and end-user partners through email, ad hoc teleconferences and the weekly work team robotised scrubbers teleconference.

- Use of ISO 13482 as a reference for hazards identification: Annex A of this norm typically presents the main hazard categories in autonomous robots. We cross-referenced the robotised scrubber parts and functions to this set of categories and checked which items fit in which category. We also performed a ranking per category.

- Use of ISO 13482 as a reference: we went through the norm in a sub-clause by sub-clause fine grain approach. Each sub-clause of ISO 13482 considers generalities, inherently safe design, safeguarding and complementary protective measures, information for use, verification and validation.

A main matrix was produced containing each relevant sub-clause bullets, failure modes, actions and recommendations.

Hardware components, software modules and functions of the robotised scrubber were crisscrossed with the sub-clauses.

Relevant components and modules with possible impact on safety were identified.

- Use of ISO 13482 as a reference: identification of the performance level for relevant safety-related functions.

- Production of a matrix listing all the hardware components having relevance in relation to the identified hazards. Ranking of the items for severity, occurrence and detectability.

- Production of a matrix listing all the software components and functions having relevance in relation to the identified hazards. Ranking of the items for severity, occurrence and detectability.

- Production of a synthesis of the estimated risks for each hazards category (Table 8.2).

8.5.13 Synthesis of Hazards Identification and Risk Assessment

The histogram presents the results of the ranking activities with the computed RPN per category of hazards.

The autonomous mode, the joystick mode and the mapping mode were considered (Figure 8.2).

The orange colour identifies hazards with RPN between 101 and 300. This level of risk is defined as not acceptable and calls for correction or mitigation actions. Therefore, recommendations have been issued. Action to reduce RPN is mandatory.

The yellow colour identifies hazards with RPN between 51 and 100. This level of risk is defined as tolerable but requests monitoring of the product. Action is advisable but not mandatory.

The green colour identifies hazards with RPN between 1 and 50. This level of risk is defined as not relevant. Action is not needed.

8.5.13.1 Details About "Orange" Level Hazards

The category hazards due to robot start-up, according to the present design of the robotised scrubber are quite low. The robot upon start-up will check its own status, after which it can start operation in autonomous mode and start moving. Its capacity to identify human beings and the navigation and safety software prevent collisions. Nevertheless, at this stage of product development, we were still lacking additional tests and resulting data and information about the performance of the software modules implied.

In autonomous mode, another situation occurs while the robotised scrubber is moving out of the docking station. This procedure takes place moving backwards. The robotised scrubber does not have sensors monitoring the rear operational space. Only the Lidar would be able to provide obstacle related data. This is a hazardous situation for the possible collision of the robot with humans or objects.

Additionally, in cases where the robotised scrubber was started and then used in joystick or autonomous mode, we have the hazardous situation related to manual driving by a

TABLE 8.1 Categories Considered in the Risk Assessment

ISO 13482:2014(E)		
Safety functions	Performance level for safety-related parts of control systems (PL)	Robotised scrubber component/issue
Emergency stop	D Provides capability for controlling hazards controlled by the robot system	Robotised scrubber has two physical emergency stop button; their optimal position has been defined as a trade-off between ease of access and possible accidental activation.
Protective stop	D Stop function using stop category 2, as described in IEC 60204-1	Bumpers category 2
Limits to workspace (including forbidden area avoidance)	D Software limits are permitted as a means to define and reduce the restricted space, provided they can affect a stop of the robot at full rated load and speed	The robotised scrubber has limits to workspace in that a monitoring zone, a speed reduction zone and a stop zone are defined in relation to the presence of humans or moving objects. It is possible to define forbidden spaces that are related to navigation risk towards objects or humans (exclusion zones such as stairs or the presence of other special situations). This is done during the mapping process according to mapping procedures.
Safety-related speed control	D Risk assessment shall determine the safety-related speed limit of the personal care robot, beyond which the robot might cause harm	The robotised scrubber design includes dynamic speed limitation adjusted to moving humans and objects.
Safety-related environmental sensing (Hazardous collision avoidance)	D Safety-related object sensing Travel surface sensing	UOl module Human tracking/ moving objects Lidar Visual floor inspection Object detection
Safety-related force control	Not applicable	
Singularity protection	Not applicable	
Design of user interface	ISO 13482 does not prescribe a performance level (PL)	Tablet application as graphical user interface
Stability control	D	Control of velocity, acceleration, deceleration, braking during autonomous navigation

human operator, who could be prone to errors depending on subjective stress and fatigue, environmental conditions and training.

The hazards due to robot shape are related to the sharp edges present on the body at the front of the first prototype made of metal. Since the design may undergo changes, for example, in relation to the position of the sensors, this hazard shall be re-evaluated after the testing of the first prototype and for the future conformation of a plastic body.

TABLE 8.2   Hardware Components Included Within the Risk
Assessment Boundaries

1	Velodyne VLP16 (mapping laser)
2	Lidar Sick S300 Certified safety sensor
3	Incremental encoders for wheels DFS60
4	Incremental encoder for traction motor
5	Controller: McDSA-E25
6	Controller: McDSA-E65
7	Sonars- Mic+130/IU/TC
8	Sonars- Mic+340/IU/TC Left and Right Controller number 1
9	Cliff sensor Sick G6 (to avoid stairs when moving backwards)
10	Cliff cable
11	Asus XTION (for human tracking and TUW)
12	Stereo Camera: StereoLabs Zed
13	Bumpers - HAAKE (positioned on the back of the robot)
14	Sub D9 Metal cover
15	MTi-300 Xsens, IMU
16	MTi-300 Xsens cable
17	Safety switches
18	PicoStation M, PICOM2HP, Wi-Fi modem
19	POE splitter
20	PU2: Processor
21	PU2: DC/DC
22	Converter
23	PU2: Motherboard
24	Socket 1151
25	PU2: GPU
26	PU2: RAM
27	PU2: SSD HDD
28	PU2: Enclosure
29	PU2: DC/DC
30	Converter Housing – M4ATX enclosure
31	PU2: Case Fan
32	PU1: PC Advantec
33	PU1: Graphic card GEFORCE GTX 750
34	Proactive safety microcontroller (Raspberry Pi)
35	Front right amber light (RS 721-6423)
36	Front left amber light (RS 721-6423)
37	Rear right amber light (RS 721-6423)
38	Rear left amber light (RS 721-6423)
39	Line laser left with pan/tilt mechanism
40	Line laser right with pan/tilt mechanism
41	Line laser front with pan/tilt mechanism
42	Line laser rear with pan/tilt mechanism
43	Line laser for Arrows projection (APINEX JTA Arrow laser), mounted on rotation plate
44	Servo used to rotate: ROB-09065 + ROB-10335

(Continued)

TABLE 8.2 (CONTINUED)   Hardware Components Included
Within the Risk Assessment Boundaries

45	Brush motor
46	Vacuum motor
47	Traction motor
48	Steering motor (with incremental encoder)
49	Pump
50	Solenoid valve
51	Basement actuator
52	Battery pack
53	Charger
54	Doser (mechanical system based on Venturi effect)
55	Pumps for docking station
56	Solenoid valve for docking station
57	PCB docking station
58	DC/DC 12 V
59	DC/DC 5 V
60	Fusible 100 A
61	Emergency button
62	BMV
63	Contactor 100 A
64	B9 connexion (for S300, IMU and CAN to PU)

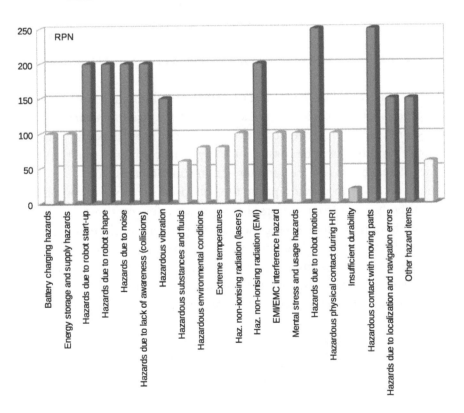

FIGURE 8.2   Histogram of the risk priority number for the category of hazard as per ISO 13482.

The hazards due to noise have a high RPN because its occurrence is the highest (the noise is always present during cleaning operations due to the brush rotation). Mitigation is quite easy anyway, in case it was needed, with the last resource being individual protection measures.

The hazards due to lack of awareness refers to the robot's possible limitations in interpreting the environmental data collected by the sensors.

The hazards due to vibrations do not refer directly to the effects on a human being. The operators of the robotised scrubber are not in contact with the robot during operations in autonomous, joystick or mapping mode. Therefore, no hazard for their health can be identified. At least this is according to ISO 13482. This norm does not consider the possible interference of vibrations with the sensors. This was part of our testing and validation evaluation.

The category non-ionising radiations – EMI refers to possible interference from external sources affecting the robotised scrubber electronics. Currently, no specific shielding is foreseen. The possible effect of EMI shall be considered especially if the robot Was used in industrial or facilities environment in which powerful sources of EMI may be present, a condition excluded from the safety assessment.

Mental stress and usage hazards are related to human factors and the interfaces for control by the human operator, so far typically in joystick and mapping modes. In mapping mode, apart from steering errors and consequent possible collisions, errors may occur regarding the area mapped (that will be the operational area of the robotised scrubber). This may lead to accidents if the area includes zones not suited for the robotised scrubber operation.

Hazards due to robot motion are essentially related to the possible mechanical instability of the robot.

The category of hazards due to physical contact during human–robot interaction (HRI) in the case of the robotised scrubber is not applicable because it has no arms or other external actuators for HRI. Physical contact can anyway occur in joystick and mapping modes, but the robotised scrubber will be passive and only some components of the safety control loops will be active. So this is more a matter of non-functional aspects.

Hazardous contact with moving parts: the robotised scrubber is completely covered by its external body apart from sensors that protrude a few centimetres outside and the emergency stop button. All the moving mechanical parts are enclosed with the exception of the brush and rear wheel. In the current design, there is an arch like opening on the left and right rear side that exposes the brush and the rear wheels. This kind of design is also present in some manned similar brushers. Anyway, this represents a possible point of contact with moving parts of the robot. A recommendation to provide a flap or other cover was issued.

Hazards due to navigation and localisation errors. This is related to the autonomous mode, at least in the present design of the software architecture that excludes reactive navigation and part of the safety enabled by software during operations in joystick and mapping mode.

8.6 TRACKING THE COMPLETION OF RECOMMENDED ACTIONS AND ENSURE RISK REDUCTION TO AN ACCEPTABLE LEVEL

The technical partners were directly involved in risk assessment activities. They received continuous feedback in relation to the identified hazards and related risk evaluation. Recommendations were forwarded to them.

The FMECA results were also used as input for the validation and testing plan that included specific safety-oriented testing activities.

Results of the validation and testing were used to confirm/disconfirm risk reduction following corrective and/or mitigation actions following the issued recommendations (action items list).

8.7 RENDITION, PRACTICAL COMMENTARY AND CONCLUSIONS

The hazards identification and risk assessment covered the design phase and the initial phase of prototype implementation, laboratory testing, testing and validation in collaboration with end users in the actual environment of use, with minor updates of design.

One practical difficulty in applying ISO 13482 is the lack of pre-existing commercial software tools to keep track of the standards requirements and the robot's components and modules during the hazard identification and risk assessment process and tracking different issues during the different phases of development and testing.

So far, we had to spend time on implementing our own tool, simply as a huge matrix (a table). We manually entered all ISO 13482 requirements and then filled the matrix and kept track of the design elements, components, modules and their ratings and then again for the first prototype following the testing and validation phases.

For each sub-clause of the norm, we ended up having about 20 cells of the matrix to be filled with information and to be updated with tracking project design and implementation evolution and of related documentation.

Another relevant issue is that some safety-related aspects are midway between functional and non-functional safety issues. For example, the intended use of the robotics scrubber includes locations and settings such as warehouses and supermarkets. This means that there are many occasions in which the robot will approach the corner of an aisle and then turn around. In this situation, a passer-by that is walking close to the corner could have a close encounter with the robot, at so close quarters so to come to a collision. Mitigation measures had to be defined and implemented. Mitigation measure one is that the robot will slow down whenever approaching a corner. Additionally, the second mitigation measure was already defined at the design stage to include a so-called proactive safety module that projects laser symbols and warnings on the floor in front of the robot. This module also issues vocal warnings through a set of loudspeakers.

A general issue for a robotics product to be marketed is the trade-off between the sale price that ensures viability and the cost of the safety sensors. The best ideal situation would be to have one certified Sick Laser S300P on each of the four sides of the robot, plus proximity sensors (sonars) on each side and bumpers on each side. Of course, this configuration would be quite costly. Redundancy appears to be an extra cost not justified by performance and by the level of risk as it was ascertained by our safety and risks assessment.

The final set of safety-related sensors included the certified Sick Laser S300P, a 3D laser for mapping, two sonars, a rear bumper (positioned on the back of the robot) and a cliff sensor (positioned on the back of the robot). All of them are part of the safety loop and cause an immediate emergency stop.

One of the weak points that involve residual risk (mitigation measure: training and instruction) is the movement in reverse motion. The system includes a docking station. When the robot leaves the docking station, it moves backwards. The 3D Lidar that is located on top of the robot in this situation cannot spot objects on the floor or a human that is kneeling behind it.

As the scrubber robot is a professional machine, its docking station is typically hosted in a secluded non-public space (usually the room where the traditional human-driven floor cleaning machines are parked and recharged). So far, the access to the room and the exposure to the risk is limited to expert personnel. Therefore, it was rated as a tolerable risk because of the rarity of occurrence of dangerous human behaviour, the risk is to be mitigated through training and instructions. As an additional mitigation measure, the reverse motion has strict lower speed limits. At that speed, the action of the rear bumper will stop the robot just because of a soft touch.

One issue in performing this risk evaluation is the lack of data about the admissible contact forces at low speed for contact with a rubber part (the bumper)

Another issue in using ISO 13482 is that it "provides guidance for the assurance of safety in the design and construction of the non-medical personal care robot, as well as the integration, installation and use of the robots during their full life cycle".

Actually, this is not true. The standard barely mentions maintenance. In our analysis for our robotics scrubber, we found that some items entail hazards and consequently risk in the case of maintenance operations.

Also, the entire life cycle is generally intended as including remanufacturing, recycling or disposal. None of these possible end of life processes is diffusely considered in the standard.

Another small issue is related to the performance level or safety integrity level of control systems. The respective section 6 of the standard is not straightforward. The rationale is not clear behind the classification and choice of PLs in the presented table.

Therefore, we had to build our own educated rationale for the application to our robot, which was similar to the object categories of the standard but not identical.

Finally, there is a risk in common to many robotics systems related to mapping. The mapping operation is done manually. Then the map is manually edited. In this process, the human can introduce errors that add up to the known limitations of the technology. This is a non-functional risk. The safety-related controls and sensors shall be able to counteract occurrences due to map errors.

In general, we can affirm that ISO 13482 is a good reference for service robots that are within similar weight and speed specifications to those considered by the standard itself. Actually, we proved that it covers all the requirements for safety (with the proviso provided in these conclusions) that we were able to identify in the robotised scrubber.

CHAPTER 9

Safety of Medical Robots, Regulation, and Standards

Kiyoyuki Chinzei

CONTENTS

9.1	Introduction	124
9.2	Regulation of Medical Devices	124
	9.2.1 In the USA	125
	9.2.2 In the EU	125
	9.2.3 Global Harmonization	125
	9.2.4 Definition of a Medical Device	126
	9.2.5 The Essential Principles	126
9.3	Safety of Medical Robots	127
	9.3.1 Definition of a Medical Robot	127
	9.3.2 Boundary of Applicable Regulations	128
	9.3.3 Safety Requirements and Standards	128
9.4	Particular Standards for Medical Robots	129
9.5	Particular Standards for Rase, IEC 80601-2-77	130
	9.5.1 Scope and Key Definitions	130
	9.5.2 Safety Requirements and Relaxation	131
9.6	Particular Standards for RACA ROBOTS, IEC 80601-2-78	132
	9.6.1 Scope and Key Definitions	132
	9.6.2 Safety Requirements	133
9.7	Future of Medical Robot Safety	133
	9.7.1 What Is Autonomy?	134
	9.7.2 Assessing the Degree of Autonomy	135
References		136

9.1 INTRODUCTION

Whilst safety is one of the key concerns of any robot, it is paramount for medical robots due to the nature of the way they are used: in most cases, they are directly applied to the patient – attached to, working at the proximity of, or even inserted into the patient's body.

Although we will introduce the definition of medical robots later, here we consider them this way:

> *Medical robots are robots intended to be used for medical purposes, which are attached to or inserted into the patient's body or working at the proximity of the patient.*

Assistive robots for elderly and disabled people are excluded here since those individuals are not considered as patients unless they are under medical treatment. Also, robots for labor and task automation or assistance in medical services are excluded if patients are not involved.

Knowing safety standards for medical robots are of key importance because conformity to standards is mandated in all major markets in the world.

Amongst many possible medical uses of robots, safety standards for robots for surgery, radiotherapy, and rehabilitation already exist or are under development. In this chapter, we look at the regulations of those robots in different nations and regions.

Medical robots are under regulatory control in many nations and regions as medical devices. The requirements and standards for medical robots are different from other robots. To understand the difference, we need to learn the regulatory system applied to medical robots. In this section, we look at the regulatory system and requirements of those robots.

9.2 REGULATION OF MEDICAL DEVICES

Regulation rules and regulatory bodies of medical devices are similar to those of medicine in most nations and regions of the world. Although the detail of regulation differs by nations and regions, general requirements can be summarized as the following (but with certain exceptions and differences).

- Quality control: Manufacturers need to maintain and record the process of product quality control.

- Marketing approval: Manufacturers need to put the product on the market.

- Post-market vigilance and surveillance: The manufacturer needs to watch adverse events and incidents related to their products. Once such an event is observed, the manufacturer investigates the event, and if needed, applies the necessary countermeasures such as reporting to the relevant authorities and recalling the product.

Requirements for the marketing approval process vary by nations and regions.

9.2.1 In the USA

In many nations, governmental regulatory agencies issue premarket approvals. The most typical example is the approval system of the Food and Drug Agency (FDA) of the USA.

Medical device approvals are classified as Premarketing Approval (PMA) and Premarket Notification, also known as 510(k). To obtain FDA approval, manufacturers need to demonstrate the medical benefits and safety of the product in the intended market. The benefits should outweigh the residual risks. Clinical trials are required to validate the benefit depending on the novelty of the device, particularly for PMA devices.

The FDA maintains a list of national and international standards that the agency recognizes as applicable for conformity assessment, called **recognized standards**. There were over 1,200 recognized standards in April 2018. The recognized standards can be searched on the FDA webpage [1].

In many nations, the government is in charge of reviewing and approving medical devices before entering the market.

9.2.2 In the EU

The European Union, due to special political circumstances and history, has a unique system. EU Medical Device Regulation (MDR) requires manufacturers to obtain a certificate for each medical device, a **CE marking**, issued by a notified body. The notified body conducts the conformity assessment by auditing the quality system of the manufacturer and reviewing the product and relevant technical documents provided by the manufacturer to assess the safety of the product. The clinical benefit is not mandated to be demonstrated except for certain groups of medical devices such as active implants. Details of the EU product safety system can be found in [2].

EN standards and international standards are referenced to assess conformity.

9.2.3 Global Harmonization

To minimize the difference of requirements by nations and regions, regulatory bodies in the world aim to harmonize and converge their requirements for medical devices. The International Medical Device Regulators Forum (IMDRF) is a group of regulatory authorities of nine nations and a region. It was established in 2011 on the basis of achievements of its former organization, the Global Harmonization Task Force (GHTF). IMDRF and GHTF documents are the foundation of the harmonized scheme of medical device regulation. They include

- **Key definitions** such as "medical device"
- **Classification** of medical devices
- **The essential principles**, the essential requirements of safety and performance of medical devices
- The role of standards in assessments

- The principle of the labeling of medical devices

- Unique Device Identification (UDI)

- The regulation of software as a medical device (SaMD)

9.2.4 Definition of a Medical Device

The definition of the term "medical device" is harmonized by the GHTF [3].

> *'Medical device' means any instrument, apparatus, implement, machine, appliance, implant, reagent for in vitro use, software, material or other similar or related article, intended by the manufacturer to be used, alone or in combination, for human beings, for one or more of the specific medical purpose(s) of:*
>
> - *diagnosis, prevention, monitoring, treatment or alleviation of disease*
>
> - *diagnosis, monitoring, treatment, alleviation of or compensation for an injury*
>
> - *investigation, replacement, modification, or support of the anatomy or of a physiological process*
>
> - *supporting or sustaining life*
>
> - *control of conception*
>
> - *disinfection of medical devices*
>
> - *providing information by means of in vitro examination of specimens derived from the human body*
>
> *and does not achieve its primary intended action by pharmacological, immunological or metabolic means, in or on the human body, but which may be assisted in its intended function by such means.*

This definition is commonly cited by international standards for medical devices.

9.2.5 The Essential Principles

To understand what is required to put a medical device onto the market, it is useful to look at **the essential principles**. A GHTF document [4] has a list of the essential principles (numbers in parentheses are the numbers of subitems in each item).

1. General requirements (6)

2. Chemical, physical, and biological properties (5)

3. Infection and microbial contamination (7)

4. Incorporated medicinal product/drug (1)

5. Incorporated biological origin materials (3)

6. Environmental properties (5)

7. Devices with a diagnostic or measuring function (3)

8. Protection against radiation (4)

9. Software (2)

10. Active medical devices (7)

11. Protection against mechanical risks (6)

12. Protection against the risks posed to the patient by supplied energy or substances (3)

13. Protection against the risks posed by medical devices intended by the manufacturer for use by lay persons (3)

14. Labels and instructions for use (1)

15. Clinical evaluation (2)

These illustrate what you need to consider before placing a medical device on the market. For example, the last subitem in the general requirement is regarding the principle of **risk management**.

> *All known and foreseeable risks, and any undesirable effects, should be minimised and be acceptable when weighed against the benefits of the intended performance of medical devices during normal conditions of use.*

Some requirements may not be applicable to a specific medical device. For example, a surgical robot that does not use X-rays does not need to meet the requirements for X-ray radiation.

Most importantly, many of these requirements can be associated with related standards. In practice, the manufacturers need to identify which requirements in the essential principles are covered by which standards, and to identify the means to mitigate and validate the remaining requirements.

9.3 SAFETY OF MEDICAL ROBOTS

9.3.1 Definition of a Medical Robot

Previously, we defined a medical robot by using this definition, medical robots can be defined very concisely as

> *robots intended to be used as medical devices.*

Indeed, a medical robot is defined by an International Electrotechnical Commission (IEC) technical report [5] as

> ROBOT* *intended to be used as* MEE *or* MES.

---

* IEC standards use a convention to apply SMALL CAPITAL type to defined terms. This chapter follows this convention.

Here, MEE and MES are **medical electrical equipment** and **system**. Those are IEC 60601 series standards terms, roughly corresponding to "active medical device using electric energy."

9.3.2 Boundary of Applicable Regulations

Since medical robots are both robots and medical devices by definition, they are on the border. It is a question – which regulation, medical device regulation or robot regulation, applies?

The short answer is "primarily regulated as medical devices, but the robot regulation (if there is one) also applies." Robot regulations in many nations do not require approval like medical devices. However, nations still directly or indirectly require conformity to relevant standards. In the EU, both the Medical Device Regulation and the Machinery Directive should be satisfied.

9.3.3 Safety Requirements and Standards

The safety requirements for medical robots are basically derived from the essential principles. And from the applicable essential principles, the applicable standards are determined.

To determine which standards are applicable, it is necessary to identify the indication – the intended use, the intended clinical functions, the intended patients and intended users, and so on. Medical robots can include many different robots for different purposes. Here we consider common aspects of medical robots. Most commonly, the following standards are applied:

- ISO 14971 (risk management of a medical device);

- ISO 10993 series (biocompatibility);

- IEC 60601 series (electrical safety, EMC, mechanical safety applicable to MEE);

- IEC 62366-1 (usability engineering of a medical device);

- IEC 62304 (software lifecycle of a medical device).

There are many other standards to apply, but you can find them cited or referenced in the above standards.

You may wonder – where are the robot safety standards? There are standards for robots, for example,

- ISO 10218-1 (industrial robot safety);

- ISO 13842 (personal care robot safety).

And there are many numbers of standards for mechanical safety, but none of them are here!

The main reason is that machinery safety and medical device safety standards are established independently so that they have own hierarchies. Two hierarchies are basically not interchangeable. For example, the risk management standards for machinery and medical devices are ISO 12100-1 and ISO 14971. These are at the top of the hierarchy and any sublevel standards are written under their mother risk management standard. Applying two different risk management standards is costly and painful. When a robot is a medical device, it is sufficient to only apply ISO 14971. Some exceptions are rehabilitation robots that can be used as non-medical devices, which also requires the application of ISO 12100 (Figure 9.1).

9.4 PARTICULAR STANDARDS FOR MEDICAL ROBOTS

IEC and ISO are currently working to develop new safety standards for two groups of medical robots:

- IEC 80601-2-77 (safety of surgical robots)

- IEC 80601-2-78 (safety of rehabilitation robots)

They are scheduled to be issued by early 2019.* Both standards are being developed under the joint projects of IEC and ISO, where IEC/TC 62 manages safety standards of MEE and ISO/TC 299 manages standards for robotics. These standards will be a part of the safety standards series IEC 60601 for MEE.

Like other IEC 60601 standards, these will be mandated. Therefore, the title and scope are carefully defined. As a result, these medical robots are renamed as:

- ROBOTICALLY ASSISTED SURGICAL EQUIPMENT (RASE)

- REHABILITATION, ASSESSMENT, COMPENSATION AND ALLEVIATION ROBOT (RACA ROBOT)

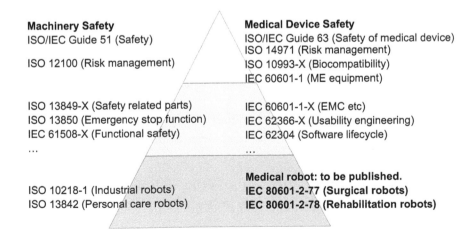

FIGURE 9.1   Hierarchies of machinery safety standards and medical device standards.

---

* This book is based on the final drafts which are subject to minor (editorial) changes.

Both robots can have a wide variety of intended uses, medical procedures, mechanical structures, control algorithms, and human-machine interfaces. Standardization projects were initially addressed to capture the common aspects in each robot.

9.5 PARTICULAR STANDARDS FOR RASE, IEC 80601-2-77

RASE is used for different disciplines of surgeries with a variety of mechanical structures and end effectors [6], for example:

- A master–slave manipulator for endoscopic surgery, such as the da Vinci Surgical System

- A numerical control machine for orthopedic surgery, such as the Robodoc

- A motion compliant robot for orthopedic surgery, such as the Mako System

- A micro-motion manipulator for eye surgery

- A hair implantation system

There are two common characteristics.

- RASE are combinations of surgical instruments and robotic bodies. The former can be forceps, mono- and bi-polar electrosurgical blade, milling drill, endoscope, and so on. Other existing standards may be applicable to the surgical instruments. The robot body facilitates the placement and manipulation of surgical instruments.

- RASE is used with other medical devices with electrical and other functional connections interacting together. In other words, safety should be achieved as a system.

- RASE is used in operating rooms where only trained staff move around.

9.5.1 Scope and Key Definitions
The draft definition is currently:

> **RASE:** MEDICAL ELECTRICAL EQUIPMENT that incorporates a PEMS actuated mechanism intended to facilitate the placement or manipulation of ROBOTIC SURGICAL INSTRUMENTS

> **ROBOTIC SURGICAL INSTRUMENT:** INVASIVE DEVICE with an APPLIED PART, intended to be manipulated by RASE to perform tasks in SURGERY

A new term, RASE, was introduced without using the term robot. It is used to avoid possible confusion and to emphasize that it is to assist surgeons, not to replace them with automation. The definition does not refer to a specific mechanical structure, means of actuation, or a control algorithm. The definition of ROBOTIC SURGICAL INSTRUMENT limits the scope of RASE to those that are invasive, at least in the current revision. This means that the following cases are excluded.

1. Energy is only administered to the patient, such as laser ablation or a bone fracture relocation device attached to the skin surface.

2. It is not intended to touch the patient's body; for example, a mechanical pointing device to display the orientation of the incision.

9.5.2 Safety Requirements and Relaxation

Some safety requirements in IEC 80601-2-77 and relaxation of requirements of IEC 60601-1 characteristic to RASE are

- **Information** essential to perform surgery shall be maintained.

- **Motion control** of the robotic surgical instruments shall be maintained.

- These two are considered as part of **the essential performance** of typical RASE surgeries (Figure 9.2).

- Continuous activation (an operator, the main surgeon in the case of RASE surgery, continuously monitors the movement and reacts to reduce the risk, including stopping when a hazardous situation is expected) is extended to allow other OPERATORS (e.g., the assistant surgeon or nurses) to also take the role of monitoring and reacting. In the case of endoscopic surgery, the main surgeon needs to concentrate on watching the endoscopic view, while other staff are expected to monitor and react to hazardous situations outside the patient body.

- If an equipment drape (drapes to cover the RASE) is necessary, its effects shall be considered in the risk management. Such a drape may be used to maintain sterility, including the prevention of contamination by liquid entering the sterile field. The drape should be durable against mechanical movement. Also, any side effects of the drape should be considered, for example, the temperature goes up under the drape, the IP classification assumes the use of drape, and so on.

- Attachment of robotic surgical instruments and RASE shall be tested.

- Interaction between surgical instrument shall be considered in the risk management. In particular, electrosurgical equipment that uses a high-frequency current can be

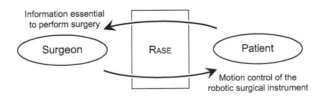

FIGURE 9.2 Essential performance of RASE.

hazardous because of the capacitive coupling leakage and electromagnetic disturbance to the robot control system.

- Narrow size robotic surgical instruments can be allowed by providing two means of operator protection and pollution level.

IEC 80601-2-77 does not include the following requirements:

- Requirements for robotic surgical instruments – use other related standards
- Testing methods of mechanical performance
- Requirements specific to **image guidance**
- Requirements specific to RASE with some **autonomy**

Autonomous surgical robots, or surgical robots with artificial intelligence, are recent topics [7], although we need more experience before introducing requirements for mandatory standards.

9.6 PARTICULAR STANDARDS FOR RACA ROBOTS, IEC 80601-2-78

RACA ROBOTS can be used for rehabilitation, assessment, compensation, and alleviation purposes, with a variety of mechanical structures and end effectors, for example:

- Walking, lower limb exoskeleton links using a motion-related biosignal, for example, HAL
- A cane-type mobile machine for the rehabilitation of walking
- A bodyweight support machine for gait following function

The common aspect between them is:

- The patient body is actuated by a mechanical attachment, with active control. It is the main clinical function to achieve rehabilitation and other purposes. The purposes do not include the daily use, for example, as prosthetic devices.
- A RACA robot may be used in an environment where non-staff individuals with different characteristics may co-exist, including lay people and children.

9.6.1 Scope and Key Definitions
The draft currently defines the following.

> **RACA ROBOT**: MEDICAL ROBOT intended by its MANUFACTURER to perform REHABILITATION, ASSESSMENT, COMPENSATION, or ALLEVIATION, comprising an ACTUATED APPLIED PART

REHABILITATION: Treatment to improve movement functions related to an impairment of a PATIENT

ALLEVIATION: Treatment to ease symptoms due to an impairment of a PATIENT

COMPENSATION: Mitigation of IMPAIRMENT of a PATIENT through support of body structures or through support or replacement of body functions

ASSESSMENT: Procedure to quantify or to aid in the qualification of the level of IMPAIRMENT of a PATIENT

ACTUATED APPLIED PART: subcategory of APPLIED PART that is intended to provide actively controlled physical interactions with the PATIENT that are related to the PATIENT'S MOVEMENT FUNCTIONS, to perform a CLINICAL FUNCTION of a RACA ROBOT

A new term ACTUATED APPLIED PART was the key definition to characterize RACA ROBOTS. The definition of a RACA ROBOT does not include

- Prosthetic devices
- Daily use devices (e.g., an electric wheelchair)
- Diagnostic imaging equipment
- (Non-medical use) personal care robots

9.6.2 Safety Requirements

Some of the safety requirements in IEC 80601-2-78 are

- Loss of situation awareness shall be considered in the risk management process. A detailed informative guidance was included.
- Misalignment of the actuated applied part from the intended patient body, movement beyond the preset limit for an individual patient are considered as mechanical hazards.
- Unintended movements in various situations shall be considered in risk management, e.g., an unexpected release of energy, a shared control between the RACA ROBOT and a human, and stopping functions.
- Test fingers for children shall be used when applicable.

The IEC issued a Technical Report (TR) on this topic [5], and there will be an informative annex on situational awareness in another medical robot standard being developed now.

9.7 FUTURE OF MEDICAL ROBOT SAFETY

Robot is defined in ISO 8373:2012, and it is agreed to be revised as:

Programmed actuated mechanism with a degree of autonomy, moving within its environment, to perform intended tasks

This definition is more focused on the **degree of autonomy** (DoA). As artificial intelligence (AI) emerges and automatic vehicles appear in the near future, medical robots will also have some degree of autonomy in the future. Since autonomy is considered as a characteristic of the AI, understanding and properly mitigating the possible safety issues of autonomy will become the key issue.

IEC TR 60601-4-1 [5] was published in May 2017. It is the first ISO/IEC document about autonomy of medical electrical equipment and systems. Not only that, it is the first of its kind in ISO/IEC documents. The technical report mainly provides the following:

- The definition of terms of autonomy in DoA

- Three methods of classification in DoA

- The relationship between DoA and risk, basic safety, and essential performance

- Usability engineering considerations for MEE with higher DoA

- Operator's situational awareness

- Examples of DoA in MEE, classification, and risk assessment

The TR does not provide the following:

- Risk level determined by DoA

- Conversion of DoA classified by one method to another

One of the TR's most important messages is that **increasing DoA does not necessarily increase risk and decreasing DoA does not necessarily decrease risk**. Motivations and benefits to adopting DoA can be various; DoA may be applied to improve the usability of MEE – but it may unintentionally introduce a new hazardous situation, such as the loss of the operator's situation awareness. It can happen by a "misunderstanding" between the human operator and the MEE with DoA. The aviation industry has already experienced fatal accidents related to situational awareness (SA). The medical equipment industry can face this issue when the DoA is high, possibly by the introduction of artificial intelligence (AI).

9.7.1 What Is Autonomy?

Concisely defining autonomy is not easy. The TR defines autonomy as the

> *capacity to monitor, generate, select and execute to perform a clinical function with no or limited operator intervention.*

Autonomy of MEE can be partial, or MEE can have a degree of autonomy. The TR defines degree of autonomy as

> *taxonomy based on the properties and capabilities of the MEE or MES related to autonomy.*

To clarify further, a note says that

> *the term autonomy in common language has been used to indicate 'null DoA' or 'full DoA' without allowing intermediate capability. It is recommended that the term autonomy be used carefully, and whenever possible, to use the term DoA instead.*

9.7.2 Assessing the Degree of Autonomy

DoA in MEE today is generally not high. The TR provides three methods to classify the DoA of the clinical function in MEE. One method is the descriptive classification method, which was adopted from Kaber [8].

The M-G-S-E columns of Table 9.1 are the four generic functions: monitoring; generating options; selecting an option (decision making); and executing the selected option. Although Table 9.1 resembles the levels of driving automation [9] or the levels of autonomy of robotic surgery [7], the methods in the TR are generalized so that it can be applied to any clinical functions of any MEE by introducing generic functions. It is another advantage of this TR – it is IEC 60601 friendly. The classification methods first look at the clinical functions of the MEE, which is the same manner in applying the IEC 60601 series standards.

TABLE 9.1   Descriptive Classification of DoA

Description	M	G	S	E
1. Full manual (FM): No autonomy involved. Operator performs all tasks to monitor the state of the system, generates performance options, selects the option to perform (decision making), and executes the decisions made.	H	H	H	H
2. Teleoperation (TO): MEE assists the operator to execute the selected action, although continuous operator control is required.	H/C	H	H	H/C
3. Preprogrammed execution (PE): Operator carries out the generation and selection activities without any analysis or selection carried out by MEE.	H/C	H	H	C
4. Shared decision (SD): Both operator and MEE generate possible options. Operator retains full control over the selected task.	H/C	H/C	H	H/C
5. Decision support (DS): MEE performs the generate options task, which the operator can select from or the operator can generate alternatives.	H/C	H/C	H	C
6. Blended decision (BD): MEE generates options, which it selects from and executes if the operator consents. The operator can also do so.	H/C	H/C	H/C	C
7. Guided decision (GD): MEE presents a set of actions to the operator. The operator's role is to select from among this set.	H/C	C	H	C
8. Autonomous decision (AD): MEE selects the best option and executes it based on the generated task.	H/C	H/C	C	C
9. Operator monitoring (OM): MEE generates options, selects the option to implement, and executes it. Operator intervenes if necessary.	H/C	C	C	C
10. Full autonomy (FA): MEE carries out all MGSE actions. Operator does not intervene except to emergency-stop MEE.	C	C	C	C

Note: Table 9.1 is simplified based on Table C.1 in the TR. C: Computer, H: Human.

REFERENCES

1. FDA, CDRH Recognized Consensus Standards Search Database, www.accessdata.fda.gov/scripts/cdrh/cfdocs/cfStandards/search.cfm (2016), accessed March 2019.
2. Czitán G. et al., Product Safety in the European Union, TÜV Rheinland Akadèmia, Budapest, (2008).
3. Global Harmonization Task Force (GHTF), Definition of the Terms 'Medical Device' and 'In Vitro Diagnostic (IVD) Medical Device', SG1/N71:2012 (2012).
4. Global Harmonization Task Force (GHTF), Essential Principles of Safety and Performance of Medical Devices, SG1/N68:2012 (2012).
5. IEC TR 60601-4-1:2017, Guidance and Interpretation – Medical Electrical Equipment and Medical Electrical Systems Employing a Degree of Autonomy (2017).
6. Hoeckelmann M. et al., Current capabilities and development potential in surgical robotics. *Int J Adv Robot Syst* 12(5), pp. 1–39 (2015). doi: 10.5772/60133
7. Yang G.-Z. et al., Medical robotics – Regulatory, ethical, and legal considerations for increasing levels of autonomy. *Sci Robot* 2, eaam8638, (2017).
8. Kaber D.B. and Endsley M.R., The effects of level of automation and adaptive automation on human performance, situation awareness and workload in a dynamic control task. *Theor Issues Ergon Sci* 5(2), pp. 113–153, (2004).
9. SAE International, Taxonomy and Definitions for Terms Related to On-Road Motor Vehicle Automated Driving Systems, SAE J3016 (2016).

CHAPTER **10**

The Other End of Human–Robot Interaction

Models for Safe and Efficient Tool–Tissue Interactions

Árpád Takács, Imre J. Rudas, and Tamás Haidegger

CONTENTS

10.1 Introduction   137
10.2 Types of Tool–Tissue Interaction   139
10.3 Review of Control Aspects of Tool–Tissue Interactions   143
10.4 Haptic Feedback in Telesurgery   145
10.5 Soft Tissue Models   147
10.6 Methods for Modeling Soft Tissues   149
    10.6.1 Mass–Spring–Damper Models   149
    10.6.2 Data Collection Methods   153
    10.6.3 Indentation Tests   154
    10.6.4 The Proposed Nonlinear Mass–Spring–Damper Model   158
10.7 Results   160
    10.7.1 Model Verification Methods   161
    10.7.2 Model Verification Results   163
10.8 Usability of the Proposed Model   164
10.9 Discussion   165
Acknowledgment   165
References   165

10.1 INTRODUCTION

In the past few years, research activities related to robotic surgery have gained attention due to the rapid development of interventional systems, representing a fine example of Human–Robot Interaction (HRI) [1]. Along with the development of novel technologies, engineers and robotic experts are facing new challenges, as a completely new type of interaction has appeared between humans and robots: human tissues manipulated by a robotic arm. Contrary to traditional HRI approaches, in the case of tool–tissue interaction, different types of models need to be used during the design and development processes, which can be reliably and safely used in manipulation-specific ranges of force values and tool movement. The new challenges carry unprecedented risks as well, especially during invasive interventions, remote surgeries, or automated task execution. While many surgical maneuvers have already been implemented with a degree of autonomy, most of today's robotic surgery devices are still used as teleoperation systems. This means that a human surgeon as an operator is always required to be present in the control loop. Parallel to the evolution of telesurgery, different model-based control methods have been developed and experimentally tested for enhancing transparency and increasing latency-tolerance, both in terms of long distance (space robotics, intercontinental operations) and short distance (local on-Earth scenarios) teleoperation. The effectiveness of traditional real-time control methods decreases significantly with the increase of time-delay, while time-varying latency introduces new challenges. A suitable control design can ensure high-quality control signals and improved sensory feedback. This can only be achieved by suitable models for all components of the telesurgical systems, including models of the human operator, the slave robot, and the mechanism of tool–tissue interaction. Using bilateral haptic devices, and accounting for tissue dynamics, can handle issues arising from communication latency. Stability and accuracy deterioration caused by latency and other external disturbances, such as contacting hard tissues or elastic tool deformation, can also be addressed using realistic soft tissue models, their integration into model-based force control algorithms largely increases the robustness and reliability of robot-assisted interventions.

Automation in the field of medicine is already present in many forms, providing a solid background to the medical robotics domain to nurture on. Most medico-surgical processes follow specific guidelines, such as generic diagnostic and treatment plans, supporting medical decision making and practice. On this highest level of abstraction, automation is part of the surgical field as well, with predefined treatment plans for common diseases, and with the rapid development of computer-integrated surgery (CIS), automation is penetrating into the fundamental layers of surgical practice, addressing the current issues of HRI from the robot-patient perspective.

Probably the most important characteristic of many surgical robots is spatial accuracy—inherently determining their applicability, functionality, and safety. Precision of robotic systems can be represented by the accuracy and repeatability of the device to characterize the overall effect of the encoder's fineness, the compliance of the hardware elements (e.g., the servos), and the rigidity of the structure. Generally, the absolute positioning accuracy shows the error of the robot when reaching for a prescribed position. This expresses the mean difference between the actual pose and the pose calculated from the mathematical model of the robot. Repeatability is the standard deviation of the positioning error acquired through multiple trials to reach the same joint values. Repeatability is typically smaller for manipulators than accuracy, and both numbers can largely depend on speed, payload, and range of motion.

Followed by the discussion of the importance of tool–tissue interaction modeling, control aspects, and haptic feedback in telesurgery, this chapter presents a methodology for soft tissue modeling. The motivation is to present tool–tissue interaction scenarios, from the HRI point of view. We present a specific but generalizable use-case, where the tissue deformation is uniform along the surface, verifying the proposed soft tissue model and highlighting the limitation of linear heuristic models. Then, we discuss a more complex approach, utilizing nonuniform surface deformation, estimating the force response from the previously verified model. The mechanical parameters of the soft tissue model, including stiffness and damping values of the elements, are estimated from measurement data, taken from the experiments described in the sections in detail.

10.2 TYPES OF TOOL–TISSUE INTERACTION

Tool–tissue interaction is the phenomenon when the surgical tool in some physical way interacts with the tissue to be manipulated during the intervention. Depending on the circumstances of the interaction, there are many types of manipulations that can be distinguished based on the instrument geometry, biological properties of the tissue, invasiveness of the interaction, and the mathematical modeling approach of the intervention.

When the surgical intervention is assisted by a robotic system, from the HRI point of view, some of the basic types of tool–tissue interactions are the following. In terms of invasiveness, the manipulation can be carried out using *blunt* instruments (tissue palpation for tumor detection, moving of organs for accessing the surgical area), *sharp* instruments (cutting, suturing, needle insertion), or *special* instruments (coagulation, ablation). In terms of the available feedback, the operator may receive *visual* information (endoscopic cameras, tool position mapping to pre-operative images), *haptic* feedback (direct on indirect force feedback, tactile feedback, haptic guidance), or *audio/audiovisual* feedback (forbidden region restriction, virtual fixtures, proximity information of the tool to the area of interest). Types of tool–tissue interaction can be approached from the mechanical properties and modeling of the participating mediums. We can differentiate between *soft tissue* interaction (organs, skin, muscles) and *hard tissue* interaction (primarily bones in drilling tasks or collision warning), while from the tool modeling aspect, *rigid tools* (scalpel blade), *elastic tools* (needles, MIS instruments), and *hybrid flexible tools* (snake-like tools, cable-driven manipulators). The modeling of tool/tissue deformation, reaction forces and biomechanical transitions (rupturing, chemical reactions) is a complex coupled problem, therefore, the *model complexity* also plays an important role in addressing a type of tool–tissue interaction. The most popular approaches—not restricted to the tissue models—include *continuum-mechanics based* models (complex deformations, highly nonlinear systems, finite elements analysis [FEA] modeling), *heuristic* models (low degree of freedom tasks, simple manipulations, high-level behavior estimation), and *hybrid* models.

A comprehensive study about the existing soft tissue models used in most MIS applications and virtual surgical simulators was presented by Famaey and Sloten [2], introducing three major categories of deformation models: heuristic models, continuum-mechanics models, and hybrid models. The complexity of each model mentioned above varies on a wide scale, although it is commonly accepted that approaches based on continuum-mechanics provide a more realistic response but requires significantly higher computational capacity. An analytical solution to the used mathematical laws generally does not exist. On the contrary, heuristic models that consist of lumped, linear mass–spring–damper elements, sometimes also called mechanical models, can be used for describing simple surgical tasks like needle insertion. The derived equations can usually be solved analytically.

While the modeling of soft tissue behavior has been the focus of research for a long time, the challenging field of gaining information about the interactions of the robot arm and the tissue has only reached popularity recently. Among the arising issues, it is important to mention the problem of force feedback, the modeling of tools, and the interaction with organs itself. A comprehensive review on current tool–tissue interaction models was carried out in [3], providing a survey on research focusing on interactions described by models, following the principles of continuum mechanics and finite element methods. The focus of interest can also be extended to models of telesurgical applications, without strict boundaries of categories, giving an overview of model properties. In [4], a simple 1 degree-of-freedom (DoF) model of a rigid master and flexible slave connection was introduced. Here, the problem of tool flexibility is addressed as one of the greatest issues in the case of tool–tissue interactions, since the force sensing can only be applied at the fixed end of the tool and its deflection can only be estimated. Besides tool flexibility, the compliant parameters of the robotic arm and the tissue model are also important and are significant parts of the tool–tissue interaction system. Other extensions of the model exist for rigid slave, flexible joint, and flexible master descriptions, and the complexity of the model of the whole system can be high. The great advantage of this approach is that not only the tool flexibility but the whole transparency of the system is addressed. It is important to mention, though, that no detailed tissue modeling is provided, the use of rigid specimen model indicates that this approach is rather focusing on teleoperation. Basdogan et al. [5] addressed the importance of tool–tissue interaction modeling in medical training through simulation in virtual reality, focusing on issues in haptics in minimally invasive surgery. When working with soft tissues, the elastic behavior of the tool can usually be omitted, using rigid models of surgical accessories. In their work, they introduced two new approaches to tissue modeling: the mesh-based FEA model, using modal analysis and the real-time meshless method of finite spheres. In the virtual environment, collision detection and perception of multiple tissue layers were created, accompanied with force and torque feedback to the user's hand. This feature is supported by force and position sensors mounted on the tool, which is held by the user instead of a robotic arm. The complexity of the above-mentioned methods is in connection with the required computational effort. In simple problems, the use of the method of finite spheres is suggested. Another approach to meshless methods was introduced by Bao et al., where several layers were used as the model of the soft tissue, their interaction modeled with a heuristic Kelvin model [6]. Modeling of two important viscoelastic properties, the creep and relaxation is possible with this new three-parameter viscoelastic model, improving the performance of conventional mass–spring–damper approaches. Yamamoto suggested a method for the detection of lumps in organ tissues such as the kidney, liver, and heart [7]. The importance of this work was a comprehensive comparison of seven different tissue models used in point-to-point palpation. The aim of the tests and model validations was to create a graphical overlay system that stores data on palpation results, creating a color scale overlay on the actual tissue, processing the acquired data using several tissue models, with a single 1 DoF force sensor at the fixed end of the tool. Yamamoto et al. also created an interpolable interface with haptic feedback and augmented visual feedback and performed palpation and surface detection tasks using vision-based forbidden-region virtual fixtures [8]. The tests were carried out on manufactured artificial tissues based on existing commercially available artificial prostate, using a complex, but—based on previous measurements—accurate Hunt–Crossley model. Position, velocity, and force sensors were mounted on a slave manipulator and the visual feedback to the human user was generated with a stereo-vision system.

When dealing with viscoelastic materials interacting with tools, coupled problems arise where additional mechanical models are required to describe the system response. It is important to mention that even when the best-suited mathematical models are employed, material properties (Young-modulus, Poisson-ratio, etc.) can only be estimated. Validation of their values requires circumstantial physical experiments. When using heuristic, mechanical tissue models, the acquisition of explicit, but general material properties are omitted. Instead of using tables and possible ranges of these properties, spring and damping coefficients must be obtained from measurements even when nothing else but the tool shape is changed. In their work, Leong et al. introduced and validated a mechanical model of liver tissue and its interaction with a scalpel blade, creating a distributed model of mechanical viscoelastic elements [9]. With the serial connection of a Maxwell and a Kelvin element, they introduced the Maxwell–Kelvin viscoelastic body. The primary aim of their work was to account for the tissue surface deformation due to the extensive shape of the tool, validating with the cutting experiment where a 1 DoF force sensor was placed at the scalpel blade holder integrated with position measurement. Besides many constitutive ideas, a great number of deficiencies can be found in the model that still needs to be improved, including mathematical errors in modeling, contradictions in the measurement result evaluation, inappropriate use of Laplace transformation, and the overall pertinence of experimental results. Liu et al. introduced a method for force control for robotic-assisted surgery on a beating heart, thus applying motion compensation for the periodic motion of the organ [10]. By installing a force sensor at the end of the instrument and tracking the 3D motion of the beating heart, they compared four different models from the viewpoint of tracking performance of the desired force. Besides the conventional viscoelastic models, a fourth, fractional derivative model of viscosity was examined. One of the relevant results of this experiment was to underline the importance of the right choice of tissue model.

In the past few years, much focus has been drawn on needle insertion modeling. Due to the simplicity of the tool geometry, needle insertion problems were much discussed using Finite Element modeling. The Finite Element Method is a widely used approach for tool–tissue interaction modeling, where commercially available FEA software packages are used to aid and simulate the operation area. The great many built-in mechanical models can provide incredibly accurate and realistic solutions for simulation. One of the largest drawbacks of this method is the sensitivity of computational time length with respect to the parameters used in FE simulations. These parameters are determined solely by the user, including spatial and time resolutions, thus, many simulations need to be carried out on the same model to achieve the desired level of reliability. Goksel et al. introduced a novel technique to use real-time remeshing in the case of FEA modeling [11]. A mesh-based linear elastic model of both the needle and tissue was used, applying remeshing in order to compensate organ shift due to the invasiveness. The importance of the model is that both tool and tissue deformation were accounted for, although the motion models were the simplest possible in 3D. Continuum mechanics also provides numerous models that can be used for modeling organ and tissue deformations and kinetics.

Approaches using linear and nonlinear models of elasticity are widely used in practice. Linear models have limited usability despite the many advantages they carry (simplicity, easy-calculation, and small requirements on computational capacity) due to inhomogeneous, anisotropic, nonlinear characteristics of tissues and large relative deformations and strains. However, nonlinear models in continuum mechanics lead to moderately complex models even in simple surgical tasks. Misra et al. introduced a detailed complex mechanical model of continuum mechanics for the analytical modeling and experimental validation of needle bending at insertion into soft tissues [12]. A hyperelastic neo-Hookean rupture model was used to describe the material properties and behavior of the soft tissue simulant (gel), assuming linear elasticity in case of the needle. Experiments were carried out using different bevel-tipped needles and the needle bending curvature was validated using unfiltered camera data. The importance of the work lays in the area of needle insertion path planning.

In the area of tool–tissue interaction research, one might be interested in rapture modeling. While most of the existing mechanical models assume reversible tissue deformation, even in the case of minimal invasive surgery (MIS), tissue rupture cannot be avoided. Mahvash and Dupon developed an analytical model of tissue rapture during needle insertion, focusing on the calculation of required insertion force [13]. The great advantage of this model is that despite the complex mechanical structure, the insertion events are divided into four different models, decomposing the process into moderately complex parts. Tissue modeling was aided with a modified Kelvin model, making the parameters of the linear components dependent of the deformation rate. The analytical model validated the experiments showing that the required insertion force is inversely proportional to the insertion speed.

It is important to mention models that are not directly describing insertion and cutting problems, but are rather used for investigating interaction of cable-driven manipulators controlled by human operators, acting on soft tissues. Kosari et al. introduced an adaptive parameter estimation and model predictive control (MPC) method on cable-driven surgical manipulators, developing a 1 DoF mechanical model, concentrating on the problem of trajectory tracking [14]. Therefore, instead of the estimation of tissue reaction forces, focus was drawn to the response of the cable-driven manipulator in order to create a realistic force feedback to the human user. The moderately complex model accounts for numerous mechanical properties and solves an optimal control problem for automating tissue compression.

The proper modeling of tool–tissue interactions is a relevant topic in standardization methods. With the help of initial calculations and simulations, efficient control methods can be chosen to avoid undesired pain and injury levels. Pain and injury onset levels for static contact force and peak pressure values are deeply researched and standardized in the literature [15].

10.3 REVIEW OF CONTROL ASPECTS OF TOOL–TISSUE INTERACTIONS

The general concept of teleoperation has long been used in various fields of robotics, including manufacturing, logistics, and service robotics scenarios [16]. Today, long-distance teleoperation is an actively discussed topic in space exploration [17] and for intervention in hazardous environments [18]. Where traditional control algorithms might fail, latency-induced challenges can be addressed by novel ideas, including soft computing methods, neural control [19], supervisory control through Internet communication [20], passivity based control [21], and various types of MPC for transparent teleoperation [22] and hybrid MPC solutions to neural network (NN)-based control methods [23].

Commercially available telesurgical systems utilize the concept of unilateral teleoperation, where the position and/or force data from the master console are transmitted to the slave system, whereas the operator only receives visual feedback from the environment through the mounted camera system. However, in bilateral teleoperation, there is a communication of force and position data in both directions of the teleoperation system. This structure allows haptic feedback to the operator, therefore, an extended virtual presence can be established in the physical surgical environment, increasing the *transparency*, which gives an answer to what level the master operator feels that the slave-side environment is being manipulated [24]. In telesurgery, the term *transparency* mostly refers to the level of match between the mechanical impedance of the manipulated environment encountered by the slave and the mechanical impedance transmitted to or felt by the operator at the master [25]. The general concept of bilateral teleoperation is shown in Figure 10.1 [26]. There is a vast literature of control architectures addressing challenges and proposing solutions to bilateral teleoperation systems, emphasizing the effect of time-delay caused by the communication latency between the master and slave sides. A large percentage of these approaches are variations of position–position teleoperation [27], position–force [28], or force–force teleoperation [29]. Other approaches include a special group of linear controllers, robust H_{inf} control, system dynamics assessment, and adaptive nonlinear controllers [30, 31, 32]. Obstacle avoidance, motion guidance, and inertia scaling also play an important role in describing the dynamics of the specific teleoperation task, where passive decomposition [33] and time-domain passivity controllers [34] can enhance the performance of actions.

Depending on the nature of the applications, the latency in communication can range between milliseconds (Internet-based teleoperation in terrestrial conditions) to several minutes (space exploration). Therefore, the magnitude of time-delay is determined by the distance between the master and slave devices and the medium of communication. It is a common view that in robotic systems, time-delay causes a trade-off between teleoperation stability and the control performance of the system. Local force feedback at the master side largely affects the performance and transparency of time-delayed teleoperation systems,

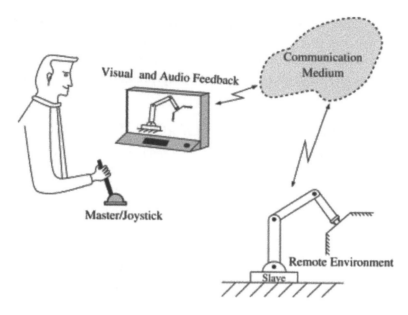

FIGURE 10.1 The concept of bilateral teleoperation by Hokayem and Spong [26].

which varies for different bilateral teleoperation architectures and the magnitude of the latency [35]. A common approach to increase the robustness of delayed teleoperation is to apply additional damping on both the master and slave side of the system, however, this often leads to a slow response of the system [36], degrading its control performance. As the transparency of the system decreases, some methods can compensate for the performance decay in bilateral teleoperation by using scattering theory [37], wave-variable control [38], or passivity control [39]. Other approaches include the telemonitoring of force feedback under low latencies [40].

In the past few decades, it has become a common view that large delays require accurate models of the operation environment based on prediction, creating a quasi-real-time simulated response to the operator [41]. One of the most successful approaches to predictive control methods utilizes the Smith predictor [42], while several approaches combine the Smith predictor with Kalman filtering for achieving better performance results [43, 44]. The linear approximation of the effect of time-delay is also a common modeling approach in teleoperation control, utilizing the state-space representation of the system based on the first-order Taylor-expansion of the system [45, 46].

In order to summarize the challenges and current possibilities in teleoperation with time-delay in the range of a few seconds, a detailed report has been published by NASA [47] in 2002. The report lists some of the most important tools and guidelines in teleoperation, highlighting the importance of predictive displays, where a realistic model of the environment is shown to the operator, which responds to the master console input in real-time. This approach has proven to be very efficient if the latency is under one second, however, it requires a reliable model of the task environment, including the slave and slave-environment interaction models [48]. Another frequently discussed issue is related to the compliance of the slave side, as it can reduce the execution time and the overall forces acting on the environment during manipulation [49]. From the haptics point of view, force reflection in bilateral teleoperation is critical in terms of stability. In real-life applications, direct force feedback can only be applied reliably with latencies under two seconds, however, in this range, high performance in completing teleoperation tasks, in terms of stability and transparency, can only be achieved with force feedback [50]. This feedback can be achieved in numerous ways, directly or indirectly, such as using a visual feed on the force magnitude or reflection of the force of the hand of the operator that does not take part in the teleoperation. The best solution is considered to be when the interaction force is simulated and fed back to the operator based on the system model. This work gives a proposal for modeling methodology of the interaction environment during teleoperation, more precisely, the modeling of tool–tissue interaction in case of telesurgical manipulations on soft tissues, since it is a key element of HRI in surgery.

10.4 HAPTIC FEEDBACK IN TELESURGERY

In recent years, the number of MIS procedures has increased significantly. MIS allows shorter patient recovery time and the decrease of surgical trauma. However, due to the long, rigid design of MIS tools, limited vision and confined operation space, several ergonomic difficulties and technological limitations have arisen that are yet to be solved. These include the deprivation of dexterity, loss of depth perception due to the two-dimensional video image feedback, distributed hand–eye coordination and special tool manipulation, and most importantly, the loss of tactile feedback [51]. Most of these limitations were addressed and partially solved with the introduction of robot-assisted surgery and telesurgery. By using stereo visual feedback, tremor filtering and ergonomic human–machine interfaces (HMIs), the lack of force feedback limits the ability of the surgeon during organ palpation, tumor localization, and the location of other abnormalities [52].

The role of haptic feedback in telesurgery is twofold: 1) restoring tactile information is essential for assessing the surface properties of the investigated organs. This feature is generally useful for artery and lump detection, therefore, the lack of tactile feedback leads to a more difficult localization of palpable anomalies, such as kidney stones; 2) haptics may provide a realistic force feedback to the robot operator, giving information about the mechanical characteristics of the tissue. This may improve the quality of basic surgical maneuvers (grabbing, palpation, cutting), and allows collision detection, which opens new opportunities toward virtual fixtures and the design of surgical simulators [53]. Tissue characterization also requires complex perception of the operating environment, where, besides tissue stiffness (hardness), relaxation properties and other viscoelastic phenomena can be investigated and accounted for when using haptic feedback. It was also shown that for tissue characterization tasks, utilizing force feedback leads to better results than only visual feedback, while with the combination of the two, superior results can be achieved [54].

While the lack of haptic feedback is still common to modern robot-assisted MIS procedures, the solutions provided by today's commercially available telesurgical systems are still limited. Increased cost, sterilization difficulties, and the sizing limitations of force sensors at the end effector are the key limiting factors to introducing haptic feedback to these systems through direct force sensing at the tool tip. To address these issues, several approaches were investigated for indirect force estimation, for example, accounting for joint flexibility [4], the dynamics of cable-driven manipulators [14], or force estimation through soft tissue modeling [55].

There is no general consensus among laparoscopic surgeons, if, and at what level would haptic feedback improve the quality of procedures. According to many surgeons, having visual feedback alone provides adequate information about the tissue palpation force for safe and reliable operation, however, the lack of haptic feedback is often considered as a major limitation in robot-assisted MIS procedures [56]. Clearly, an experienced surgeon finds the lack of haptic feedback less disturbing than a novice. However, in haptic guidance, learning spatiotemporal trajectories, contrary motion compensation (Fulcrum-effect), and strategy planning, the presence of haptic feedback and/or surgical simulators can enhance force skill learning for trainees [57].

Providing a complex and reliable perception for the operators of haptic devices could not only enhance intra-operative performance, but it may also become an essential tool in surgical training and pre-operative planning. In recent years, the use of surgical software simulators has largely increased, offering different training scenarios, anatomical variations, and conditions in the operating environment [58,59]. Using haptic devices, a new dimension opened in performance evaluation during procedures. Moreover, due to the complex mechanical behavior of soft tissues, augmented simulations require reference data from real surgical scenarios and should be tested by human operators to validate the usability of the virtual models [60].

The problem of distinguishing between soft tissues by testing their mechanical properties is often referred to as the cognitive role of haptic devices in simulation environments [61]. Today's surgical simulators that are using haptic interfaces are both relying on simple mechanical models of soft tissues and complex, parameterized finite element models. However, for enhancing real-time operation and focusing on the most representative mechanical effects, simple models are preferred in order to keep the transparency of the operation at maximum. Besides high computational requirements, using bilateral haptic devices and accounting for tissue dynamics can also handle issues arising from communication latency [62]. Stability and accuracy deterioration caused by latency and other external disturbances, such as contacting hard tissues or elastic tool deformation, can also be addressed using realistic soft tissue models. Their integration into model-based force control algorithms largely increases the robustness and reliability of robot-assisted interventions [63]. The integration of soft tissue properties to robot-assisted and virtual reality-based MIS procedures is an actively researched topic within the field of surgical robotics. Methods for acquiring useful measurement data use a combined experimental procedure of measuring tissue relaxation force under step-like tissue compression and force measurement during constant compression rate indentation input. Samur et al. proposed a method for tissue parameter estimation using a custom indenter during laparoscopic surgery by means of inverse finite element solution to estimate optimum values of nonlinear hyperelastic and elastic properties [64]. Beccani et al. developed a tool for intra-operative wireless tissue palpation, using a cylindrical palpation probe and estimating local volumetric stiffness values, assuming linear elastic behavior of the tissue [65].

A deformable model based on nonlinear elasticity and the finite element method for haptic surgical simulators was proposed in [66], validated on real-time simulations of laparoscopic surgical gestures on virtual liver models. Trejos et al. suggested an augmented hybrid impedance control scheme to perform force control, providing model-based control background for a tactile sensing instrument in intra-operative tissue palpation [67]. Endoscopically guided, minimally invasive cannulation tasks were investigated by Wagner et al. to test the hypothesis that force feedback can improve surgical performance, finding that applied forces by surgeons can be decreased for those with adequate training background [68]. In [51], Tholey et al. developed an automated laparoscopic grasper with force feedback capability in order to aid the surgeons in differentiating tissue stiffness through the PHANToM (Sensable Technologies, Woburn, MA) haptic device. Participants were asked to differentiate between tissues, having provided visual and/or haptic feedback to complete the task.

Alternative approaches are also popular in general force feedback for laparoscopic training and procedures. Horeman et al. developed a training system that provided visual haptic feedback of the interaction forces during a procedure [69]. They found that providing haptic feedback through visual representation considerably improved the quality of the solved tasks. A detailed feasibility study of lung tumor detection using kinesthetic feedback was published by McCreery et al., creating an *ex vivo* experimental environment, modeling various tissue stiffness values, injecting agar into healthy tissues, and substituting haptic feedback with recorded force data [70].

10.5 SOFT TISSUE MODELS

A detailed investigation about the most widely used tool–tissue interaction models was published by Famaey and Sloten, sorting the soft tissue models into three distinguished categories:

- *Continuum mechanics-based* tissue models, utilizing concepts of finite element analysis (FEA) and continuum-mechanics approaches

- *Heuristic* models, which represent a combination of linear and/or nonlinear spring and damping elements

- *Hybrid* models, usually representing the combination of FEA/continuum mechanics-based and heuristic approaches [71]

It is a common view that continuum mechanics-based tissue models allow one to provide a realistic behavior description function during the tissue manipulation, although the vast computational requirements, the high complexity of the geometry, and the highly generic approach limit their usability in real-time surgical applications and simulation environments. On the other hand, heuristic models, which are also often mentioned as rheological models or mass–spring–damper models, are proven to be useful in modeling basic surgical manipulation tasks, including indentation and tissue grabbing [72]. In many cases, mass–spring–damper models also provide an analytical solution to the problems, allowing a more straightforward mathematical description of the tool–tissue interaction phenomenon [3]. There is extensive literature about the description of soft tissue behavior both in fixed compression rate indentation [6] and tissue relaxation phases [73], providing raw measurement data on the force response. The use of heuristic models for soft tissue representation was deeply discussed by Yamamoto, listing and assessing numerous basic models during point-to-point palpation for hidden lump detection [7]. The mechanical properties of human adipose tissues were investigated by Alkhouli et al. using a viscoelastic linear soft tissue model, focusing on the stress relaxation phase of the indentation [74]. The nonlinear viscoelastic mass–spring–damper model created by Troyer et al. was also verified based on relaxation tests, bearing in mind that the model can be later integrated in FEA approaches in order to speed up the computational process [75].

In a wider perspective, the heuristic soft tissue models can be integrated into image-based surgical guidance systems, aiding accuracy and stability of the interventions [76], while applying them as visual cues, the performance of haptic feedback devices can also be improved significantly. A fine example of such virtual soft tissue models was presented by Li et al., introducing a pseudo-haptic feedback-based method for the investigation of embedded hard incisions in a silicone phantom tissue [77]. Another complex tissue model was proposed by Leong et al. [9], where a curve fitting method was proposed for the acquisition of the soft tissue mechanical parameters, based on measurement data from [78]. While the initial idea of Leong was feasible, the correct mathematical derivation of the results was missing. The corrected mathematical description, improved measurement data, and detailed model verification was presented by Takács et al., concluding that the proposed nonlinear Wiechert heuristic model can effectively model the soft tissue behavior and quantitatively represent its mechanical properties during basic surgical manipulation tasks [55]. A comprehensive overview of the structure and usability of heuristic tissue models was presented by Wang and Hirai [79]. They investigated the force response of different commercially available clay samples and Japanese sweets materials.

Soft tissue manipulation requires sophisticated techniques and precise surgical tools, particularly during tissue indentation, cutting, or suturing. There is a need for accurate soft tissue models, as the best performance of surgical robotic applications can only be achieved by utilizing control methods taking the tissue mechanical behavior and properties into account [16]. Furthermore, in terms of stability and transparent teleoperation, the accurate modeling of tool–tissue interaction is essential for utilizing reliable model-based control methods. The most important aspects of these model-based approaches becomes imminent in the case of force control. The reaction force during a given manipulation can be estimated, and the control signal, which directly sets the input force or the tool trajectory, can be calculated. The control signal is then transferred to the robotic arm holding or manipulating the soft tissue, increasing the efficiency, stability, and accuracy of the intervention.

10.6 METHODS FOR MODELING SOFT TISSUES

10.6.1 Mass–Spring–Damper Models

Let us consider the tool–tissue interaction model proposed by Leong et al. in [9]. As shown in Figure 10.2, mass–spring–damper models are uniformly distributed under the soft tissue surface. When the tissue surface is deformed, the total force response is calculated by adding up the force response values of each individual element, which are all infinitely small and are connected to the surface of the deformed tissue. The model assumes that the displacement of each point on the tissue surface is known at any time and the deformation is always happening in the axis of the mechanical element.

The heuristic soft tissue modeling approach is one of the simplest ways to model the behavior of soft tissues. The complex biological structure of these tissues induces unique and diverse mechanical properties for these materials, including high levels of inhomogeneity, viscoelasticity, and anisotropy, which cannot be overlooked and drastically simplified when designing robot control applications. These restrictions are usually not applied for everyday industrial and service robotics applications for material handling and machining.

The concept of this modeling approach is very simple: linear and/or nonlinear damper and spring elements are assembled together in a mixed parallel and serial connection. The assembled network of mechanical elements is typically used for describing the soft tissue behavior during uniaxial deformation, while projecting force values representing the reaction force response of the tissue. Nevertheless, the model can be extended for measurement of rheological and viscoelastic properties of multiaxial elongation as well [80].

Efficient application of this approach requires the knowledge of the $u(t)$ deformation input of each of the end points of the network of the combined mechanical elements. With this information in hand, the force response can be given by a closed-form mathematical function, called the force response function. The reaction force depends on the basic mechanical properties of the element.

- Linear spring elements represent a force response f_s, which is calculated from the specific spring stiffness coefficient k and the deformation magnitude in the spring axial direction:

$$f_s = k(x_1 - x_2). \tag{10.1}$$

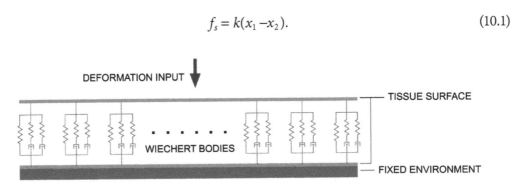

FIGURE 10.2 The proposed linear tool–tissue interaction model, where the Wiechert bodies are distributed along the tissue surface.

- Linear damper elements represent a force response f_d, which is calculated from the damping coefficient b and the relative deformation rate of the end points in the axial direction:

$$f_d = b(\dot{x}_1 - \dot{x}_2).$$ (10.2)

where x_1 and x_2 represent the end coordinates of the spring and damper elements, $\dot{x}_1$ and $\dot{x}_2$ are the deformation rates in the axial direction.

The literature of mass–spring–damper models lists three basic combinations of these elements in common application, referred to as the basic models of viscoelasticity. These are the Kelvin–Voigt, the Maxwell, and the Kelvin models, as shown in Figure 10.3 [72]. In this section, only the behavior of linear models is discussed, but the general description applies to the nonlinear models as well.

In analytical mechanics, the Kelvin–Voigt model is the most commonly used mass–spring–damper model, as it is capable of representing reversible deformation and stress relaxation simultaneously. The behavior of the system can be described using an ordinary differential equation and an analytical solution to the force response function can be given by solving this equation. The easy interpretation and simplicity of this approach makes it very popular in many fields of mechanical engineering. A strong limitation of the model arises from its difficulty of handling step-like deformations, as the reaction force on the damper element would be infinitely large in the case of a sudden deformation variation. As the Kelvin–Voigt model consists of the parallel connection of a spring and a damper element, the representation of the response function for the reaction force in the time-domain can be written as

$$f_{KV}(t) = b\dot{u}(t) + ku(t),$$ (10.3)

where $u(t)$ is the deformation function. The reaction force response function in the Laplace domain is

$$F_{KV}(s) = (bs + k)U(s).$$ (10.4)

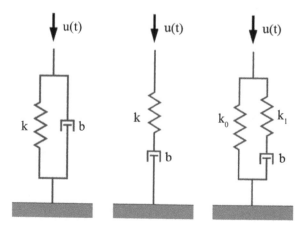

FIGURE 10.3 The most widely used viscoelastic models in soft tissue modeling: Kelvin–Voigt model (left), Maxwell model (center), and the Kelvin model (right).

In viscoelasticity, *creep* is a phenomenon that describes permanent deformation due to the applied mechanical stress, which can be straightforwardly modeled by the Maxwell model. In this approach, a spring and a damper element are connected in a serial way, representing creep and stress relaxation in the material. In practical applications, the use of this model is limited by the fact that the force response value converges to 0, when a constant deformation input is applied due to the serial connection of the damper element. The model is not capable of modeling residual stress and the deformation function of the model cannot be directly expressed as a function of the acting forces. This is due to the unknown position of the virtual mass point connecting the two elements, which can only be estimated but not directly measured. As time-domain representation of this model generally does not exist, a Laplace domain description is given below:

$$F_M(s) = \frac{khs}{bs + k} U(s).$$

(10.5)

The simplest possible solution to model residual stress, reversible deformation, and stress relaxation is provided by the Kelvin model, also often referred to as the Standard Linear Solid (SLS) viscoelastic model. The Kelvin model is constructed by the parallel connection of a single spring element and a Maxwell model. A popular time-domain representation is usually given in a closed-form formula:

$$f_K(t) + \frac{b}{k_1} \dot{f}_K(t) = k_0 \left(u(t) + \frac{b}{k_0} \left(1 + \frac{k_0}{k_1} \dot{u}(t) \right) \right),$$

(10.6)

while in the Laplace domain, the transfer function of this model is given by

$$F_K(s) = \frac{b(k_0 + k_1)s + k_0 k_1}{bs + k_1} U(s).$$

(10.7)

In modern medical technologies, the high diversity of the soft tissues and their complex behavior during manipulation tasks yielded to the need for more sophisticated viscoelastic models, relying on the modularity of the heuristic soft tissue modeling approach. Ultimately, new combinations of linear or nonlinear spring and damper elements would allow one to increase the performance of surgical robotics applications by better understanding the tissue behavior. Two of these more complex yet commonly used combinations are shown in Figure 10.4. If a Maxwell and a Kelvin model are connected serially, the so-called Maxwell–Kelvin model can be created, consisting of a total of five mechanical elements. The elastic behavior and relaxation properties can be more accurately modeled using this model, refining tissue parameters based on the experimental data using curve fitting. There exists a Laplace domain representation for this approach:

$$F_{MK}(s) = \frac{A_{2_{MK}} s^2 + A_{1_{MK}} s}{B_{2_{MK}} s^2 + B_{1_{MK}} s + B_{0_{MK}}} U(s),$$

(10.8)

where $A_{2_{MK}}$, $A_{1_{MK}}$, $B_{2_{MK}}$, $B_{1_{MK}}$, $B_{0_{MK}}$ are linear functions of the mechanical parameters k_0, k_1, k_2, b_1, and b_2.

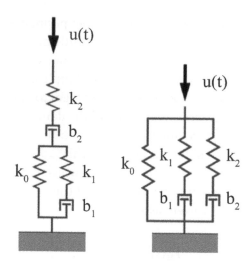

FIGURE 10.4   Advanced combinations of heuristic viscoelastic models in soft tissue modeling: the Maxwell–Kelvin model (left) and the Wiechert model (right).

More complex mass–spring–damper models do not necessary give better accuracy and performance in tissue behavior modeling. The Maxwell–Kelvin model, for example, will still have the limitation of the reaction force converging to 0, similar to the previously discussed Maxwell model. Alternatively, a Kelvin model and several Maxwell models can be connected in a parallel way in order to form a generalized Maxwell model, or, if there is only one Maxwell body connected to the system, the Wiechert model. It was shown in [9] and [55] that this assembly provides a smooth and accurate way for fine-tuning mechanical parameters for specific tissues during simple surgical manipulations.

A comparison of the Wiechert and Kelvin models was provided by Wang et al. [81], concluding that there is a significant advantage of using the Wiechert model in modeling spleen and liver organ force response estimation. A methodology for parameter estimation for the Wiechert model was also presented by Machiraju et al. [82], carrying out the investigation of tissue behavior during the stress relaxation phase. In the Laplace domain, the transfer function of the Wiechert model is as follows:

$$F_W(s) = \frac{A_{2_W}s^2 + A_{1_W}s + A_{2_W}}{B_{2_W}s^2 + B_{1_W}s + B_{0_W}}U(s) = W_W(s)U(s), \tag{10.9}$$

where

$A_{2_W} = b_1 b_2 (k_0 + k_1 + k_2),$

$A_{1_W} = (b_1 k_2 (k_0 + k_1) + b_2 k_1 (k_0 + k_2)),$

$A_{0_W} = k_0 k_1 k_2 b_2,$

$B_{2_W} = b_1 b_2,$

$B_{1_W} = b_1 k_2 + b_2 k_1,$

$B_{0_W} = k_1 k_2.$

10.6.2 Data Collection Methods

The structured collection of experimental data was motivated by the lack of general, publicly available force measurement data from tissue palpation. A frequent approach for this type of data collection aims for the palpation or indentation of *ex-vivo* tissue samples with known compression speed, creating a set of tissue deformation–reaction force characteristics. The goal of these measurements is to provide a reference data for curve fitting, where its deviation in the force response of the simulated tissue behavior is minimized for the optimal set of tissue parameters of the investigated model. With these considerations in hand, the following methodology for tissue characterization using the Wiechert model was carefully planned in order to provide sufficient data for model verification. According to the tool–tissue interaction model, infinitely small Wiechert bodies are distributed under the deformed tissue surface as shown in Figure 10.2. The model parameters are obtained by applying a uniform deformation input on the surface. During the initial experiment, six pieces of cubic-shaped fresh beef liver samples were investigated, with edge lengths of 20 ± 2 mm. The dimensions of each of the specimens were measured before and after the indentation tests. The specimens were compressed at three fixed compression rates: a slow rate of 20 mm/min, a medium rate of 100 mm/min, and a near-step input at 750 mm/min, the latter being the maximum deformation rate provided by the physical system. The indentation tests were carried out at the Austrian Center for Medical Innovation and Technology (ACMIT, Wiener Neustadt), on a Thümler GmbH TH 2730 tensile testing machine connected to an Intel Core i5-4570 CPU with 4 GB RAM, using ZPM 251 (v4.5) software. The force response data was collected with an ATI Industrial Automation Nano 17 titanium six-axis Force/Torque transducer, using the 9105-IFPS-1 DAQ Interface and the power supply at 62.5 Hz sampling time. An Intel Core i7-2700 CPU with 8 GB RAM hardware and the ATICombinedDAQFT .NET software interface was used for data visualization and storage. In the case of each specimen (marked by letters A–F), at first, the low and medium speed indentation tests were carried out, reaching 4 mm of indentation depth. The deformation input function was also recorded for validation purposes.

The uniform surface deformation was achieved by using a custom designed 3D-printed indenter head mounted on the force sensor. The starting position of the indenter was 1 mm above the surface of the specimen. During the evaluation of the measurement data, only 3.6 mm of indentation depth was investigated. This way, any nonlinearity in the ramp-input function during the compression could be filtered out. For the constant compression rate indentation test, force data was recorded during the head movement and each of the specimens was subjected to compression 12 times. The reaction force response curves did not have any systematic deviation from the first test on the same specimen. This strengthens the assumption that no substantial tissue damage was caused during the measurements that could have a depriving effect on the final results. The near-step input deformation was applied several times on each of the specimens. Evaluating the measurement data, it was found that the force response magnitude in the relaxation phase (60 seconds) decreased significantly during the second and third experiments on the same tissue, most likely from the severe damage to the internal tissue structure. Based on this observation, only the very first set of measured data points was used for the parameter estimation in the relaxation phase for each specimen. The image of the experimental setup is shown in Figure 10.5.

10.6.3 Indentation Tests

In the first phase, the force response data from the relaxation tests was evaluated. This way, an initial estimation can be given on the individual mechanical parameters of the linear Wiechert model. For the simplification of the calculations, the indentation speed of 750 mm/min was approximated with a step-input function. The analytical expression for the force response function can be easily obtained by taking the inverse Laplace transform of Eq. (10.9). In the Laplace domain, the output function is calculated by taking the product of the transfer function $W_W(s)$ and the Laplace transform of the step-input function:

$$f_{W_r}(t) = L^{-1}\left\{W_W(s)\frac{x_d}{s}\right\} = x_d\left(k_0 + k_1\left(1 - e^{-\frac{k_1}{b_1}t}\right) + k_2\left(1 - e^{-\frac{k_2}{b_2}t}\right)\right), \qquad (10.10)$$

where $f_{W_r}(t)$ is the reaction force in the relaxation phase and $x_d = 4$ mm is the compression depth at the maximum deformation. For all six specimens, the relaxation data is displayed in Figure 10.6. The average response curves are also shown in Figure 10.6 for better visualization, which were obtained by taking the average values of the response data for each of the specimens, weighted with respect to the tissue surface size, and normalized to 20×20 mm. An unexpected break can be observed in the curves for tissue samples, which is supposedly due to the effect of the deceleration of the indenter reaching the target indentation depth. For simplification reasons, this break is not taken into account during the curve fitting phase, as it does not affect the force response results significantly. The most relevant sections of the response curves are the initial relaxation slopes (force relaxation) and the

FIGURE 10.5 Experimental setup for beef liver indentation tests at the Austrian Center for Medical Innovation and Technology (ACMIT).

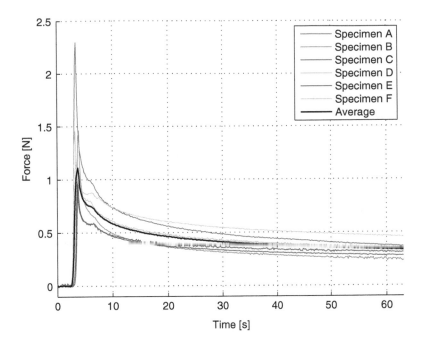

FIGURE 10.6 Force response curves for step-input relaxation tests for eight identically cut liver pieces.

steady-state values (residual stress). As previously derived, a closed-form solution to the step-input can be given and curve fitting on the original measurement can be applied. MATLAB® *cftool* toolbox was used for carrying out the curve fitting, while the parameters were independently obtained for each of the six specimens and were compensated by the tissue surface magnitude. Summarizing, the procedure resulted in six sets of parameters of stiffness and damping parameter values:

$$k_i^c = k_i \frac{A_0}{A}, i = 1,2,3 \qquad (10.11)$$

$$b_j^c = b_j \frac{A_0}{A}, j = 1,2, \qquad (10.12)$$

where A is the surface area of each specimen and $A_0 = 400$ mm^2 is the reference tissue surface value. The average parameter values are listed in Table 10.1 under the *linear* model type.

TABLE 10.1   Parameter Estimation Results from Force Relaxation and Constant Compression Rate Tests

Model Type	K_0 [N/m]	K_1 [N/m]	K_2 N/m]	b_1 [Ns/m]	b_2 [Ns/m]	k_0 [m^{-1}]	k_1 [m^{-1}]	k_2 [m^{-1}]	RMSE Combined [N]
Linear	4.86	57.81	53.32	9987	10464	–	–	–	0.1865
Nonlinear	2.03	0.438	0.102	5073	39.24	909.9	1522	81.18	0.0206

It was shown in [83] that the Wiechert model gives a reasonably good description of the soft tissue behavior in the relaxation phase. However, the verification of the model requires more indentation scenarios, which were based on two more sets of compression tests with constant compression rate. The average force response curves for each specimen for the case of 20 mm/min and 100 mm/min are displayed in Figures 10.7 and 10.8, respectively, along with the global weighted average response curve. Note that for better visualization, the curves are displayed in an *indentation depth–force* graph instead of the previously used *time–force* graph. The indentation depth was 4 mm. The figures only show the first 3.6 mm of deformation for previously discussed reasons. Utilizing the same method for obtaining the analytical force response as it was used in the step-input case, the following analytical expression was obtained for the force response:

$$f_{W_c}(t) = L^{-1}\left\{W_W(s)\frac{v}{s^2}\right\} = v\left(k_0 t + b_1\left(1-e^{-\frac{k_1}{b_1}t}\right) + b_2\left(1-e^{-\frac{k_2}{b_2}t}\right)\right), \quad (10.13)$$

where v denotes the compression rate (20 mm/min or 100 mm/min) and f_{W_c} stands for the force response magnitude. Theoretically, the substitution of the model parameters into Eq. (10.13) should give a good estimation on the measurement data for the force curves. It is important to note that the 750 mm/min indentation speed was approximated as a step-input, therefore, a minor compensation of the previously obtained mechanical parameters would still be needed. However, the constant compression rate indentation test results showed that the qualitative behavior of the analytical response curve largely differs from the measured response curve. Therefore, the validity of the linear Wiechert model in this

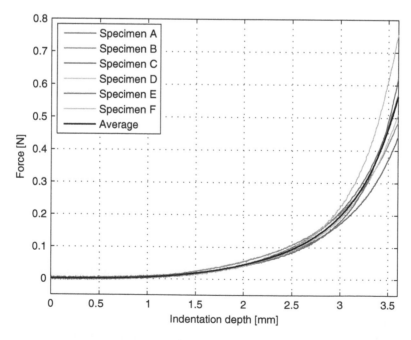

FIGURE 10.7   Force response curves for constant compression rate indentation tests at 20 mm/min.

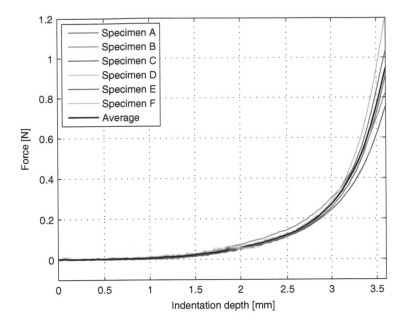

FIGURE 10.8   Force response curves for constant compression rate indentation tests at 100 mm/min.

indentation phase is limited, while from the haptics application point of view, it is more relevant to have a good soft tissue model during constant compression rate indentation. The estimated response curves and the average measurement data for the constant compression rate of 100 mm/min are shown in Figure 10.9. The best fitting curve derived by the MATLAB® *cftool* toolbox, assuming positive mechanical parameter values, is also displayed in Figure 10.9.

The measurement data and the considerable deviation from the estimated force response implies that the reaction force during constant compression rate indentation represents progressive stiffness characteristics, contrary to the previously assumed linear one. The phenomenon is a direct consequence of the complex biomechanical structure of the liver tissue, which cannot be observed during step-response relaxation tests. There is a need for the extension of the model, keeping it as simple as possible. A possible way for addressing progressing stiffness characteristics is to introduce nonlinearities through the spring elements. A model as such, with some basic restrictions is introduced, based on several practical considerations:

$$k_i(x) \geq 0, \tag{10.14}$$

$$\frac{dk_i(x)}{dx} \geq 0, \tag{10.15}$$

for all $x > 0$ and $i = 1,2,3$. This implies that both the stiffness values and their derivatives with respect to the indentation depth must be nonnegative. The proposed nonlinear stiffness function is the following:

$$k_j(x) = K_j e^{\kappa_j x} \tag{10.16}$$

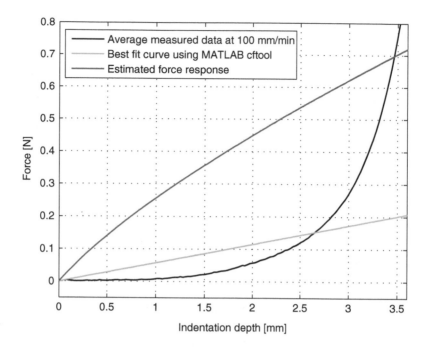

FIGURE 10.9   Verification results of the linear Wiechert model at the compression rate of 100 mm/min. The blue curve shows the predicted force response from the parameter data acquired from relaxation tests, while the measured force response is represented by the black curve. The green curve corresponds to the best fit using reasonable mechanical parameters, clearly indicating that the model is not capable of predicting the reaction force in the case of constant compression rates.

for $j = 1,2,3$, where K_j and k_j are nonnegative constants. In the proposed model, all of the three spring elements have the same exponential, nonlinear behavior. Damping elements remain linear. This representation introduces a total of eight mechanical parameters, creating an off-the-shelf model that could be used both in compression and relaxation phases.

Summarizing the findings, the experimental data indicates that the force response is a convex curve in the case of constant compression rate indentation. Figure 10.9 shows that because of the nature of Eq. (10.13), the linear Wiechert model would always estimate a concave force response curve. The proposed nonlinear Wiechert model addresses this issue by introducing progressive, exponential spring element stiffness, which, logically, would lead to a better fit with the experimental data.

10.6.4 The Proposed Nonlinear Mass–Spring–Damper Model

The nonlinear formulation of the proposed soft tissue model does not allow a closed-form analytical expression for the force response. Therefore, instead of applying the MATLAB *cftool* toolbox, the *fminsearch* optimization function was used to find the optimal set of tissue parameters [84]. The parameter values and the combined root mean square error results for fitting the experimental data are shown in Table 10.1. The curve fitting procedure was carried out simultaneously on both datasets of 20 mm/min and 750 mm/min responses, while the combined error values were calculated by summing up the individual root mean square error (RMSE) for each curve, defining the cost function for *fminsearch*. The estimated force responses, utilizing the parameters from Table 10.1, are shown in Figures 10.10 and 10.11.

Independent parameter verification was carried out by simulating the force response during the constant compression indentation rate of 100 mm/s. During the simulation, the following set of differential equations was solved:

$$\dot{x}_0 = v(t),$$

$$\dot{x}_1 = \frac{1}{b_1} K_1 (x_0 - x_1) e^{\kappa_1 (x_0 - x_1)}, \qquad (10.17)$$

$$\dot{x}_2 = \frac{1}{b_2} K_2 (x_0 - x_2) e^{\kappa_2 (x_0 - x_2)},$$

where $v(t)$ is the surface deformation rate, x_0 denotes the position of an arbitrary point at the surface, while x_1 and x_2 represent two virtual points, connecting k_1–b_1 and k_2–b_2 elements, respectively, as shown in Figure 10.12. The system output is the reaction force, $F(t)$, calculated by

$$F(t) = K_0 x_0 e^{\kappa_0 x_0} + K_1 (x_0 - x_1) e^{\kappa_1 (x_0 - x_1)} + K_2 (x_0 - x_2) e^{\kappa_2 (x_0 - x_2)}. \qquad (10.18)$$

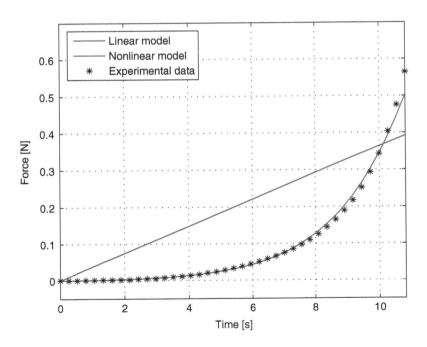

FIGURE 10.10   Force response estimation curves, utilizing the parameter sets from Table 10.1 at a constant compression rate of 20 mm/s.

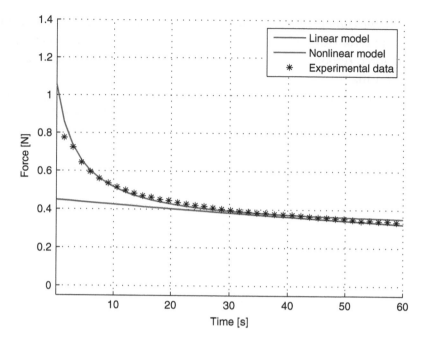

FIGURE 10.11   Force response estimation curves, utilizing the parameter sets from Table 10.1, in the case of a step-like input, focusing on stress relaxation data.

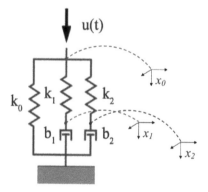

FIGURE 10.12   The proposed nonlinear soft tissue model, with the indication of the virtual mass points.

10.7 RESULTS

Figure 10.13 shows how the simulation results are mapped on the measurement data. The average RMSE was calculated separately with respect to each of the specimens, resulting with $\varepsilon_{RMSE} = 0.1748$ [N]. This proves that the model represents the tissue behavior under the given manipulation tasks very well. The simulated curve yielded a somewhat lower reaction force value than those of the experimentally obtained, which is an expected behavior. During the parameter estimation, an ideal step-response curve was used as an input function in the simulation, while, during the indentation tests, the maximum indentation speed was 750 mm/min. As a consequence, the lower-than-desired indentation speed resulted in lower stiffness values for the spring elements, partly due to the rapid relaxation during the

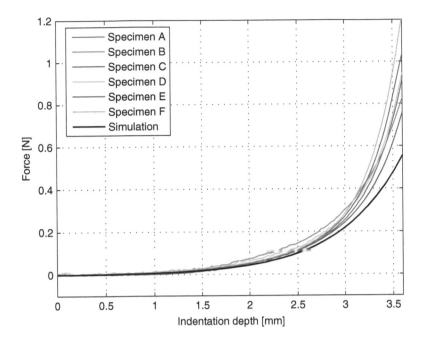

FIGURE 10.13 Force response curves for constant compression rate indentation tests at 100 mm/min, showing the simulated response of the nonlinear model using the parameters listed in Table 10.1.

compression phase. The effect can be observed in both Figure 10.10 and Figure 10.13. This does not affect the validity of the model significantly, as the qualitative behavior is still satisfying in all the simulated cases.

10.7.1 Model Verification Methods

The verification of the approach was extended to the scenario of nonuniform surface deformation, utilizing the basic concept shown in Figure 10.2. Additional experimental data was collected from indentation tests, where 3 specimens with the dimensions of $25 \times 25 \times 200$ mm from the same beef liver were palpated with a sharp instrument, taking special care not to physically damage the tissue surface. Constant rate indentations were carried out at four different indentation rates (5 mm/s, 10 mm/s, 20 mm/s, and 40 mm/s) at different points of the surface of each specimen, reaching 6 mm of indentation depth. The indenter used for the experiments was a 3D-printed piece that was mounted on the flat instrument used in the experiments for the uniform deformation. At the tip, the indenter had a bevel angle of 30° and its length was 30 mm. It was assumed that the indenter created a line-like deformation input on the surface of the specimens, perpendicular to their longest dimensions. The schematic figure of the nonuniform indentation is shown in Figure 10.14.

A few assumptions have been made prior to the verification of the estimation of the reaction force:

- The surface deformation shape is approximated as a quadratic function and is uniform along the width of the specimen.

- It is assumed that the indentation only affects the liver structure in a certain ρ distance from the indentation point.

- Only uniaxial deformation is considered, therefore, all nonvertical forces are neglected in the calculations.

The reaction force was assumed to be the sum of the reaction of infinitely small elements over the tissue surface:

$$F(t) = \iint\limits_{y,z} f(y,z,t)dydz, \tag{10.19}$$

where $f(y,z,t)$ is the force response of a single infinitely small element at the surface point (y,z) at a given time t. $f(y,z,t)$ can be calculated by solving Eq. (10.18) for each surface element using the unique deformation rate $v_{xy}(t)$ of the element and utilizing *specific* stiffness and damping values shown in Table 10.2. These specific values were obtained by normalizing the appropriate parameters to the surface size of 1 m².

The surface of the tissue was discretized using square-shaped cells $A_i = A_{y_i,z_i}$ with the edge length of 0.1 mm. The deformation rate profiles for each element, $v_i(t)$, were obtained from visual recordings. The indentation tests were recorded by a conventional video camera, fixed along the z-axis. The dislocation of seven surface points was tracked by analyzing 12 video files frame-by-frame at time intervals of 1 s. The resolution of the picture was 1980×1980 pixels, the recordings were taken at 25 frames per second. An average deformation profile was calculated by processing the data manually. It was found that a quadratic function was a good approximation for the final deformation surface (after reaching the $x_d = 6$ mm indentation depth), assuming that the deformation surface is symmetrical to the axis of indentation. Doming effects were neglected during the indentation, as these effects are more relevant at the regions far from the indentation point. Due to the progressive spring characteristics of the model, these regions contribute very little to the overall force

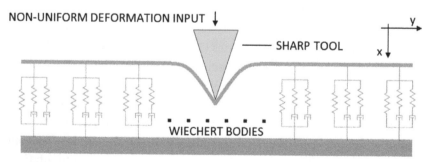

FIGURE 10.14 The schematic figure of the nonuniform indentation tests.

TABLE 10.2 Specific Parameter Values for the Use of Nonuniform Surface Deformation Model Verification

K_0^s [N/m³]	K_1^s [N/m³]	K_2^s [N/m³]	b_1^s [Ns/m³]	b_2^s [Ns/m³]	κ_0 [m⁻¹]	κ_1 [m⁻¹]	κ_2 [m⁻¹]
5075	1095	255	$127 \cdot 10^6$	$1.1 \cdot 10^6$	909.9	1522	81.189

response. With the assumptions above, the deformation rate profile $v_i(t)$ can be obtained at each surface point A_i, provided by the following equation:

$$v(y,t) = \frac{v_{in}}{\rho^2}(|y|-\rho)^2, \qquad (10.20)$$

indicating that in the case of constant indentation rate, each surface point is moving at a constant speed. Eq. (10.18) was solved for each element and the force response was obtained and summed using the velocity profiles according to Eq. (10.20).

10.7.2 Model Verification Results

The estimated force response and the results of the simulation for the third specimen at 10 mm/min indentation speed are shown in Figure 10.15. Calculations were carried out on an Intel Core i5-3337U CPU with 8 GB RAM, the simulation time varied between 0.5 and 1.5 s, depending on the indentation speed, and thus, the length of the experiment. Based on the results and the low RMSE values, it can be concluded that the method can be used in applications for real-time force estimation. As shown in Figure 10.15, the experimentally obtained force response curves initially follow the simulated curve reasonably well, both qualitatively and quantitatively (region A). At the indentation depth of 4 mm, the slope of the experimental curves increases rapidly, which is assumed to be due to the tension forces arising in the normal direction with respect to the indentation axis (region B). This is an expected behavior, indicating that at higher deformation levels, the 1 DoF approach of the problem should be handled with caution. The RMSE values for each verification case were computed, with the results varying between $\varepsilon_{RMSE,min} = 1.384$ N and $\varepsilon_{RMSE,max} = 2.821$ N. The proposed soft tissue model can also be extended to more complex

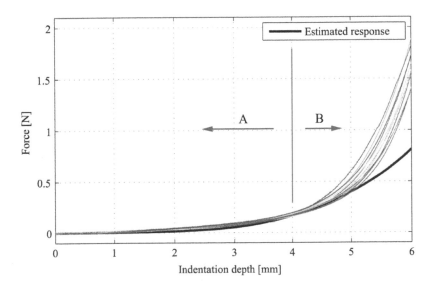

FIGURE 10.15 Measurement results and estimated force response for the case of 10 mm/min indentation for nonuniform surface deformation. The model fits the experimental data very well in region A, while in region B, this approach should be used with care.

surface deformation functions. Given that the boundary conditions are well-defined, one would find finite element modeling methods a useful tool for determining the surface deformation shape function [12].

10.8 USABILITY OF THE PROPOSED MODEL

The model proposed in this chapter can be integrated in a control scheme and the corresponding control design methodology, presented by Takács et al. in [85], regulates interaction force during autonomous manipulation of soft biological tissues. This approach gives an extensive application example for utilizing recent results of polytopic model-based control through the framework of Tensor Product Model Transformation [86]. Control of the reaction force during robotic interaction with soft tissues, for example, grasp–hold–release cycles, still remains an actively researched topic. Since biological tissues typically have highly nonlinear dynamic behavior (progressive stiffness characteristics, stress relaxation, etc.), time invariant linear controllers cannot provide ideal performance across the whole operation domain.

Based on the presented tissue model, parameter-dependent error dynamics can be utilized and system reformulation can be carried out in order to avoid the error rendered by the slow dynamics of one state variable [87]. Reformulating the system allows concentrating the 8-parameter dependency into a single parameter for a given application domain, constructing a feed forward term for the equilibrial input. The formulation opens up new possibilities in state feedback controller design, handling the unmodeled dynamics and further disturbances. Since the nonlinear model includes state variables that cannot be measured in the real process, the proposed tissue model can be also used as reference tissue model. This allows a linear matrix inequality (LMI)-based synthesis providing the variable gains as parameter-dependent polytopic tensor product (TP) functions. The implementation of the proposed method into supervised telemanipulation/telesurgical equipment enhances the performance of these systems, allowing haptic sensing to the operator.

Along with force control, the problem of haptic feedback in telesurgical systems remains an open challenge in the related fields of research. Current surgical teleoperation systems lack any haptic feedback capabilities, limiting their usability in everyday practice. Furthermore, by allowing haptic feedback from manipulated real tissue, functionality can be extended to surgical simulation using virtual tissue models created by the proposed soft tissue modeling method.

Results of our usability study showed that the proposed nonlinear tissue model mimics the mechanical behavior of the *ex-vivo* tissue very well both from the qualitative and quantitative point of view. This allows the integration of the model into virtual tissue models used in surgical simulators—virtual environments providing physical interaction with the human operator through the haptic interface—where it is critical to have a realistic haptic sensation reflected to the human operator when manipulating the tissues. This way, the quality of HRI during surgical procedures can be improved, while accuracy, stability, and thus, safety, can be increased during procedures, as shown in other parallel studies as well [88]. The study also showed that using a haptic interface made it hard to distinguish between artificial silicone tissues and real tissues during teleoperation, indicating that by creating a silicone sample according to the guidelines presented in this work, surgical training can be accelerated and enhanced by artificial tissue phantoms, yet providing realistic haptic sensation to the trainees, emphasizing the importance of introducing the concept of HRI in early medical and surgical education.

10.9 DISCUSSION

The importance of HRI in modern surgical systems is growing. In order to achieve a stable and reliable teleoperation in today's intervention systems, it is crucial to understand the mechanical behavior of manipulated tissues. Creating models for tool–tissue interaction and soft tissues can also aid model-based control methods. There is an extensive literature on various soft tissue models, however, the verification of heuristic models is mostly limited to stress relaxation tests. While the linear forms of these models are very popular in tissue behavior investigation, their practical usability is limited in general manipulation scenarios. The proposed model addressed this issue by accounting for the progressive stiffness characteristics of soft tissues, while a verification methodology was proposed using uniaxial compression tests, allowing its integration into robot-assisted surgical systems. It is important to note that lateral tension forces and their effect are not modeled in this approach, however, a quantitative representation of tissue behavior is still possible in cases of relatively small deformations. A reliable estimation of the reaction forces during telesurgical manipulation and the possibility of haptic feedback based on this model can increase the performance, accuracy, and safety of these procedures, therefore, current results open up new possibilities to a generic, uniform representation of soft tissues and artificial tissue samples, leading to more sophisticated tool–tissue interaction models representing a fine example of HRI in the medical field.

ACKNOWLEDGMENT

Authors acknowledge the financial support of this work by the Hungarian State and the European Union under the EFOP-3.6.1-16-2016-00010 project. T. Haidegger is supported through the New National Excellence Program of the Ministry of Human Capacities. T. Haidegger is a Bolyai Fellow of the Hungarian Academy of Sciences.

REFERENCES

1. Mathias Hoeckelman, Imre Rudas, Paolo Fiorini, Frank Kirchner, and Tamás Haidegger. Current capabilities and development potential in surgical robotics. *International Journal of Advanced Robotic Systems*, 12(61):1–39, 2015.
2. Nele Famaey and Jos Vander Sloten. Soft tissue modelling for applications in virtual surgery and surgical robotics. *Computer Methods in Biomechanics and Biomedical Engineering*, 11(4):351–366, 2008.
3. Árpád Takács, Sandor Jordan, Radu-Emil Precup, Levente Kovács, József Tar, Imre Rudas, and Tamás Haidegger. Review of tool-tissue interaction models for robotic surgery applications. In *Applied Machine Intelligence and Informatics (SAMI), 2014 IEEE 12th International Symposium on*, pp. 339–344, IEEE, Herl'any, Slovakia, January 2014.
4. Mahdi Tavakoli and Robert D Howe. Haptic effects of surgical teleoperator flexibility. *The International Journal of Robotics Research*, 28(10):1289–1302, 2009.

5. Cagatay Basdogan, Suvranu De, Jung Kim, Manivannan Muniyandi, Hyun Kim, and Mandayam A Srinivasan. Haptics in minimally invasive surgical simulation and training. *IEEE Computer Graphics and Applications*, 24(2):56–64, 2004.

6. Yidong Bao, Dongmei Wu, Zhiyuan Yan, and Zhijiang Du. A new hybrid viscoelastic soft tissue model based on meshless method for haptic surgical simulation. *The Open Biomedical Engineering Journal*, 7:116, 2013.

7. Tomonori Yamamoto. *Applying Tissue Models in Teleoperated Robot-Assisted Surgery*. PhD Dissertation, Johns Hopkins University, Baltimore, 2011.

8. Tomonori Yamamoto, Niki Abolhassani, Sung Jung, Allison M Okamura, and Timothy N Judkins. Augmented reality and haptic interfaces for robot-assisted surgery. *The International Journal of Medical Robotics and Computer Assisted Surgery*, 8(1):45–56, 2012.

9. Florence Leong, Wei-Hsuan Huang, and Chee-Kong Chui. Modeling and analysis of coagulated liver tissue and its interaction with a scalpel blade. *Medical & Biological Engineering & Computing*, 51(6):687–695, 2013.

10. Chao Liu, Pedro Moreira, Nabil Zemiti, and Philippe Poignet. 3D force control for robotic-assisted beating heart surgery based on viscoelastic tissue model. In *Engineering in Medicine and Biology Society, EMBC, 2011 Annual International Conference of the IEEE*, pp. 7054–7058, IEEE, Boston, MA, USA September 2011.

11. Orcun Goksel, Septimiu E Salcudean, and Simon P Dimaio. 3D simulation of needle-tissue interaction with application to prostate brachytherapy. *Computer Aided Surgery*, 11(6):279–288, 2006.

12. Sarthak Misra, Kyle B Reed, Benjamin W Schafer, KT Ramesh, and Allison M Okamura. Mechanics of flexible needles robotically steered through soft tissue. *The International Journal of Robotics Research*, 29(13): 1640–1660. 2010.

13. Mohsen Mahvash and Pierre E Dupont. Mechanics of dynamic needle insertion into a biological material. *IEEE Transactions on Biomedical Engineering*, 57(4):934–943, 2010.

14. Sina Nia Kosari, Srikrishnan Ramadurai, Howard Jay Chizeck, and Blake Hannaford. Robotic compression of soft tissue. In *Robotics and Automation (ICRA), 2012 IEEE International Conference on*, pp. 4654–4659, Saint Paul, MN, USA, IEEE, May 2012.

15. ISO. ISO 10218-2: 2011: Robots and robotic devices—safety requirements for industrial robots—part 2: Robot systems and integration. Geneva, Switzerland: International Organization for Standardization, 2011.

16. Tamás Haidegger, Levente Kovács, Radu-Emil Precup, Balázs Benyó, Zoltán Benyó, and Stefan Preitl. Simulation and control for telerobots in space medicine. *Acta Astronautica*, 81(1):390–402, 2012.

17. Alex Ellery. Survey of past rover missions. In *Planetary Rovers*, pp. 59–69. Springer, Berlin2016.

18. Seunghwan Park, Yu-Cheol Lee, and Gon-Woo Kim. Implementation of spatial visualization for a tele-operated robot in a complex and hazardous environment. In *2014 IEEE International Conference on Automation Science and Engineering (CASE)*, pp. 285–289, Taipei, Taiwan August 2014.

19. John K Chapin, Karen A Moxon, Ronald S Markowitz, and Miguel AL Nicolelis. Real-time control of a robot arm using simultaneously recorded neurons in the motor cortex. *Nature Neuroscience*, 2(7):664–670, 1999.

20. Ren C Luo and Tse Min Chen. Development of a multi-behavior based mobile robot for remote supervisory control through the internet. *IEEE/ASME Transactions on Mechatronics*, 5(4):376–385, 2000.

21. Jaeheung Park and Oussama Khatib. A haptic teleoperation approach based on contact force control. *The International Journal of Robotics Research*, 25(5–6):575–591, 2006.

22. Shahin Sirouspour and Ali Shahdi. Model predictive control for transparent teleoperation under communication time delay. *IEEE Transactions on Robotics*, 22(6):1131–1145, 2006.

23. Ian Lenz, Ross Knepper, and Ashutosh Saxena. Deepmpc: Learning deep latent features for model predictive control. In *Robotics Science and Systems (RSS)*, pp. 1–9, 2015.

24. Dale A Lawrence. Stability and transparency in bilateral teleoperation. *IEEE Transactions on Robotics and Automation*, 9(5):624–637, 1993.

25. Ilia G Polushin, Peter X Liu, and Chung-Horng Lung. A force-reflection algorithm for improved transparency in bilateral teleoperation with communication delay. *IEEE/ASME Transactions on Mechatronics*, 12(3):361–374, 2007.

26. Peter F Hokayem and Mark W Spong. Bilateral teleoperation: An historical survey. *Automatica*, 42(12):2035–2057, 2006.

27. G Jagannath Raju, George C Verghese, and Thomas B Sheridan. Design issues in 2-port network models of bilateral remote manipulation. In *1989 IEEE International Conference on Robotics and Automation*, pp. 1316–1321, IEEE, Scottsdale, AZ, USA, May 1989.

28. Gary MH Leung, Bruce A Francis, and Jacob Apkarian. Bilateral controller for teleoperators with time delay via μ-synthesis. *IEEE Transactions on Robotics and Automation*, 11(1):105–116, 1995.

29. Homayoon Kazerooni, T-I Tsay, and Karin Hollerbach. A controller design framework for telerobotic systems. *IEEE Transactions on Control Systems Technology*, 1(1):50–62, 1993.

30. Shahin Sirouspour. Modeling and control of cooperative teleoperation systems. *IEEE Transactions on Robotics*, 21(6):1220–1225, 2005.

31. Wen-Hong Zhu and Septimiu E Salcudean. Stability guaranteed teleoperation: An adaptive motion/force control approach. *IEEE Transactions on Automatic Control*, 45(11):1951–1969, 2000.

32. József K Tar, János F Bitó, Imre J Rudas, Kristóf Eredics, and José A Tenreiro Machado. Comparative analysis of a traditional and a novel approach to model reference adaptive control. In *International Symposium on Computational Intelligence and Informatics (CINTI)*, pp. 93–98, Budapest, Hungary IEEE, November 2010.

33. Dongjun Lee and Perry Y Li. Passive bilateral control and tool dynamics rendering for nonlinear mechanical teleoperators. *IEEE Transactions on Robotics*, 21(5):936–951, 2005.

34. Jee-Hwan Ryu, Dong-Soo Kwon, and Blake Hannaford. Stable teleoperation with time-domain passivity control. *IEEE Transactions on Robotics and Automation*, 20(2):365–373, 2004.

35. Keyvan Hashtrudi-Zaad and Septimiu E Salcudean. Transparency in time-delayed systems and the effect of local force feedback for transparent teleoperation. *IEEE Transactions on Robotics and Automation*, 18(1):108–114, 2002.

36. Takashi Imaida, Yasuyoshi Yokokohji, Toshitsugu Doi, Mitsushige Oda, and Tsuneo Yoshikawa. Ground-space bilateral teleoperation of ets-vii robot arm by direct bilateral coupling under 7-s time delay condition. *IEEE Transactions on Robotics and Automation*, 20(3):499–511, 2004.

37. Hubert Baier and Günther Schmidt. Transparency and stability of bilateral kinesthetic teleoperation with time-delayed communication. *Journal of Intelligent and Robotic Systems*, 40(1):1–22, 2004.

38. Da Sun, Fazel Naghdy, and Haiping Du. Application of wave-variable control to bilateral teleoperation systems: A survey. *Annual Reviews in Control*, 38(1):12–31, 2014.

39. Romeo Ortega, Julio Antonio Lora Perez, Per Johan Nicklasson, and Hebertt Sira-Ramirez. *Passivity-Based Control of Euler-Lagrange Systems: Mechanical, Electrical and Electromechanical Applications*. Springer Science & Business Media, London, 2013.

40. Sukhan Lee and Hahk Sung Lee. Modeling, design, and evaluation of advanced teleoperator control systems with short time delay. *IEEE Transactions on Robotics and Automation*, 9(5):607–623, 1993.

41. G Hirzinger, J Heindl, and K Landzettel. Predictive and knowledge-based telerobotic control concepts. In *IEEE International Conference on Robotics and Automation*, pp. 1768–1777, IEEE, Scottsdale, AZ, USA May 1989.

42. Paolo Arcara and Claudio Melchiorri. Control schemes for teleoperation with time delay: A comparative study. *Robotics and Autonomous systems*, 38(1):49–64, 2002.

43. Saghir Munir and Wayne J Book. Internet-based teleoperation using wave variables with prediction. *IEEE/ASME Transactions on Mechatronics*, 7(2):124–133, 2002.

44. Andrew C Smith and Keyvan Hashtrudi-Zaad. Smith predictor type control architectures for time delayed teleoperation. *The International Journal of Robotics Research*, 25(8):797–818, 2006.

45. José Maria Azorn, O Reinoso, Rafael Aracil, and Manuel Ferre. Generalized control method by state convergence for teleoperation systems with time delay. *Automatica*, 40(9):1575–1582, 2004.

46. Dai Hanawa and Tatsuhiro Yonekura. A proposal of dead reckoning protocol in distributed virtual environment based on the taylor expansion. In *2006 International Conference on Cyberworlds*, pp. 107–114, Lausanne, Switzerland, IEEE, November 2006.

47. Luis F Penin and Kotaro Matsumoto. Teleoperation with time delay: A survey and its use in space robotics. Technical report, National Aerospace Laboratory (NAL) Japan, 2002.

48. Thomas B Sheridan. Space teleoperation through time delay: review and prognosis. *IEEE Transactions on Robotics and Automation*, 9(5):592–606, 1993.

49. Won S Kim, Blake Hannaford, and AK Fejczy. Force-reflection and shared compliant control in operating telemanipulators with time delay. *IEEE Transactions on Robotics and Automation*, 8(2):176–185, 1992.

50. Blake Hannaford, Laurie Wood, Douglas A McAffee, and Haya Zak. Performance evaluation of a six-axis generalized force-reflecting teleoperator. *IEEE Transactions on Systems, Man, and Cybernetics*, 21(3):620–633, 1991.

51. Gregory Tholey, Jaydev P Desai, and Andres E Castellanos. Force feedback plays a significant role in minimally invasive surgery: results and analysis. *Annals of surgery*, 241(1):102–109, 2005.

52. Maria V Ottermo, Marit Øvstedal, Thomas Langø, Øyvind Stavdahl, Yunus Yavuz, Tor A Johansen, and Ronald Mårvik. The role of tactile feedback in laparoscopic surgery. *Surgical Laparoscopy Endoscopy & Percutaneous Techniques*, 16(6):390–400, 2006.

53. Mohsin I Tiwana, Stephen J Redmond, and Nigel H Lovell. A review of tactile sensing technologies with applications in biomedical engineering. *Sensors and Actuators A: Physical*, 179:17–31, 2012.

54. Carol E Reiley, Takintope Akinbiyi, Darius Burschka, David C Chang, Allison M Okamura, and David D Yuh. Effects of visual force feedback on robot-assisted surgical task performance. *The Journal of thoracic and cardiovascular surgery*, 135(1):196–202, 2008.

55. Árpád Takács, Imre J Rudas, and Tamás Haidegger. Surface deformation and reaction force estimation of liver tissue based on a novel nonlinear mass–spring–damper viscoelastic model. *Medical & Biological Engineering & Computing*, 54(10):1553–1562, 2016.

56. Allison M Okamura, Lawton N Verner, CE Reiley, and Mohsen Mahvash. Haptics for robot-assisted minimally invasive surgery. In Kaneko M, and Nakamura Y. (eds.) *Robotics Research. Springer Tracts in Advanced Robotics, vol 66.*, pp. 361–372, Springer, Berlin, Heidelberg2010.

57. Dan Morris, Hong Tan, Federico Barbagli, Timothy Chang, and Kenneth Salisbury. Haptic feedback enhances force skill learning. In *Second Joint EuroHaptics Conference and Symposium on Haptic Interfaces for Virtual Environment and Teleoperator Systems (WHC'07)*, pp. 21–26, Washington, DC, USA, IEEE, March 2007.

58. Kevin Montgomery, Cynthia Bruyns, Joel Brown, Stephen Sorkin, Frederic Mazzella, Guillaume Thonier, Arnaud Tellier, Benjamin Lerman, and Anil Menon. Spring: A general framework for collaborative, real-time surgical simulation. *Studies in Health Technology and Informatics*, pp. 296–303, IOS Press, Amsterdam, 2002.

59. Yonghang Tai, Lei Wei, Hailing Zhou, Saeid Nahavandi, and Junsheng Shi. Tissue and force modelling on multi-layered needle puncture for percutaneous surgery training. In *Proceddings of the 2015 IEEE International Conference on Systems, Man, and Cybernetics*, pp. 2923–2927, Budapest, IEEE, October 2016.

60. Iman Brouwer, Jeffrey Ustin, L Bentiey, A Dhruv, and F Tendick. Measuring in vivo animal soft tissue properties for haptic modeling in surgical. *Medicine Meets Virtual Reality (MMVR)*, 81:69, 2001.

61. Herve Delingette. Toward realistic soft-tissue modeling in medical simulation. *Proceedings of the IEEE*, 86(3):512–523, 1998.

62. Mahdi Tavakoli, Arash Aziminejad, Rajni V Patel, and Mehrdad Moallem. High-fidelity bilateral teleoperation systems and the effect of multimodal haptics. *IEEE Transactions on Systems, Man, and Cybernetics, Part B (Cybernetics)*, 37(6):1512–1528, 2007.

63. Árpád Takács, Levente Kovács, Imre J Rudas, Radu-Emil Precup, and Tamás Haidegger. Models for force control in telesurgical robot systems. *Acta Polytechnica Hungarica*, 12(8):95–114, 2015.

64. Evren Samur, Mert Sedef, Cagatay Basdogan, Levent Avtan, and Oktay Duzgun. A robotic indenter for minimally invasive measurement and characterization of soft tissue response. *Medical Image Analysis*, 11(4):361–373, 2007.

65. Marco Beccani, Christian Di Natali, Levin J Sliker, Jonathan A Schoen, Mark E Rentschler, and Pietro Valdastri. Wireless tissue palpation for intraoperative detection of lumps in the soft tissue. *IEEE Transactions on Biomedical Engineering*, 61(2):353–361, 2014.

66. Guillaume Picinbono, Herve Delingette, and Nicholas Ayache. Nonlinear and anisotropic elastic soft tissue models for medical simulation. In *Robotics and Automation, 2001. Proceedings 2001 ICRA. IEEE International Conference on*, volume 2, pp. 1370–1375, Seoul, South Korea, IEEE, May 2001.

67. Ana Luisa Trejos, Jagadeesan Jayender, MP Perri, Michael D Naish, Rajnikant V Patel, and RA Malthaner. Robot-assisted tactile sensing for minimally invasive tumor localization. *The International Journal of Robotics Research*, 28(9):1118–1133, 2009.

68. Christopher R Wagner and Robert D Howe. Force feedback benefit depends on experience in multiple degree of freedom robotic surgery task. *IEEE Transactions on Robotics*, 23(6):1235–1240, 2007.

69. Tim Horeman, Sharon P Rodrigues, John J van den Dobbelsteen, Frank-Willem Jansen, and Jenny Dankelman. Visual force feedback in laparoscopic training. *Surgical Endoscopy*, 26(1):242–248, 2012.

70. Greig L McCreery, Ana Luisa Trejos, Michael D Naish, Rajni V Patel, and Richard A Malthaner. Feasibility of locating tumours in lung via kinaesthetic feedback. *The International Journal of Medical Robotics and Computer Assisted Surgery*, 4(1):58–68, 2008.

71. KJ Parker. A microchannel flow model for soft tissue elasticity. *Physics in Medicine and Biology*, 59(15):4443–4457, 2014.

72. Walter Maurel, Yin Wu, Daniel Thalmann, and Nadia Magnenat Thalmann. *Biomechanical Models for Soft Tissue Simulation*. Springer, Berlin, Heidelberg,1998.

73. Jacob Rosen, Jeffrey D Brown, Smita De, Mika Sinanan, and Blake Hannaford. Biomechanical properties of abdominal organs in vivo and postmortem under compression loads. *Journal of Biomechanical Engineering*, 130(2):210201–210217, 2008.

74. Nadia Alkhouli, Jessica Mansfield, Ellen Green, James Bell, Beatrice Knight, Neil Liversedge, Ji Chung Tham, Richard Welbourn, Angela C Shore, Katarina Kos, et al. The mechanical properties of human adipose tissues and their relationships to the structure and composition of the extracellular matrix. *American Journal of Physiology-Endocrinology and Metabolism*, 305(12):E1427–E1435, 2013.

75. Kevin L Troyer, Snehal S Shetye, and Christian M Puttlitz. Experimental characterization and finite element implementation of soft tissue nonlinear viscoelasticity. *Journal of Biomechanical Engineering*, 134(11):114501–114508, 2012.

76. Csaba Urbán, Peter Galambos, Gyorgy Györök and Tamás Haidegger Simulated medical ultrasound trainers a review of solutions and applications. *Acta Polytechnica Hungarica*, 15(7): 111–131, 2018.

77. Min Li, Jelizaveta Konstantinova, Emanuele L Secco, Allen Jiang, Hongbin Liu, Thrishantha Nanayakkara, Lakmal D Seneviratne, Prokar Dasgupta, Kaspar Althoefer, and Helge A Wurdemann. Using visual cues to enhance haptic feedback for palpation on virtual model of soft tissue. *Medical & Biological Engineering & Computing*, 53(11):1177–1186, 2015.

78. Florence Ching Leong. *Modelling and Analysis of a new Integrated Radiofrequency Ablation and Division Device*. PhD Dissertation, National University of Singapore, Singapore, 2009.

79. Zhongkui Wang and Shinichi Hirai. Modeling and parameter estimation of rheological objects for simultaneous reproduction of force and deformation. In *International Conference on Applied Bionics and Biomechanics*, Venice, Italy, October 2010.

80. A Constantinesco, H Schwerdt, and J Chambron. Testing device to determine the dynamic rheological properties of soft tissues in biaxial elongation. *Medical and Biological Engineering and Computing*, 19(2):129–134, 1981.

81. Xin Wang, Jonathan A Schoen, and Mark E Rentschler. A quantitative comparison of soft tissue compressive viscoelastic model accuracy. *Journal of the Mechanical Behavior of Biomedical Materials*, 20:126–136, 2013.

82. C Machiraju, A-V Phan, AW Pearsall, and S Madanagopal. Viscoelastic studies of human subscapularis tendon: relaxation test and a wiechert model. *Computer Methods and Programs in Biomedicine*, 83(1):29–33, 2006.

83. Árápad Takács, József K Tar, Tamás Haidegger, and Imre J Rudas. Applicability of the maxwell-kelvin model in soft tissue parameter estimation. In *2014 IEEE 12th International Symposium on Intelligent Systems and Informatics (SISY)*, pp. 115–119, IEEE, Subotica, Serbia September 2014.

84. Arpad Takacs, Péter Galambos, Péter Pausits, Imre J Rudas, and Tamás Haidegger. Nonlinear soft tissue models and force control for medical cyber-physical systems. In *2015 IEEE International Conference on Systems, Man, and Cybernetics (SMC)*, pp. 1520–1525, Hong Kong, ChinaIEEE, September 2015.

85. Árpád Takács, József Kuti, Tamás Haidegger, Péter Galambos, and Imre Rudas. Polytopic model based interaction control for soft tissue manipulation. In *2016 IEEE International Conference on Systems, Man, and Cybernetics*. IEEE, Budapest, Hungary October 2016.

86. P Baranyi, Y Yam, and P Varlaki. Tensor Product model transformatoin in polytopic model-based control. *Automation and Control Engineering*. CRC Press, Boca Raton, FL, 2017.

87. Árpád Takács, Tamás Haidegger, Jozsef Galambos, Peter, and Imre J Kuti Rudas. Nonlinear soft tissue mechanics based on polytopic tensor product modeling. In *2016 IEEE 14th International Symposium on Applied Machine Intelligence and Informatics (SAMI)*, pp. 211–215, IEEE, Herl'any, Slovakia January 2016.

88. Lőrinc Márton, Zoltán Szántó, Tamás Haidegger, Péter Galambos, and József Kövecses. Internet-based Bilateral Teleoperation using a revised time-domain passivity controller. *Acta Polytechnica Hungarica* 14 (8): 27–45, 2017.

CHAPTER 11

Passive Bilateral Teleoperation with Safety Considerations

Márton Lőrincz

CONTENTS

11.1 Introduction   171
    11.1.1 Safety Considerations During Human–Robot Interaction and Its
        Implications on Telerobotics   173
11.2 Bilateral Teleoperation: Basic Notions   174
11.3 Passivity Controller–Passivity Observer Design   175
11.4 Passivity Controller with Bounded Force and Velocity Signals   178
    11.4.1 Bounds for Control Signals   178
    11.4.2 Passivity Controllers   178
    11.4.3 Transparency with Rate-Limited Signals   180
11.5 Experimental Results   182
    11.5.1 Experimental Measurements with the Proposed Bilateral
        Teleoperation Control Method   182
11.6 Conclusions   184
Acknowledgments   184
References   184

11.1 INTRODUCTION

Bilateral teleoperation is a promising technique to execute supervised robotic tasks in remote environments. In these systems, a distant robot (slave) reproduces the human operator's action. The master robot, which is in contact with the operator, reflects the slave-environment interaction through haptic feedback, i.e. the operator feels the reaction force of the remote environment.

The design and implementation of reliable bilateral teleoperation systems present a number of challenges when there is a considerable physical distance between the master and slave. The most important problem is the *stability* of the teleoperator in the presence of communication delay [1]. The second problem is related to the *transparency* of the tele-operation, i.e. to couple the human operator as well as possible to the task by providing a faithful transmission of the force and velocity signals.

Various bilateral control approaches were proposed to deal with the communication delay, which could induce instability in networked teleoperation systems. The wave variable-based teleoperation applies a transformation on the force and velocity signals to obtain the wave signals that are transmitted through the communication channel. In [2], it was shown that, by applying the wave transformation, the passivity of the teleoperation system can be guaranteed in the presence of time-varying delays if the rate of the delay in the communication channel is upper bounded. In [3], a communication strategy for teleoperation systems is described, according to which the measurements are sent over the communication channels only if the difference between the current measurement and the most recently sent value exceeds a certain threshold. It was shown that the passivity of the teleoperation systems can be guaranteed with sign function type control laws. Another survey of environment-, operator- and task-adapted controllers for teleoperation systems can be found in [4]. The problem of bilateral teleoperation was analysed in robotic systems with constant communication delay in [5] and [6]. It was shown that PD (Proportional – Derivative) controllers implemented both on the master and slave side can ensure the passivity of the teleoperation systems. The dissipation parameters in the control law of the robot have to be chosen in the function of the communication delay.

The time-domain passivity approach is a popular framework for guaranteeing the passivity of teleoperation systems. The method is based on observing the energy of the tele-operator using a so-called passivity observer. When the observer shows that the passivity of the teleoperation system is compromised, the passivity controller is switched on to dissipate the energy excess of the system. The method was originally introduced for haptic interfaces to achieve a stable interaction with virtual environments [7]. The applicability of the method for bilateral teleoperation systems was demonstrated in [8]. In [9], a method was proposed to extend the concept to multi-DOF (Degree of Freedom) robotic systems. In [10], the time-domain passivity framework was applied for such cases when there is a considerable communication delay between the master and the slave. Based on the time-domain passivity approach, in [11], a general network-based analysis and design framework for teleoperation systems was introduced.

Due to the specific structures of the passivity controllers introduced in previous works, in certain operating conditions, near zero force and velocity signals appear in the denominator of the relation which is used to compute the control signal, i.e. the calculated control signals can take excessively large values. In a control system, it should always be taken into consideration that the actuators have saturation limits. The control signal is truncated when its magnitude is greater than the saturation limit. The problem related to the boundedness of the control signals in time-domain passivity-based control algorithms was mentioned in [7] as a potential limitation. The energy bounding approach [12, 13] is a possible improvement of the time-domain passivity framework for stable haptic interaction. The energy-dependent parameters of the resulting passivity controller are bounded, but the calculated bounds also depend on force and position and can take large values.

From the enumerated bilateral control approach, it can be concluded that the stability in the presence of communication delay can be assured by including additional damping terms into the control algorithms. The higher the delay the more accentuated damping effect is necessary. However, the additional damping compromises the tracking performances. This effect can be mitigated by applying the time-domain passivity approach for bilateral control. In this bilateral control scheme, the damping term is switched on only when it is necessary. However, the original time-domain passivity control design does not guarantee the boundedness of the control signals.

11.1.1 Safety Considerations During Human–Robot Interaction and Its Implications on Telerobotics

In order to display the forces sensed by the distant robot to the human operator, most of the telerobotic applications involve direct human–master robot contact. Generally, haptic devices are used as master robots. The actuators of many commercial haptic devices, such as the Geomagic Touch™ or the Novint Falcon™, have reduced mechanical power and they can hardly cause serious injury to the human operator. However, special telerobotic applications require such haptic devices with sizes that are comparable with the size of human limbs, see, for example [14]. In this case, similar safety standards for telerobotic systems that were developed for human–robot interaction in an industrial environment are necessary.

The standard ISO 10218 has two parts and deals both with the safe usage of industrial robots and their safe integration as well [15, 16]. It includes several regulations and principles related to the human–robot collaboration. The safety-rated monitored stop principle allows the operator to interact with the robot only when the robot is stopped. The speed and separation monitoring prescribes that the robot's speed has to be reduced when an operator is close to the robot. The most important functional regulation is related to power and force limiting, as an incidental contact between the robot and a person should not result in harm to the person.

The newly introduced technical specification, ISO/TS 15066: Safety requirements for industrial robots – Collaborative operation, provides a comprehensive guidance for safe collaborative robot applications [17]. This standard allows human–robot contact, but this contact shall not yield to injury. It provides a list of force and pressure levels, power and speed limits to guide robot designers. Based on a pain onset study, it outlines different force and pressure limits for different body areas.

The ISO 13482 presents the safety requirements for personal care robots [18]. These robots are classified into three types:

1. Mobile servant robots capable of traveling to perform serving tasks in interaction with humans.

2. Physical assistant robots that physically help the user to perform required tasks by providing supplementation or augmentation of personal capabilities.

3. Person carrier robots with the purpose of transporting humans.

The medical applications represent one of the most important utilization fields of telerobotic systems. In spite of the fact that the autonomy and complexity of applied medical robots increased in the last decade [19], dedicated medical robotics standards are nowadays still under development, see IEC/DIS 80601-2-77 [20] and IEC/DIS 80601-2-78 [21].

Form the different standards, it can be concluded that the most important functional requirements for safe robotic applications are related to limiting the forces, speed and the power of the robot. As an example, according to the ISO 10218 standard (see, e.g., [22] and the references therein), the following conditions always have to be fulfilled for allowing human–robot interaction: either the TCP (Tool Centre Point) or robot's flange velocity needs to be under 0.25 m/s, and the maximum static force has to be under 150 N or the maximum dynamic power has to be under 80 W. These requirements can be achieved through appropriate robot actuation design [23] or through suitable controller design using extra force/torque sensors in the robot joints [24].

Telerobotic applications require special control algorithms in order to assure the stability of the networked control system in the presence of time-varying communication delays. To guarantee both stability and safety, the development of such control algorithms that can ensure stability with bounded control signals is necessary.

In this chapter, a controller design is presented for telerobotic systems that assures the passivity of the teleoperation and produces control signals, with bounds that can be prescribed by the designer. The bilateral control architecture, originally proposed in [25], is a modified passivity observer–passivity controller scheme, which is suitable for safe bilateral teleoperation. It is shown that the passivity of the teleoperation system in the presence of communication delays can be guaranteed with bounded force and velocity signals, if the rates of the signals, which are sent through the communication channel, are bounded. A passivity condition was derived which is a relation between the maximum delay in the communication channel, the rate of change of the signals sent through the communication channels and the bounds of the control signals.

The rest of this chapter is organized as follows. In Section 11.2, the basic notions related to the passivity and transparency of teleoperation systems are recalled. The classic passivity observer–passivity controller framework is presented in Section 11.3. The proposed algorithm for passive teleoperation with bounded control signals is described in Section 11.4. In Section 11.5, experimental measurements are presented. Finally, Section 11.6 concludes this work.

11.2 BILATERAL TELEOPERATION: BASIC NOTIONS

In this study, the velocity–force type bilateral teleoperation architecture is applied. Consider the bilateral teleoperation system in Figure 11.1. The human operator (H) moves the master device (M). The velocity of the master device (v_m) is sent through the communication channel and it serves as a reference for the slave controller (SC). The slave controller is responsible for tracking the master's velocity by the slave (S). The force f_s calculated by the slave controller (SC) is sent back to the master side. When the slave (S) is in contact with the environment (E), the environment exerts a force (f_e) on the slave device and the following approximation can be assumed: $f_s \approx -f_e$. Through f_s the human operator "feels" the effect of the environment on the slave device.

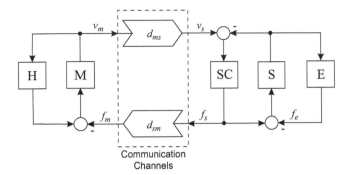

FIGURE 11.1   Networked velocity-force type bilateral teleoperation system – block diagram.

Consider the two-port network block in Figure 11.2 representing the communication channels. At the ports of the network, we have the power correlated force and velocity values f_s, v_s and f_m, v_m respectively. The two-port network formed from the communication channels is considered passive if and only if the energy function (E) defined below is always positive, i.e.,

$$E(t)= \int_0^t \big(f_s(\tau)v_s(\tau)+ f_m(\tau)v_m(\tau)\big)d\tau+ E(0)\geq 0, \qquad (11.1)$$

where $E(0)$ is the energy in the time instant $t=0$. In the rest of this work, it is assumed that $E(0)=0$.

Assume that the *Human + Master* and the *Slave Controller + Slave + Environment* networks in Figure 11.2 are passive. The power continuous interconnection of passive systems is also passive. Hence, for the passivity of the teleoperation system, it is sufficient to show that the *Communication* network in Figure 11.2 to be passive.

The *control objectives* for teleoperation systems can be summarized as follows (see also e.g., [6]):

1. *Passivity*:

   The two-port network containing the communication channels is passive.

2. *Position Coordination*:

   If the forces developed by human operator and the environment are zero, then $x_s \to x_m$ if $t \to \infty$. Here x_s is the slave position and x_m is the master position.

3. *Static Force Reflection*:

   If $v_s, \dot{v}_s, v_m, \dot{v}_s \to 0$ then $f_m \to -f_s$.

11.3 PASSIVITY CONTROLLER–PASSIVITY OBSERVER DESIGN

In the passivity controller–passivity observer approach, in order to guarantee the passivity of the teleoperation systems, both on the master and the slave side a passivity controller is placed, which additively modifies the received velocity and force signals that arrive

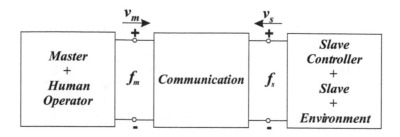

FIGURE 11.2   Velocity-force type bilateral teleoperation system – network representation.

through the communication channels. However, these controllers are active only when the passivity observer indicates that the teleoperation system starts losing its passivity. Otherwise, the control signals are 0.

In order to design the passivity observer, one should consider that in the teleoperation system the applied sampling time is substantially smaller than the time constants of the master and slave devices. In this case, the energy at the ports of the *Communication* network in Figure 11.2 can be approximated as

$$E[k] = T \sum_{i=0}^{k} \left(f_m[i]v_m[i] + f_s[i]v_s[i] \right), \tag{11.2}$$

where $T > 0$ is the sampling time and $k = \lceil t/T \rceil$. As it was presented in [7], if $E[k] > 0$, the network is passive. Otherwise, the network generates energy and the amount of the generated energy is $-E[k]$.

In the presence of a delay in the communication channel, the relation (11.2) is not computable. Due to the delay, in the sample k at a port of the communication channel, there is no information about the velocity and force measured at the other port of the network.

To solve this problem, in [10], the energy on the slave side was decomposed on input (*IN*) and output (*OUT*) energy as follows:

$$E_{IN}^s[k] = \begin{cases} E_{IN}^s[k-1] + Tv_s[k]f_s[k], & \text{if } v_s[k]f_s[k] > 0, \\ E_{IN}^s[k-1], & \text{otherwise.} \end{cases} \tag{11.3}$$

$$E_{OUT}^s[k] = \begin{cases} E_{OUT}^s[k-1] - Tv_s[k]f_s[k], & \text{if } v_s[k]f_s[k] < 0, \\ E_{OUT}^s[k-1], & \text{otherwise.} \end{cases} \tag{11.4}$$

The energy on the master side can also be decomposed into E_{IN}^m and E_{OUT}^m in the same way:

$$E_{IN}^m[k] = \begin{cases} E_{IN}^m[k-1] + Tv_m[k]f_m[k], & \text{if } v_m[k]f_m[k] > 0 \\ E_{IN}^m[k-1], & \text{otherwise.} \end{cases} \tag{11.5}$$

$$E_{OUT}^m[k] = \begin{cases} E_{OUT}^m[k-1] - Tv_m[k]f_m[k], & \text{if } v_m[k]f_m[k] < 0, \\ E_{OUT}^m[k-1], & \text{otherwise.} \end{cases} \tag{11.6}$$

Both on the master and the slave side of the *Communication* network in Figure 11.2, the total observed energy is $E_{IN} - E_{OUT}$. If in each sampling time at either ports of the network $E_{OUT} \leq E_{IN}$, there is no energy flow out of the network. This passivity condition also holds if the delayed input energies are considered [10], i.e. the passivity of the teleoperation system holds if

$$E_{OUT}^m[k] \leq E_{IN}^s[k - d_{sm}[k]] \tag{11.7}$$

and

$$E_{OUT}^s[k] \leq E_{IN}^m[k - d_{ms}[k]], \tag{11.8}$$

where d_{sm} denotes the discrete-time delay in the communication channel from the slave to the master and d_{ms} denotes the discrete-time delay in the channel from the master to slave. The discrete time delays d_{sm} and d_{ms} are positive integer values, they are equal to the integer parts of the continuous delays in the corresponding channel divided with the sampling time T.

The condition (11.7) is verifiable on the master side, the condition (11.8) is verifiable on the slave side.

The IN and OUT statements in the relations (11.3) to (11.6) are actually two registers that record the energy per sampling time, and depending on the power sign, it is added to either one of them. As E_{IN} and E_{OUT} increase in time, the registers could overflow after long operating time. The registers can be reset when the passivity conditions hold and the force and velocity values are zero. However, in modern robot control equipment, the implementation of large registers can easily be solved, the safe realization of the passivity observer based bilateral control is not compromised.

In order to satisfy the passivity conditions (11.7) and (11.8), additional energy dissipation terms (passivity controllers) should be placed to the ports of the communication channels.

On the slave side, the passivity controller is formulated as

$$v_s[k] = \hat{v}_s[k] + \begin{cases} v_{PC}[k], & \text{if } E_{OUT}^S[k] > E_{IN}^m[k - d_{sm}[k]], \\ 0, & \text{otherwise.} \end{cases} \tag{11.9}$$

Here, $\hat{v}_s$ denotes the received velocity signal from the slave side, and v_{PC} is the output of the passivity controller on the slave side.

The master side controller has the form

$$f_m[k] = \hat{f}_m[k] + \begin{cases} f_{PC}, & \text{if } E_{OUT}^m[k] > E_{IN}^s[k - d_{ms}[k]], \\ 0, & \text{otherwise.} \end{cases} \tag{11.10}$$

Here, $\hat{f}_m$ denotes the received force signal from the slave side, and f_{PC} is the output of the passivity controller on the master side.

The detailed design of the passivity controller, which also assures the safe teleoperation (the boundedness of the force and velocity signals in the teleoperation system), is presented in the next section.

11.4 PASSIVITY CONTROLLER WITH BOUNDED FORCE AND VELOCITY SIGNALS

11.4.1 Bounds for Control Signals

The ISO 10218 standard specifies concrete maximum velocity and force values for robotic systems, which work in the same workspace with humans. However, some authors suggest that in the case of lightweight robots, if special sensors and control architectures are applied in the robot control system, the prescribed maximum values are too restrictive and compromise the tracking performance of the robot control system [22].

In the case of teleoperation systems, the force and velocity values prescribed by this standard cannot be applied directly. For example, to avoid possible finger/hand injuries of the human operator, stricter constraints for the force values are necessary. In this study, the maximum velocity and force values are taken as adjustable parameters and accordingly their values can be set during teleoperator design in the function of the specifics of the application. The values of the transmitted force and velocity signals can be bounded by placing saturation blocks at the inputs of the communication channels. However, according to (11.10) and (11.9), the force received by the master device and the velocity received by the slave device, the control signals calculated by the passivity controllers are added. These control signals have to be bounded as well.

Accordingly, the following bound values are considered:

$$|\hat{v}_s| \le V, \quad |v_{PC}| \le V, \tag{11.11}$$

$$|\hat{f}_m| \le F, \quad |f_{PC}| \le F. \tag{11.12}$$

If the signals in the teleoperation system are bounded (to satisfy the safety constraints), the bandwidth of the velocity control loop has to be designed narrower compared with the case when no control signal bound is assumed during controller design. We assume that the slave side velocity controller guarantees precise tracking within this bandwidth, i.e. the absolute value slave velocity error remains under a prescribed limit. The bounded velocity tracking error can be achieved by applying suitable robot control algorithms, see, for example [26].

11.4.2 Passivity Controllers

The outputs of the passivity controllers, meant to guarantee the passivity of the teleoperation system in the presence of delay in the communication channels, have to respect the relations (11.11) and (11.12).

In this view, for the slave side passivity controller (11.9), the control signal v_{PC} is defined as

$$v_{PC} = V \, \text{sgn}(f_s[k]). \tag{11.13}$$

Similarly, for the master side controller (11.10), the control signal f_{PC} is taken as

$$f_{PC} = F \, \text{sgn}(v_m[k]). \tag{11.14}$$

Proposition: The control laws (11.9), (11.13) and (11.10), (11.14) guarantee the passivity of the teleoperation system if the rates of the signals v_m and f_s are bounded, i.e.,

$$\frac{|v_m[k]-v_m[k-1]|}{T}\leq\delta_v, \quad \frac{|f_s[k]-f_s[k-1]|}{T}\leq\delta_f \tag{11.15}$$

and the rate bounds are chosen as

$$\delta_v=\frac{V}{TD_{ms}}, \quad \delta_f=\frac{F}{TD_{sm}}, \tag{11.16}$$

where D_{ms} and D_{sm} are the maximum values of the discrete-time delays in the communication channel, i.e. $d_{ms}[k]\leq D_{ms}$ and $d_{sm}[k]\leq D_{sm}$, $\forall k$.

To prove the affirmation of the Proposition, consider the block diagram of the proposed bilateral control system, shown in Figure 11.3. The blocks *PCM* and *PCS* are the applied passivity controllers. The saturation blocks assure that the signals which are sent through the communication channels are bounded. The rate limiters (*RL*) at the inputs of the communication channels guarantee that the absolute difference between two consecutively sent values is upper bounded.

To show that the two-port network representing the communication channels with rate bounded inputs is passifiable with bounded control signals, the energy function (11.2) is written in recursive form as follows:

$$E[k]=E[k-1]+T\left(f_m[k]v_m[k]+f_s[k]v_s[k]\right). \tag{11.17}$$

By assuming $E(0)\geq 0$, if the increment on the right hand side of the equation above is positive in each sample, the function E is non-decreasing and accordingly the energy always remains positive.

If the passivity conditions (11.7) and (11.8) are satisfied, then $E[k]>0$. Otherwise the relation (11.17) with the control laws defined in (11.9), (11.13) and (11.10), (11.14) reads as

$$E[k]=E[k-1]+T((\hat{f}_m[k]+F\,\mathrm{sgn}(v_m[k]))v_m[k]+(\hat{v}_s[k]+V\,\mathrm{sgn}(f_s[k]))f_s[k]). \tag{11.18}$$

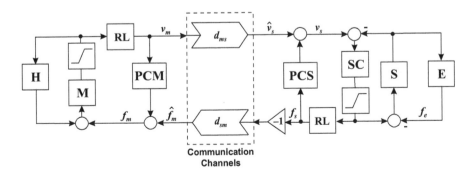

FIGURE 11.3 Networked bilateral teleoperation system with bounded control signals – block diagram.

The equation above can be rewritten as

$$E[k] = E[k-1] + T((f_s[k] - f_s[k] + \hat{f}_m[k] + F\,\mathrm{sgn}(v_m[k]))v_m[k]$$
$$+ f_s[k](v_m[k] - v_m[k] + \hat{v}_s[k] + V\,\mathrm{sgn}(f_s[k])))$$
$$= E[k-1] + T((f_s[k] + \hat{f}_m[k] + F\,\mathrm{sgn}(v_m[k]))v_m[k] \qquad (11.19)$$
$$+ f_s[k](-v_m[k] + \hat{v}_s[k] + V\,\mathrm{sgn}(f_s[k]))).$$

Since $\hat{v}_s[k] = v_m[k - d_{ms}[k]]$ and $\hat{f}_m[k] = -f_s[k - d_{sm}[k]]$ it yields

$$E[k] = E[k-1] + T((f_s[k] - f_s[k - d_{sm}[k]])v_m[k] + F\,|v_m[k]|$$
$$+ f_s[k](-v_m[k] + v_m[k - d_{ms}[k]]) + V\,|f_s[k]|). \qquad (11.20)$$

By taking into consideration the conditions (11.15) we have

$$|f_s[k] - f_s[k - d_{sm}[k]]| \le \delta_f T D_{sm} \qquad (11.21)$$

and

$$|v_m[k] - v_m[k - d_{ms}[k]]| \le \delta_v T D_{ms}. \qquad (11.22)$$

From the inequalities above, and from (11.15) and (11.16), it yields that the increment in (11.20) is positive. Accordingly, the bilateral control system is passive.

11.4.3 Transparency with Rate-Limited Signals

The position coordination can be compromised when the rate of the velocity signal is upper bounded. The slave side position (x_s) is legged from the master side position (x_m), when the absolute value of the velocity rate is upper bounded. It happens because the position is the integral of the velocity and the modifications, even in the transient state of the velocity, compromise the steady state of the position signal.

To deal with this problem, an extended velocity rate limiter is proposed. Let us denote the rate limiter function with $RL(\cdot)$, which assures that the first order derivate of the input velocity is upper bounded with a prescribed bound. In continuous time, if the input velocity signal is $v(t)$, the position signal corresponding to it is $x(t) = \int_0^t v(\tau)d\tau$. Let the rate-limited velocity signal be $v_{RL}(t) = RL(v(t))$. The corresponding position is $x_{RL} = \int_0^t v_{RL}(\tau)d\tau$.

To guarantee that the position signal (x_{RL}) corresponding to the rate-limited velocity converges the input position signal (x) in steady state, a corrector algorithm can be applied. The input of the rate limiter function $RL(\cdot)$ is extended as follows:

$$x_{RL} = \int_0^t v_{RL}(\tau)d\tau, \qquad (11.23)$$
$$v_{RL} = RL\left(v + \frac{1}{T_I}(x - x_{RL})\right),$$

where T_I is a strictly positive time constant.

When the rate of the velocity v does not reach its limit, the equality $x_{RL}=x$ holds and the error term is zero. When the rate limitation is active, in steady state the error term guarantees the convergence of x_{RL} to the real position.

The discrete time implementation of the algorithm (11.23) is straightforward, the integral can be approximated using, for example, the Euler method with a step size equal to the sampling time T:

$$x_{RL}[k]= x_{RL}[k-1]+ Tv_{RL}[k],$$

$$v_{RL}[k]= RL\left(v[k]+ \frac{1}{T_I}\left(x[k]-x_{RL}[k]\right)\right). \tag{11.24}$$

The modification above guarantees that the velocity sent through the communication channel is rate limited and the position coordination is preserved.

Example: To illustrate the effects of the rate limitation and the benefits of the proposed corrector algorithm, simulation experiments were performed applying a velocity Rate Limiter with $\delta_v=1.66$ m/s^2 rate bound. The input of the rate limiter is a velocity signal the rate of which is 3.33 m/s^2, see the first graph in Figure 11.4. The second graph in Figure 11.4 shows the effect of velocity rate limitation. The output of the rate limiter increases with δ_v rate until the input is smaller than the output. However, the position corresponding to the rate-limited

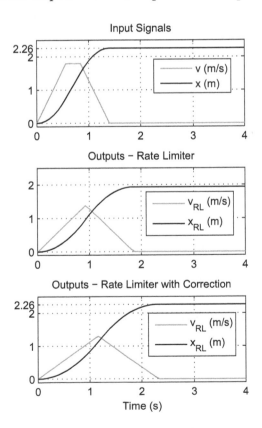

FIGURE 11.4 Rate-limited velocity signals and the resulting position signals with and without correction.

velocity does not reach the value of the input position in steady state, compromising the position transparency. The third graph in Figure 11.4 shows the effect of the corrector term on the output of the rate limiter (Eq. 11.23 with $T_I = 0.5$ s). In this case, the input correction assures the position transparency in the presence of rate-limited velocity as well.

11.5 EXPERIMENTAL RESULTS

The proposed control algorithm was tested on a 1 DOF teleoperation system. Direct current servo motors served as actuators both on the master and the slave side. The supply voltages of the motors were 48 V, the maximum motor current was 4 A. Perpendicular to the motor axes, plastic rods were fixed both on the master and the slave side. On the master side, the human operator can generate the motion for the master by moving the rod. On the slave side, a cylinder made of steel was placed in the path of the rod to test the behaviour of the teleoperation system when it is in contact with the environment [27].

The position and velocity were measured using identical incremental encoders on the master and the slave side. The applied encoders give 65536 pulses per turn. The motor torques are measured using torque sensors with a ±2.4 Nm measurement domain. The analogue signals corresponding to the torque values are sampled using 10-bit analogue–digital converters.

The control software was implemented on a PC with the QNX operating system. The master and slave side observers and controllers were implemented with $T = 1$ ms sampling time.

For a safe usage of the teleoperation system, the actuator outputs on the master and the slave side were limited to ± 0.7 Nm. The maximum output value of the master side passivity controller was also taken as $F = 0.7$ Nm. The bound of the slave side controller output was chosen as $V = 2$ m/s.

During the experiments the round-trip time in the communication channels was 250 ms with 125 ms delay in one direction. Hence, by the relation (11.16), the rate bounds of the signals were calculated as $\delta_f = 0.7/0.125 = 5.6$ Nm/s and $\delta_v = 2/0.125 = 16$ m/s^2.

The energy was observed both on the master side and the slave side of the communication channel using the observers described in Section 11.3. When the passivity conditions (11.7) or (11.8) are not satisfied, the passivity controllers (11.9), (11.13) and (11.10), (11.14) are switched on with the previously presented parameters. During controller implementation, it should also be taken into consideration that the calculated energy difference by the passivity observer is influenced by measurement noise. The effect of the measurement noise on the control can be avoided by introducing a small threshold value, in order of the measurement noise, for testing the passivity conditions (11.7) and (11.8). The passivity controller is switched on only when the energy difference overpasses this threshold level. The value of the threshold was determined by observing the computed energies (E_{IN}, E_{OUT}) when there is no slave robot–environment contact, i.e. the passivity controllers are not active.

11.5.1 Experimental Measurements with the Proposed Bilateral Teleoperation Control Method

Experimental measurements are presented in Figure 11.5. During measurements, the slave contacted the environment in $t = 0.95$ s and $t = 5.2$ s. Displacement error during the contact occurs, since, due to the delay in the communication channels, the operator can still push the rod whilst the slave cannot move because of the hard contact. The operator stops only when the master receives the delayed reaction force. The slave side passivity controller activates when the slave hits the steel obstacle. The master side controller activates when the operator pulls back the master's rod from the contact position. The calculated control signals are also presented in Figure 11.5.

With the proposed control strategy, the teleoperation system shows stable behaviour with bounded control signals. Whenever the passivity observers indicate that the difference between the output energy and delayed input energy is positive, the corresponding controller switches on and dissipates the extra energy of the teleoperation system. By stable behaviour, the measurements also show good position coordination and reliable force reflection when the master side passivity controller is not active.

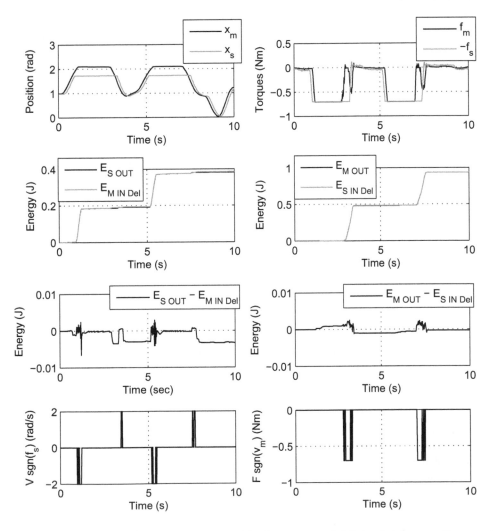

FIGURE 11.5 Experimental measurements with the proposed bilateral teleoperation control method.

11.6 CONCLUSIONS

In concordance with the currently available safety standards, the functional safety during human–robot interaction can be assured by limiting the magnitude of the force and velocity signals in the robot control system. On the other hand, if communication delays are present in a telerobotic system, the passivity has to be assured using control laws that depend on force and velocity values. The control approach presented in this chapter relates the passivity and safety problems in bilateral teleoperation systems implemented over communication channels with time-varying delay. It was shown that the passivity of a bilateral teleoperation system in the presence of delay can be guaranteed with such controllers that outputs are bounded with predefined limit values. This fact can be exploited to design such bilateral teleoperation systems in which the functional safety requirements related to the boundedness of the force and velocity signals are fulfilled. In the proposed bilateral control approach, to fulfil the requirements related to the limits of the control signals, the rates of the force and velocity signals, which are sent through the communication channels, are bounded. Due to the rate limitation, the transparency and tracking performances can only be guaranteed in the low-frequency domain. The presented theoretical result leads back to the normal restriction that safe and stable bilateral control is possible if rapid motions and abrupt force variations are avoided during the teleoperation task. The rate limiter terms in the proposed bilateral control scheme are able to cancel the abrupt signal variations. A modified velocity rate limiter algorithm was also proposed to assure improved position coordination in the controlled bilateral teleoperation system. According to the proposed approach, the input of the rate limiter is extended with an additive corrector term representing the difference between the position corresponding to the original velocity and the position corresponding to the rate-limited velocity. The performed real-time experimental measurements show that the proposed control algorithm assures stable bilateral teleoperation with bounded control signals and the teleoperation system also has good position coordination and force reflection property.

ACKNOWLEDGMENTS

The author's research work was supported by a grant of the Romanian National Authority for Scientific Research, CNCS UEFISCDI, project number PN-II-RU-TE-2011-3-0005. The experimental measurement results were performed during the research visit of the author at the DLR – Institute of Robotics and Mechatronics. The author acknowledges Jordi Artigas Esclusa, DLR – Institute of Robotics and Mechatronics, for his support during the research visit.

REFERENCES

1. P.F. Hokajem, M.W. Spong, Bilateral Teleoperation: An historical survey. *Automatica* **42**, 2025, (2006).
2. N. Chopra, P. Berestesky, M. Spong, Bilateral teleoperation over unreliable communication networks. *IEEE Transactions on Control Systems Technology* **16**(2), 304, (2008).
3. S. Hirche, M. Buss, Human-oriented control for haptic teleoperation. *Proceedings of the IEEE* **100**(3), 623, (2012).

4. C. Passenberg, A. Peer, M. Buss, A survey of environment, operator, and task-adapted controllers for teleoperation systems. *Mechatronics* **20**(7), 787, (2010).
5. E. Nuno, R. Ortega, N. Barabanov, L. Basanez, A globally stable PD controller for bilateral teleoperators. *IEEE Transactions on Robotics* **24**(3), 753, (2008).
6. D. Lee, M.W. Spong, Passive bilateral teleoperation with constant time delay. *IEEE Transactions on Robotics* **22**(2), 269, (2006).
7. B. Hannaford, J.H. Ryu, Time-domain passivity control of haptic interfaces. *IEEE Transactions on Robotics and Automation* **18**(1), 1, (2002).
8. J.H. Ryu, D.S. Kwon, B. Hannaford, Stable teleoperation with time-domain passivity control. *IEEE Transactions on Robotics and Automation* **20**(2), 365, (2004).
9. C. Ott, J. Artigas, C. Preusche, Subspace-oriented distribution for the time domain passivity approach. *IEEE/RSJ International Conference on Intelligent Robots and Systems* (2011), pp. 177–183. San Francisco/USA 25-30 Sept. 2011.
10. J.H. Ryu, J. Artigas, C. Preusche, A passive bilateral control scheme for a teleoperator with time-varying communication delay. *Mechatronics* **20**, 812, (2010).
11. J. Artigas, J.H. Ryu, C. Preusche, G. Hirzinger, Network representation and passivity of delayed teleoperation systems. *IEEE/RSJ International Conference on Intelligent Robots and Systems* (2011), pp. 177–183. San Francisco/USA 25-30 Sept. 2011.
12. J.P. Kim, J. Ryu, Robustly stable haptic interaction control using an energy-bounding algorithm. *The International Journal of Robotics Research* **29**(6), 666, (2010).
13. S. Park, C. Seo, J.P. Kim, J. Ryu, Robustly stable rate-mode bilateral teleoperation using an energy bounding approach. *Mechatronics* **21**(1), 176, (2011).
14. T. Hulin, K. Hertkorn, P. Kremer, S. Schätzle, J. Artigas, M. Sagardia, F. Zacharias, C. Preusche, The DLR bimanual haptiice with optimized workspace. *Proceedings IEEE International Conference on Robotics and Automation* (2011), pp. 3441–3442. Shanghai/China, 9–13 May 2011.
15. ISO 10218-1:2011, Robots and robotic devices – Safety requirements for industrial robots – Part 1: Robots. www.iso.org/standard/51330.html
16. ISO 10218-2:2011, Robots and robotic devices – Safety requirements for industrial robots – Part 2: Robot systems and integration. www.iso.org/standard/41571.html
17. ISO/TS 15066:2016, Robots and robotic devices – Collaborative robots. www.iso.org/standard/62996.html
18. ISO 13482:2014, Robots and robotic devices – Safety requirements for personal care robots. www.iso.org/standard/53820.html
19. S. Avgousti, E.G. Christoforou, A.S. Panayides, S. Voskarides, C. Novales, L. Nouaille, C.S. Pattichis, P. Vieyres, Medical Telerobotic Systems: Current Status and Future Trends, *BioMedical Engineering OnLine* **15**(1):96,(2016).
20. IEC/DIS 80601-2-77, Medical electrical equipment – Part 2-77: Particular requirements for the basic safety and essential performance of robotically assisted surgical equipment. www.iso.org/standard/68473.html
21. IEC/DIS 80601-2-78, Medical electrical equipment – Part 2-78: Particular requirements for the basic safety and essential performance of medical robots for rehabilitation, assessment, compensation or alleviation. www.iso.org/standard/68474.html
22. S. Haddadin, A. Albu-Schäffer, G. Hirzinger, Approaching Asimov's 1st law: The 'Impact' of the Robot's weight class. *Proceedings of the Robotics: Science and Systems*: 1–8 Atlanta/USA, 27–30 June 2007.
23. M. Zinn, O. Khatib, B. Roth, *The International Journal of Robotics Research* **23**, 379, (2004).
24. S. Haddadin, A. Albu-Schäffer, G. Hirzinger, Requirements for safe rRobots: Measurements, analysis and new insights. *The International Journal of Robotics Research* **28**, 1507, (2009).

25. L. Marton, J.A. Esclusa, P. Haller, T. Vajda, in *IEEE International Conference on Industrial Informatics* (2013), pp. 337–342.Bochum/Germany, 29–31 July 2013.
26. F.L. Lewis, D.M. Dawson, C.T. Abdallah, *Robot Manipulator Control*, Marcel Dekker, Inc., New York, (2004).
27. Lőrinc Márton, Zoltán Szántó, Tamás Haidegger, Péter Galambos, and József Kövecses. Internet-based Bilateral Teleoperation using a revised time-domain passivity controller. *Acta Polytechnica Hungarica* 14 (8): 27–45, 2017.

CHAPTER 12

Human–Robot Interfaces in Autonomous Surgical Robots

Paolo Fiorini and Riccardo Muradore

CONTENTS

12.1 Introduction   187
12.2 The I-SUR Robotic System   191
12.3 HRI During the Pre-Intervention Phase   191
12.4 HRI During the Intervention Execution   195
12.5 Conclusions   197
Acknowledgments   198
References   198

12.1 INTRODUCTION

This chapter addresses a very complex problem that can be expressed in a very simple form: is it possible to automate surgery? We believe that, if a solution can ever be approached, it would lie in the intersection of robotics, automation, and cognition, since factors such as experience, knowledge, and intuition are as important as mechanism design and control algorithms in successful surgery. The feasibility of a solution to this problem was analyzed during the European project Intelligent Robotic Surgery (I-SUR), a project of the Seventh Framework Programme during the period 2011 to 2014. In this project, we developed general methods for cognitive surgical robots capable of combining sensing, dexterity, and cognitive capabilities to carry out autonomously simple surgical actions, such as puncturing and suturing. To narrow further the scope of this research, we addressed the well-known surgical area of kidney interventions, whose variability and uncertainty are limited, but still representative of general situations and requiring strong cognitive capabilities to ensure the correct execution of the surgery. We examined the reasoning aspects of these domains, the control capabilities needed to carry out these surgical actions, and we integrated them into a robotic test bed performing autonomous surgical actions on anatomically correct phantoms [HOE15].

To make the problem tractable, we defined the automation of the above tasks in a very precise way, as shown in Figure 12.1. We addressed the complete execution of simple

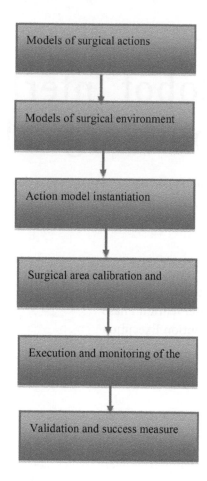

FIGURE 12.1   Surgical automation concept.

surgical actions by representing them as a sequence of different states, each state characterized by specific pre and post conditions and by several possible outcomes. Medical
and surgical knowledge were used to define the models of abstract surgical actions and to
identify the possible outcomes of each action state. Pre-operative data, for example, CAT
and MRI scans, were used to generate the virtual anatomy of the patient. An expert surgeon planned the surgical action in the virtual environment and her/his plan was used to
instantiate the abstract action model into a specific procedure for the given environment.
We developed a novel robotic system endowed with the necessary dexterity and sensing
capabilities, together with control algorithms to execute the specific instance of the surgical act. During the execution of the surgical act, two types of cognitive functions were
activated. The first measured the environment geometric and physical characteristics to
update the pre-operative models. The second function monitored the medical situation
by fusing operation parameters with medical knowledge to select the best state transition
or to ask the surgeon for help. The surgical action execution was monitored and evaluated
by an expert surgeon who interacted with the robotic instrument using an interface that
minimized the cognitive load.

Surgical interventions are among the most challenging activities performed by humans. They require years of training and education, coupled with practice, intuition, and cognitive as well as manual abilities. However, in spite of technological advances, surgical practice is still constrained by the limitations of human capabilities. In some cases, this limitation is due to a lack of basic knowledge of the anatomical structures to be operated on, as in the case of certain brain interventions. In many cases though, the limitations are due to a surgeon's inability to operate in the confined space of the human body, to perform the correct diagnosis of the patient pathology, or to quickly react to sudden situation changes.

Cognitive robotic systems can help to overcome these limitations by bringing to the surgical scenario actuators, sensors, control algorithms, and knowledge that could potentially extend the limits of human perception and manual dexterity. However, it is obvious that the cognitive abilities of human surgeons are not matched by any current computerized systems. Furthermore, it is also clear that even sophisticated control systems cannot carry out a task in this domain without accessing specific knowledge and reasoning capabilities. Thus, the overall scientific objective of the I-SUR project was to explore the connection between control and reasoning in this complex domain and to acquire basic knowledge about the integration of complex, domain-specific knowledge, with task-level control systems. We demonstrated the feasibility of this concept by developing methods that permitted the automatic execution of two simple surgical actions, i.e., puncturing and suturing, in two different anatomical areas, kidneys and skin.

The introduction of minimally invasive surgery (MIS) first and, more recently, of surgical robots, has brought new perspectives to surgery and has significantly improved the quality of many surgical procedures. However, current surgical robots are not the final answer to a surgeon's accuracy demands. In fact, they are teleoperated devices without any embedded autonomy, i.e., sophisticated versions of scalpels and scissors, and therefore performance-bound by the perception and dexterity of their human operators. Although it is well known that automation has been successfully used to enhance a great variety of human activities from aircraft control to manufacturing, the whole area of autonomous interaction of surgical tools with biological tissues is rather unexplored. In the applications where it has been used, automation has increased safety, accuracy, reproducibility, and has decreased human fatigue. Thus, we hypothesize that similar benefits could also be gained by introducing automation to specific aspects of surgery, provided that we can successfully solve the challenges of this concept. Surgical procedures are complex sequences of actions, which are difficult to formalize for automation. The environment in which such actions take place is highly variable and uncertain. The knowledge needed to carry out an intervention includes the "a priori" surgical knowledge and the "on line" perception processing. The selection of the specific surgical action does not depend only on the preoperative patient data, but it relies on the surgeon's experience, training, and intuition. All this knowledge is difficult to formalize in a computer-compatible form and it is represented in a variety of different formats, which are often incompatible with each other and with current robot controllers. During the intervention, this knowledge must be integrated with the information acquired in real time by the surgeon and by her/his understanding of the medical condition of the patient.

Thus, to start addressing this complex web of requirements, we developed the following key technological areas:

1. Representation. This area is concerned with the development of formal and quantitative methods for surgical action characterization. It required the integration of different competencies with different languages. The main aspects of surgery, i.e., biomechanics, anatomy, and physiology, relative to the selected surgical areas were described with methods from computer science and analyzed with tools from system theory.

2. Communication. This area addressed the creation of a seamless flow of information in the diagnosis-planning-execution of an intervention. Unlike current practices, where the surgeon is the holder of all the specific knowledge relevant to an intervention, we established a formal link between all the surgical phases, thus enabling the transfer of commands to a surgical robot in a format understandable by the surgical team members.

3. Perception. This area refers to the augmentation of surgeons' capabilities. The monitoring and interpretation of surgical parameters are key elements of a successful surgeon, and any autonomous system must be aware of the evolution of the surgical procedure. Furthermore, the situation understanding by the robot must be communicated to the surgeon. Thus, perception in this context refers to the enhancement of the surgeon perception thanks to the sensing and data processing of the surgical robot.

4. Planning and Execution. In this area, we developed a safe and robust controller for the selected surgical actions. During today's intervention, no computer support is provided to the surgeon relative to the progress of the surgery according to the plan defined earlier. Unlike current teleoperated surgical robots, an autonomous surgical robot must store and monitor the intervention plan, adapt it to the specific situations (anatomy, pathology, biomechanics), and ensure the safety of the complete process.

Specifically, the I-SUR project has developed the following innovative technologies:

- New methods for representing the medical knowledge relevant to soft organ surgery

- New methods for the interactive planning of surgery in deformable environments

- New designs of dexterous, sensorized instruments for robotic surgery

- New methods for intervention execution and monitoring

- New methods for real-time data processing and medical situation awareness

- New communication methods between the robotic instrument and the operating surgeon

We refer to the many papers published during the project, and listed in the references, to have an in-depth understanding of the technical details of each of the above areas, and in this chapter, we give a unified presentation of the issue related to human–robot interaction in the context of the execution of an autonomous puncturing tasks. The rest of the chapter is organized as follows. Section 12.2 presents an overview of the robotic hardware developed for the project. Section 12.3 summarizes the interaction and communication aspects of the pre-operative phases that include task and organ modeling and planning. Then, Section 12.4 describes the interaction aspects during task execution, for example, approach verification in simulation, the presentation of sensory data processing and reasoning, and the physical interaction of the surgeon with the robot by teleoperation. Finally, the last section presents some of the issues identified and left open by the project [MUR16].

12.2 THE I-SUR ROBOTIC SYSTEM

The automation of multiple surgical actions required the design of the versatile and dexterous robotic platform shown in Figure 12.2. The commercial robot UR5 [UR5] holds the US probe that detects on the US images the motion of the needle to guarantee the safety of the procedure. The I-SUR robot holds the needle and performs the puncturing according to the planned trajectory. To achieve the necessary workspace, dexterity and insertion forces, the robot consisted of two units:

1. A *macro unit* with four degrees of freedom (DOF) to perform the large displacement of the needle, consisting of a 3-DOF linear delta robot [MB2010] since this parallel kinematics offers a rigid platform capable of carrying the weight of the needle driver while ensuring high stiffness and positioning accuracy.

2. A dexterous *micro unit* capable of positioning the needle with the required accuracy. The micro unit has 4-DOF, mimicking the human arm (shoulder flexion/extension, shoulder rotation, elbow flexion/extension, and forearm pronation/supination).

Figure 12.2 shows the anatomical phantom used in the tests.

12.3 HRI DURING THE PRE-INTERVENTION PHASE

The modeling and planning phases of an autonomous surgical action are more complex than for human intervention since the task must be described in algorithmic form to the robot. In this chapter, we describe the puncturing action carried out in the context of a cryoablation procedure, that is, the killing of cancer cells by repeated cycles of freezing and thawing. Thus, the guidance commands of the puncturing needles must be carried out according to this procedure's requirements. Cryoablation must preserve the healthy tissues around the tumor and the surrounding anatomical structures (liver, bowel, spleen, ureters) according to [DMC07]. This technique is a valuable alternative to open surgery or laparoscopy, ensuring safety with low morbidity and high efficacy on oncological results, as reported in [CA09]. The main requirement for the correct execution of this procedure is the accuracy in the needle displacement: during the planning phase, the optimal target points for the cryoprobes must take into account both dimension/location of the lesion and the temperature distribution of the generated ice ball (irreversible tissue destruction

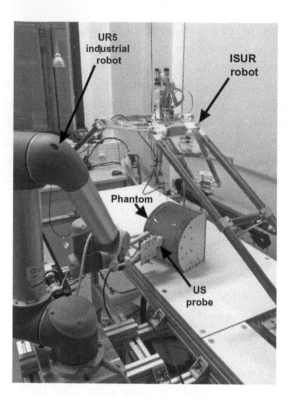

FIGURE 12.2 The I-SUR robot with the ultrasound probe.

occurs from −20°C to −40°C). To make the procedure understandable to the human user, i.e., surgeon or interventional radiologist, planning software was developed to compute the position of the needles so that the ice balls formed at the end of the needles could completely cover the volume of the tumor.

The tumor volume was extracted from the segmentation of the kidney of anonymous patients. The models of the organs were segmented from images taken when the cryoablation needles were already inserted into the kidney tumor to account for tissue deformation. The reconstruction of the organs was done by using open source software 3D Slicer. The CT scan with the visible first needle was first cropped down for a faster segmentation process and then the segmented layers were assembled into 3D models by using the Model Maker module in 3D Slicer, as shown in Figure 12.3. From this phase, we derived the geometrical constraints of the needle placement as well as the model of the anatomical phantom that was used during the tests. The needle positions were analyzed using the graphical interface shown in Figure 12.4.

The other key element of pre-operative planning is the development of the surgical action model and its instantiation on the specific patient, i.e., our phantom, anatomy. The surgical task model must allow for supervision, reasoning, and control, and it was formalized using a requirements engineering approach, following the validation-oriented methodology described in [MB12]. The used methodology collects human knowledge about the desired surgical procedures and related safety issues, translates it into a formal model and automatically generates control-oriented specifications of the prescribed system behavior.

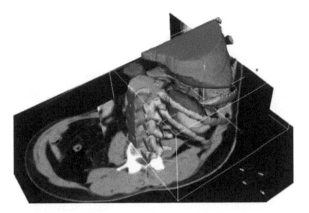

FIGURE 12.3   3D model of patient anatomy.

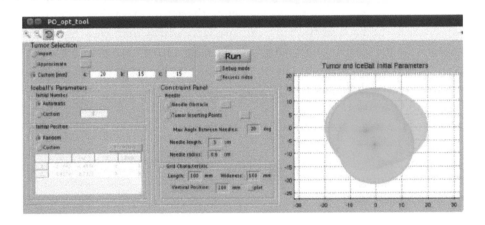

FIGURE 12.4   Planning needle positions.

The latter is then mapped into the supervision logic of the final software architecture, where the correctness properties can be further verified using formal tools.

From the HRI point of view, the surgical task structure is represented with graphs of increasing detail, ending up in the pseudo-code of the task. This approach allows a good visual and conceptual understanding of the task structure. In the initial phase of the model generation, the knowledge of expert surgeons, for example, urologists practicing cryoabla-tion tasks, is captured to define the main procedures, i.e., "best practices" to be performed, the elements of the domain, i.e., tools, gestures, pre-operative and intra-operative data, the critical events related to the surgical actions, and how they could be addressed to preserve safety. In the I-SUR case, this phase required interviews of the surgeons, participation of developers and engineers to real surgical interventions, and execution of such operations on artificial phantoms and augmented reality simulators developed during the project, as described in [RM12]. Then, surgical requirements can be expressed using a goal-oriented methodology called FLAGS (Fuzzy Live Adaptive Goals for Self-adaptive systems [LB10]), which is focused on the essential objectives of an operation and on complications that may arise during its execution. The result of the knowledge formalization is a goal model, technically defined as a set of formal properties expressed in the Alloy language [DJ12], which is a specification language expressing structural and behavioral constraints for complex software systems, based on first-order logic (FOL) and linear temporal logic (LTL [CB08]). For example, a leaf goal of the cryoablation procedure, related to its safe completion, requires avoiding forbidden regions, for example, bones, nerves, and other organs, during needle insertion.

The state model obtained after goal-oriented analysis is finished can be used for modular software design by applying decomposition methods from classical discrete system theory and using UML (Unified Modeling Language [OMG]) as a modeling tool, the latter being the current gold standard in object-oriented and component-based software design. Finally, the UML model of the modular system is verified using formal tools for Model Checking [RM15] to prove that the design model preserves the properties expressed by the goal model. The resulting UML diagram is shown in Figure 12.5, which represents the "conceptual" interface to the robotic system before the actual execution takes place.

This diagram is the basis of the Surgical Interface, which manages the interaction of the surgeons with the system by showing the intra-operative images and the 3D rendering of the full robotics system in its current pose and accepts commands and inputs when required to progress with the task. When the surgeon needs to take control of the task, the teleoperation node activates a PHANTOM Omni haptic device, which then becomes the master device of the surgical system.

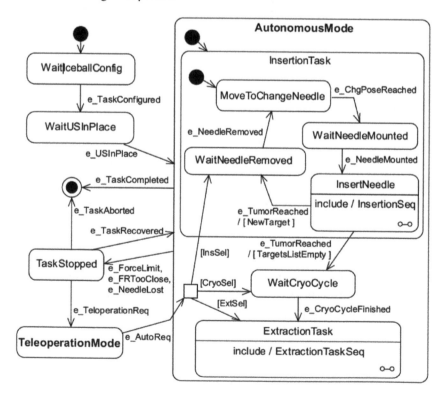

FIGURE 12.5 The UML state diagram of the behavioral specification for cryoablation needle insertion.

12.4 HRI DURING THE INTERVENTION EXECUTION

The surgeon can use a very extensive graphical interface to examine the motion sequence of the autonomous needle insertion before the action is performed. The surgeon can adjust the motion parameters and verify the correct position of the robot and of the patient before the surgical task starts and then he/she can monitor in real time all the robot parameters using the interface shown in Figure 12.6. The interface includes panels, buttons, and windows that have been organized to increase usability and grouped into logical sections:

- Surgery presentation: CAD model view, setting functions for CAD model view (organs, objects/tools, view angle), CT views (axial, coronal and sagittal)

- Commands: cryoablation planning tool, ice ball configured, new needle, ask extraction

- Background information: e.g., robot applied forces

Important task information is placed in the center of the interface, all data screens are located on the right side to help the surgeon focus on the important parts of the cryoablation procedure. Additionally, task-related buttons are placed at the bottom to avoid the hand covering the screen while "turn off" buttons for each robot are placed at the top. Furthermore, patient information is added on the top of the screen for a consistent interface, and each component (windows, buttons, texts) is aligned for faster visual grouping and directing of attention.

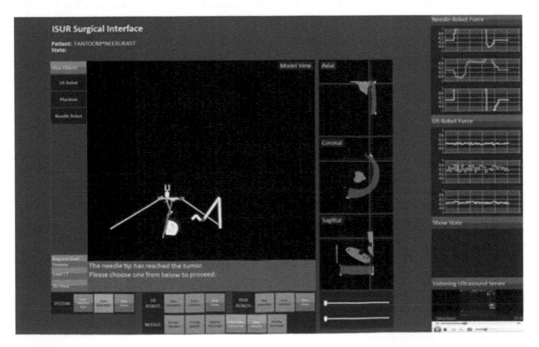

FIGURE 12.6   The surgical interface of I-SUR.

One innovative aspect of the interface of a cognitive system, such as I-SUR, refers to the ability to convey the decisions made by the system during the intervention and to provide the rationale of those decisions in an understandable format. Also, in this case, graphical rendering of the data and of the interpretation has been used to give feedback to the surgeon. During needle insertion, the critical element to assess the correct task execution is the needle position: it must not collide with critical structures and reach the target position to deliver the freezing therapy. This information is best shown to the surgeon by displaying the echographic images of the patient anatomy, with the current needle position superimposed to its planned position, as shown in Figure 12.7. This picture shows a section of an anatomical structure (top part) and the kidney with a superficial tumor (bottom part). The planned needle trajectory is superimposed with high accuracy to the actual trajectory of the needle. However, the autonomous controller is faced with the difficult task of separating correct needle insertion from the incorrect insertions. This reasoning aspect of the system interface is carried out by processing the task states estimated by a Hidden Markov Model with a Bayesian network. The robot base distance to the target is computed using the I-SUR robot kinematics and the path planning information. The needle tip distance to the target and the angle to the target were estimated by the needle tracking algorithm from the tip position and the needle orientation. Making use of this information, the Bayesian network computed the probability of the reasoning event "tumor hit." If the probability is below an empiric threshold, the insertion is considered failed and the needle should be extracted.

However, the failure to reach the target could be attributed to many causes, including a system failure, and therefore, it may not be safe to demand the extraction of the needle and the repetition of the insertion to the robot controller. In cases such as this, it may be necessary to ask the surgeon to take over the intervention and to complete it manually. The transition from autonomous to manual control of a robotic task is a challenge that was solved successfully during the I-SUR project [FF15]. In this case, the "manual" human–robot interface is the Phantom Omni joystick shown in Figure 12.8. The challenge consists

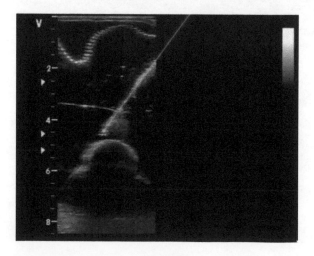

FIGURE 12.7   Echographic images of the needle insertion.

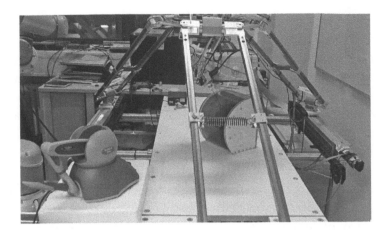

FIGURE 12.8   The manual human–robot interface of the I-SUR project.

of avoiding any jump of the position of the needle when the robot controller switches its input from the planned trajectory to the manual command. Clearly, the joystick and the needle are in two different poses and before starting the needle extraction, the position and the orientation of the joystick must match the actual position and orientation of the needle. The autonomous surgical robot has now become a teleoperated system and the surgeon must align the joystick to the needle using his/her perception of the surgical scene. The alignment can impose a high cognitive load on the surgeon and it can lead to risks for the patient because of unintentional motions transmitted to the robot. Furthermore, the manual mode is activated during critical situations and mistakes in the teleoperation can cause severe injury to the patient. Thus, the safe switch between autonomous and teleoperated modes and kinematic mismatches compensation is an essential feature in the HRI for an autonomous surgical robot. We implemented a two-layered bilateral control architecture that ensures safe behavior during the transition between autonomy and teleoperation and still retains high-performance control after the switch.

12.5 CONCLUSIONS

In this chapter, we have described the HRI aspects of the cognitive robotic platform I-SUR, designed to execute autonomously simple surgical tasks, such as needle insertion. We identified three specific interface aspects in the design of an autonomous robot. The first interface mode is a collection of the graphical renderings of modeling and planning: we model patient anatomy and task structure, and map the latter to the former. The second interface mode is more standard and is used to display the simulation of the task for the last check before the intervention, the status of the surgical task during execution, and the images of the relevant intra-operative sensors, for example, echography. Within this interface, the cognitive aspects of the surgical task are highlighted to the user: a reasoning engine detects anomalies in the task and warns the user about possible failures. The third interface mode is manual and is activated when the surgeon needs to take charge of the task, for example, when a failure is detected. Through this interface, the operator can teleoperate the robot and continue the intervention or bring the needle to a safe position.

We demonstrated that the system is able to plan an intervention of cryoablation to a kidney, execute the needle insertion, and monitor the procedure without any intervention by the operator supervising the surgical action. The experimental validation has been performed on an anatomically accurate US/CT compatible phantom of the human abdomen.

Although the ISUR project successfully reached its stated goals, the path to task autonomy in surgery is still long and difficult, in particular when a cognitive interaction between the human operator and the surgical robot is required. Our future work will aim not only at improving the robustness of the system, at better integrating the different subsystems, and at enlarging the number of tasks that could be executed autonomously (e.g., cutting and suturing), but also to improve the communication between the human user and the robot.

During the I-SUR project, we started addressing some of the key issues related to the autonomous control of complex and dangerous tasks, such as surgery, and how to communicate and exchange pre- and intra-operative knowledge between the human user and the robotic system, in particular:

- Controlled and increased patient safety. Autonomous control features and monitoring will be indispensable in more demanding surgical procedures of the future.

- Increased surgical automation. In spite of the progress in computer and robotic-assisted surgery, automation in the operating room is still not available due to the lack of basic technology and of appropriate validation methods.

- Expanding user and intervention bases. Currently, surgical robot users are surgeons with high technology awareness and training resources. In the future, autonomous features will help less technology savvy users to take advantage of robotic tools.

- Safety regulations and standards. Autonomous robots in the operating room need social acceptance and appropriate safety regulations and standards. In I-SUR, we started to address the social and legal lags between autonomous technologies and regulations.

The solution to these challenges will help with the introduction of autonomous and semi-autonomous robotic systems to operating rooms.

ACKNOWLEDGMENTS

This research was funded by the European Union Seventh Framework Programme FP7/2007-2013 under grant agreement n. 270396 (Intelligent Surgical Robotics, I-SUR).

REFERENCES

[UR5] Universal Robots. Available at www.universal-robots.com.
[MB2010] M. Bouri, and R. Clavel. The linear delta: Developments and applications. In *41st International Symposium on Robotics (ISR) and 6th German Conference on Robotics (ROBOTIK)*, pp. 1198–1205, Munich, Germany VDE, 7–9 June 2010.
[DMC07] D. M. Clarke, A. T. Robilotto, E. Rhee, R. G. VanBuskirk, J. G. Baust, Andrew A. Gage, and J. M. Baust. Cryoablation of renal cancer: Variables involved in freezing-induced cell death. *Technology in Cancer Research & Treatment*, 6(2): 69–79, 2007.

[CA09] C. Adam, A. C. Mues, and J. Landman. Current status of ablative therapies for renal tumors. *Indian Journal of the Urological*, 25(4): 499–507, 2009.

[MB12] M. Bonfè, F. Boriero, R. Dodi, P. Fiorini, A. Morandi, R. Muradore, L. Pasquale, A. Sanna, and C. Secchi. Towards automated surgical robotics: A requirements engineering approach. In *Proceedings of the IEEE RAS and EMBS International Conference Biomedical Robotics and Biomechatronics (BioRob)*, pp. 56–61, Rome, Italy, 24–27 June 2012.

[RM12] R. Muradore, D. Zerbato, L. Vezzaro, L. Gasperotti, and P. Fiorini. From simulation to abstract modeling of surgical operations. In *Joint Workshop on New Technologies for Computer/Robot Assisted Surgery*, Madrid, Spain, 9–10 July 2012.

[LB10] L. Baresi, L. Pasquale, and P. Spoletini. Fuzzy goals for requirements-driven adaptation. In *Proceedings of International Requirements Engineering Conference*, pp. 125–134, Sydney, Australia, 27 September–1 October 2010.

[DJ12] D. Jackson. Alloy, 2012. Available at http://alloy.mit.edu/.

[CB08] C. Baier, and J.-P. Katoen. *Principles of Model Checking*, MIT Press, Cambridge, MA, 2008.

[OMG] Object Management Group, UML v. 2.2 Superstructure specification Document N. formal/2009-02-02 2009. Available at www.omg.org/spec/UML/2.2/.

[RM15] R. Muradore, P. Fiorini, G. Akgun, D. E. Barkana, M. Bonfe, F. Boriero, A. Caprara, G. De Rossi, R. Dodi, O. J. Elle, F. Ferraguti, L. Gasperotti, R. Gassert, K. Mathiassen, D. Handini, O. Lambercy, L. Li, M. Kruusmaa, A. O. Manurung, G. Meruzzi, H. Q. P. Nguyen, N. Preda, G. Riolfo, A. Ristolainen, A. Sanna, C. Secchi, M. Torsello, and A. E. Yantac. Development of a cognitive robotic system for simple surgical tasks. *International Journal of Advanced Robotic Systems*, 12: 37, 2015.

[FF15] F. Ferraguti, N. Preda, A. Manurung, M. Bonf, O. Lambercy, R. Gassert, R. Muradore, P. Fiorini, and C. Secchi. An energy tank-based interactive control architecture for autonomous and teleoperated robotic surgery. *IEEE Transaction of Robotics*, 31(5): 1073–1088, 2015.

[HOE15] M. Hoeckelmann, I. J. Rudas, P. Fiorini, F. Kirchner, and T. Haidegger. Current capabilities and development potential in surgical robotics. *International Journal of Advanced Robotic Systems*, 12(5): 61, 2015.

[MUR16] R. Muradore, and P. Fiorini. A review of bilateral teleoperation algorithms. *Acta Polytechnica Hungarica*, 13(1): 191–208, 2016.

Index

ACMIT, *see* Austrian Center for Medical Innovation and Technology (ACMIT)
ACPS, 38
ADU, *see* Automated drill unit (ADU)
Aerospace manufacturing, 72–73
 human–robot collaboration in, 72–73
  activities, 75–76
  challenges, 73–75
  Industrial case studies, 76–78
 robotics in, 71–72
Agents, 27–28
AGV, *see* Autonomously guided vehicle (AGV)
Airbus A350 XWB wing skin drilling and tacking, 77
Airbus's Futurassy Project, 78
Alloy language, 194
American National Standards Institute (ANSI), 87
ANNIE mobile manipulator, 82
ANSI, *see* American National Standards Institute (ANSI)
ANSI R15.08, 87
API, *see* Application programming interface (API)
Application ontologies, 22
Application programming interface (API), 20
Arm Assist, 94
Asimov, Isaac, 14
Asimov's Laws of Robotics, 14
Assistive robots, 124
Audio/audiovisual feedback, 139
Austrian Center for Medical Innovation and Technology (ACMIT), 153, 154
Automated drill unit (ADU), 76
Automation, 138
 CORA, 20–21, 24–25, 27–28
 surgical, 187–188
Autonomously guided vehicle (AGV), 81
Autonomous system, 14
Autonomy, 27

Basel Committee on Banking Supervision (BCBS), 11
Basic safety, 99
BCBS, *see* Basel Committee on Banking Supervision (BCBS)

Bilateral teleoperation, 171–173
 architectures, 143–144
 basic notions, 174–175
 challenges, 171–172
 communication strategy for, 172, 176–177
 experimental results, 182–183
 human–robot interaction and its implications, 173–174
 networked velocity-force type, 175
 passivity of, 172–173
  controller–passivity observer approach, 175–180
  controllers, 178–180
  control signals, bounds for, 178, 179
  rate limited signals, transparency with, 180–182
Blunt instruments, 139
Boeing 777 Fuselage Automated Upright Build, 77–78
Bosch APAS, 81
British Standard Institute (BSI), 9–10
BSI, *see* British Standard Institute (BSI)

CAC, *see* Codex Alimentarius Commission (CAC)
CARLoS mobile manipulator, 82
CE-marking, 7, 92–93, 125
CENELEC, for electro-technical standardization, 1–2, 93
CEN standardization, 1–2, 93
CEN Workshop Agreement (CWA), 2
Certified safety, robotics, 13
Codex Alimentarius Commission (CAC), 11
Coexistence, 75
Collaboration, 76
Collaborative robots, 72; *see also* Human–robot collaboration, in aerospace manufacturing
Communication, 20
Complementary safety, 54–55
Components, 50
Composability, 53, 54
Composite modules, 50, 54
Continuum-mechanics models, 139–140, 142, 147

Cooperation, 75–76
Coordinate system, 31–32
CORA, *see* Core Ontology for Robotics and
  Automation (CORA)
CORAX, 28–29
CORDIS system, 4
Core ontologies, 22, 27
Core Ontology for Robotics and Automation
  (CORA), 20–21, 24–25, 27–28
  applications, 33–38
  in cargo delivery scenario, 35–36
  in robotic skill ontology, 33–35
  in surgical robot ontology, 36–38
Core Ontology for Web of Things (WoTCO), 38
Creep, viscoelasticity, 151
CWA, *see* CEN Workshop Agreement (CWA)
Cyber physical system, 14
Cyber-security, 7

Dangerous failures, 57–58
Data collection methods, 153–154
Degree of autonomy (DoA), 134–135
  classification of, 135
  defining autonomy, 134–135
1 degree-of-freedom (DoF) model, 140, 141, 142
Design object, 28
DIN EN 1525, 85, 86
DoA, *see* Degree of autonomy (DoA)
Domain ontologies, 22

EC, *see* European Commission (EC)
EC Guide, 6
Elastic tools, 139
EP, *see* European Parliament (EP)
Essential performances, 99–100
Essential principles, 126–127
ETSI, for telecommunications, 1–2
EU legislation for robotics, 6–7
European Commission (EC), 10, 15
European Parliament (EP), 10, 15
European Standards, 1–2

Failure mode, effects and criticality analysis
  (FMECA), 106–107, 110–111, 112
Failures, 57–58
FAUB, *see* Fuselage Automated Upright Build
  (FAUB)
FDA, *see* Food and Drug Agency (FDA)
FEM, *see* Finite Element Method (FEM)
Fetch mobile manipulator with Freight Base, 82
Finite Element Method (FEM), 141–142
FLAGS, *see* Fuzzy Live Adaptive Goals for
  Self-adaptive systems (FLAGS)

FLOBOT, European project, 104
FMECA, *see* Failure mode, effects and criticality
  analysis (FMECA)
Food and Drug Agency (FDA), 125
Force response function, 149, 155–160, 161
Formal standards, 1, 3
Fuselage Automated Upright Build (FAUB), 77–78
Fuzzy Live Adaptive Goals for Self-adaptive systems
  (FLAGS), 193

GCS, *see* Global coordinate system (GCS)
GDPR, *see* General Data Protection Regulation
  (GDPR)
General Data Protection Regulation (GDPR), 7
General product safety (GPSD), 6–7
Geomagic Touch™, 173
GHTF, *see* Global Harmonization Task Force
  (GHTF)
GKN Aerospace's Fokker Business, 76–77
Global coordinate system (GCS), 32
Global Harmonization Task Force (GHTF), 125, 126
GPSD, *see* General product safety (GPSD)

Haptic feedback in telesurgery, 139, 145–147
Hard tissue interaction, 139
Hardware (HW) modules, 49–50, 62–65
Harm, 108
Harmonised standards, 5–6, 7
Hazards, 108, 114–119
Heuristic models, 139, 147–148
Hierarchies, 32
HRI, *see* Human–robot interaction (HRI)
Human–robot collaboration, in aerospace
  manufacturing, 72–73
  activities, 75–76
  challenges, 73
    HRI, safety of, 74
    human factors, 75
    human–robot interface, 75
    robots, limitations of, 73–74
    working environment, 74
  industrial case studies
    Airbus A350 XWB wing skin drilling and
      tacking, 77
    Airbus's Futurassy Project, 78
    Boeing 777 Fuselage Automated Upright
      Build, 77–78
    GKN Aerospace's Fokker Business, 76–77
Human–robot interaction (HRI), 20, 74, 75,
  137–139
  control aspects of, 143–145
  importance of, 165
  I-SUR

during intervention execution, 195–197
during pre-intervention phase, 191–194
proposed model, usability of, 164–165
results, 160–161
    model verification methods, 161–163
    model verification results, 163–164
soft tissue models, 147–148
    data collection methods, 153–154
    indentations tests, 154–158
    mass–spring–damper models, 149–152
    nonlinear mass–spring–damper model,
        158–160
    telesurgery haptic feedback in, 145–147
    types of, 139–143
Hunt–Crossley model, 141
Hybrid flexible tools, 139
Hybrid models, 15–16, 139, 147, 148

IASB, *see* International Accounting Standards
        Board (IASB)
ICANN, *see* Internet Corporation for Assigned
        Names and Numbers (ICANN)
IEC, *see* International Electrotechnical Commission
        (IEC)
IEC 60204-1, 55
IEC 60335-1 and -2, 104
IEC 60601 standards series, 97, 98–99, 128
IEC 61508-1, -2, and -3, 55, 57
IEC 61800-5-1, -2, and -3, 55
IEC 62061, 55
IEC 62304, 128
IEC 62366-1, 128
IEC 80601-2-77, 129, 130–132, 174
IEC 80601-2-78, 129, 132–133, 174
IEC standards, 2, 3
IEC/TC 62, 129
IEC TR 60601-4-1, 134
IEEE, *see* Institute of Electrical and Electronics
        Engineers (IEEE)
IEEE Standard 1872-2015, 20, 21, 23–24, 42–44
    ontologies in, 25
        CORA, 27–28
        CORAX, 28–29
        POS ontology, 31–33
        RPARTS, 29–31
        SUMO, 25–26
IMDRF, *see* International Medical Device
        Regulators Forum (IMDRF)
Indentations tests, 154–158
Industrial robot systems, 72
Inherent safety, 54–55, 59
Institute of Electrical and Electronics Engineers
        (IEEE), 9

Integrated approach, 4–5
Intelligent Robotic Surgery (I-SUR), 187, 189, 190, 191
    human-robot interaction
        during intervention execution, 195–197
        during pre-intervention phase, 191–194
    innovative technologies, 190
    surgical interface of, 195
Interactions, 76
International Accounting Standards Board
        (IASB), 11
International Electrotechnical Commission (IEC),
        127–128
International Medical Device Regulators Forum
        (IMDRF), 94, 125
International standardization organizations (ISO),
        2, 3, 10, 12; *see also specific standards*
Internet Corporation for Assigned Names and
        Numbers (ICANN), 11
Interoperability, 53
Interruption, 76
Intertwinement, 12
Intervention, 76
ISO, *see* International standardization
        organizations (ISO)
ISO 8373:2012, 104, 133
ISO 10218-1, 55, 57, 83, 128, 173, 174, 178
ISO 10218-2, 55, 72, 83
ISO 10993 series, 128
ISO 12100, 55, 57, 58, 129
ISO 13482:2014, 10, 12–13, 55, 57, 104, 105–106,
        115–117, 119–121, 173
    hazards identification and, 106–109, 113–114
    risk evaluation and, 106–109
    safety assessment and, 106–109, 114
ISO 13485:2016, 97
ISO 13842, 128
ISO 13849, 55, 57, 60
ISO 13855, 86
ISO 14971, 128, 129
ISO/IEC 80601-2-78, 100
ISO/TC 299, 129
ISO TC 299 WG6, 52
ISO/TS 15066, 55, 72, 83, 85, 86, 173
I-SUR, *see* Intelligent Robotic Surgery (I-SUR)

Kelvin models, 142, 150–152
Kelvin–Voigt model, 150
KUKA FlexFellow, 81
KUKA KMR mobile manipulator, 82

Lawmaking *vs.* standard-setting, 11
LCS, *see* Local coordinate systems (LCS)
LiSA mobile laboratory assistant, 82

Local coordinate systems (LCS), 32
Lokomat®Pro V6, 94

Machinery Directive, 106
Mass–spring–damper models, 140, 148, 149–152
MATLAB® cftool toolbox, 155, 158
Maxwell–Kelvin model, 151–152
Maxwell–Kelvin viscoelastic body, 141
Maxwell model, 150–152
MDR, *see* Medical Device Regulation (MDR)
Medical Device Regulation (MDR), 92–93, 125
Medical devices, 92–93
    compliance, 96
    definitions, 94–95, 126
    manufacturer of, 96
    regulations of, 94–96, 124
        essential principles, 126–127
        in EU, 125
        global harmonization, 125–126
        in USA, 125
    regulatory systems for, 96
    robots, 96, 124
    safety for, 94–100
        environmental standards, 97–98
        in-process standards, 98
        installation standards, 97–98
        medical electrical equipment, 98–100
        process standards, 97
        product standards, 96–97
        standards, scope of, 98
Medical electrical equipment, 98–100
Medical robots, 96, 124
    applicable regulations, boundary of, 128
    definition of, 127–128
    RACA ROBOTS, 132–133
    RASE, 130–132
    safety
        future of, 133–135
        requirements for, 128–129
        standards for, 128–130
Minimal invasive surgery (MIS), 142, 145–146, 189
MIS, *see* Minimal invasive surgery (MIS)
Mobile manipulators, 81–82
    advantages, 83
    challenges, 83
        forces and speeds due to combined motions, 87
        integration of two separate systems, 87
        unplanned restart/error recovery, 87
    commercial, examples of, 82
    motivation for, 82–83
    risk analysis, 83–86
        contact, processes involving, 83, 84–85
        HRC, process without, 84, 85

pick and place, 83, 84
        process without contact with parts, 83, 85
        simple mobile manipulation, 85–86
        third-hand applications featuring
            hand-guiding, 83, 84
    safety sensors for, 86–87
    simple *vs.* true, 82
Model complexity, 139
Model predictive control (MPC), 142
Modularity of robot, 49–52
    example, 51
    hardware module, 49, 62–65
    requirements, 52–55
        composability, 53
        interoperability, 53
        reusability, 52–53
        safety, 53–55
    safety, 55–62
    software module, 49, 65–69
Modules, 49–50
    basic, 50
    composite, 50, 54
    example, 51
    hardware, 49, 62–65
    safety, 55–62
        definition, 55–56
        design procedure for, 56
        engineering approach for, 56
        levels, 55
    software, 49, 65–69
Motivation, 4–5
MPC, *see* Model predictive control (MPC)

Neo-Hookean rupture model, 142
Neurorehabilitation, 91–92
Non-formal standards, 1
Nonlinear mass–spring–damper model, 158–160
Nonuniform indentation tests, 162
Novint Falcon™, 173

Objects, 26
Occupational Safety and Health Administration
        (OSHA), 108
Ontologies, 20
    application, 22
    classes, 21
    concept of, 21–22
    core, 22
    development process, 22–24
    domain, 22
    formal axioms, 21
    in IEEE 1872-2015, 25
        CORA, 27–28

CORAX, 28–29
POS ontology, 31–33
RPARTS, 29–31
SUMO, 25–26
purpose of, 21
relations, 21
robotics and, 20–21, 23–25
Rosetta, 33
in surgeries, 36–37
task, 22
top-level, 22
Ontologies for Robotics and Automation Working Group (ORA WG), 20–21, 23–24, 38–39
Ontology engineering, 22–23
"Orange" level hazards, 114–119
ORA WG, see Ontologies for Robotics and Automation Working Group (ORA WG)
OROSU, see Orthopaedics (OROSU)
Orthopaedics (OROSU), 36–37
OSHA, see Occupational Safety and Health Administration (OSHA)

Perceived safety, robotics, 13
Personal care robots, 12–14, 104–105
PHANTOM Omni haptic device, 194
PMA, see Premarketing Approval (PMA)
Position (POS) ontology, 31–33, 36
Premarketing Approval (PMA), 125
Premarket Notification, 125
Processes, 26
Product certification, 92–93
Project approaches, 3–5
Public policymaking for robots, 14–15

Quality Management System standards, 97
Quality of life, 105

RACA ROBOTS, 132–133
definitions, 132–133
safety requirements in, 133
scope, 132–133
standard for, 100–102
RAS, see Robotics and Automation Society (RAS)
RASE, 130–132
definitions, 130–131
performance of, 131
relaxation of requirements of, 131–132
safety requirements in, 131–132
scope, 130–131
Recognized standards, 125
Regulations of medical devices, 94–96, 124
definitions, 126
essential principles, 126–127
in EU, 125
global harmonization, 125–126
in USA, 125
Rehabilitation robots, 91–92, 93
Resolution on Civil Law Rules on Robotics 2015/2103(INL), 10, 14
Reusability, 52–53
Ridgeback s.a.s., 107
Rigid tools, 139
Risk, 108–109
management, 127
reduction process, 59–61
Risk priority numbers (RPNs), 111
RMSE, see Root mean square error (RMSE)
Robot Architecture (ROA) Ontology, 39
Robot groups, 27
Robotic environments, 27, 28
Robotics, 6
in aerospace manufacturing, 71–72
certified safety, 13
EU legislation for, 6–7
and human–robot interaction, 42–44
modularity of, 49–52
ontologies, 20–21, 23–25
perceived safety, 13
personal care robots, 12–14
public policymaking for, 14–15
standard-setting in, 12–14
systems, 27
Robotics and Automation Society (RAS), 23
Robot Part, 29–30
Robots, 27
actuating part, 30
collaborative, 72
communication part, 31
industrial, 72
interface, 27
medical devices and, 96
processing part, 31
safety levels for, 55–57
sensing parts, 30
task representation effort, 39–42
Robot Task Representation (RTR) Study Group, 40–42
Root mean square error (RMSE), 159
Rosetta ontologies, 33
RPARTS, 29–31
RPNs, see Risk priority numbers (RPNs)

Safe failures, 57–58
Safety, 53–55, 92–93
control systems, parts of, 60–62
levels, 55
for medical devices, 94–100

modules, 55–62
  sensors for mobile manipulators, 86–87
  standards, 92–93, 124
  V&V procedure for, 56–57
Scrubber robots, 104, 106
  ground rules and assumptions, definition of
    background, 109
    block diagrams, 112
    capability of failure detection, 112
    criticality and ranking approach, 111
    environmental conditions, 109
    failure effects, 112
    FMECA, 110–111
    hazard analysis and risk assessment specific
      activities, 112–114, 114–119
    information basis, 111
    operating profiles, 110
    product misuse/abuse by user, 110
    safety-related functions, performance level
      of, 112, 114
  modes of operation, 109
  physical architecture, 113
  practical commentary on, 119–121
  rendition, 119–121
  system boundaries, definition of, 109
  tracking, 119
Sharp instruments, 139
Sick Laser S300P, 119–120
Simple mobile manipulation, 82
  for manipulator motion, 86
  for platform motion, 85–86
Skills, 33–34
Smart actuator, 51–52
Smart autonomous robot, 14
Smith predictor, 144
SNOMED-CT©, 36
Soft law, 11
Soft tissue interaction, 139
Soft tissue models, 139–140, 147–148
  data collection methods, 153–154
  indentations tests, 154–158
  mass–spring–damper models, 149–152
  nonlinear mass–spring–damper model, 158–160
Software (SW) modules, 49–50, 65–69
Special instruments, 139
Standardization, 1–3, 5
  concept of, 10–11
  European, 1
  intertwinement, 12
  worldwide level, 2
Standard Linear Solid (SLS) viscoelastic model, 151
Standards, 4
  characteristics, 1

concept of, 10–11
definition, 1
formal, 1, 3
harmonised, 5–6, 7
non-formal, 1
for RACA robots, 100–102
Standard-setting
  vs. lawmaking, 11
  in robot technology
    personal care robots, 12–14
Suggested Upper Merged Ontology (SUMO), 25–26
SUI/KIF, 25
Surgical automation, 187–190
Surgical procedures, 189
Surgical robots, 138

Task ontologies, 22
TCs, *see* Technical committees (TCs)
Technical committees (TCs), 3
Technical legislation, 5–7
Technical Report, 2
Technical Specification (TS), 2
Teleoperation (bilateral), 138, 171–173
  architectures, 143–144
  basic notions, 174–175
  challenges, 171–172
  communication strategy for, 172, 176–177
  experimental results, 182–183
  haptic feedback in, 145–147
  human–robot interaction and its implications
    on, safety during, 173–174
  networked velocity-force type, 175
  passivity of, 172–173
    controller–passivity observer approach,
      175–180
    controllers, 178–180
    control signals, bounds for, 178, 179
    rate limited signals, transparency with,
      180–182
Tensor Product Model Transformation, 164
TFEU, *see* Treaty on Functioning of European
    Union (TFEU)
TNEs, *see* Transnational enterprises (TNEs)
Tool–tissue interactions, 138–139
  control aspects of, 143–145
  importance of, 165
  proposed model, usability of, 164–165
  results, 160–161
    model verification methods, 161–163
    model verification results, 163–164
  soft tissue models, 147–148
    data collection methods, 153–154
    indentations tests, 154–158

mass–spring–damper models, 149–152
    nonlinear mass–spring–damper model,
        158–160
  telesurgery haptic feedback in, 145–147
  types of, 139–143
Top-level ontologies, 22; *see also* Suggested Upper
    Merged Ontology (SUMO)
TORU Cube, 82
Transformations, 32
Transnational enterprises (TNEs), 12
Transparency, 143
Treaty on Functioning of European Union (TFEU), 10
True mobile manipulation, 82
TS, *see* Technical Specification (TS)
Type-C Standard, 106

UML, *see* Unified Modeling Language (UML)
Unified Modeling Language (UML), 194

VALERI mobile manipulator, 82
Verification and validation (V&V), 56, 57, 58
Visual information, 139
V&V, *see* Verification and validation (V&V)

Wiechert model, 152, 156–158
WoTCO, *see* Core Ontology for Web of Things
    (WoTCO)

XML Schema Definition Language (XSDL), 38
XSDL, *see* XML Schema Definition Language
    (XSDL)

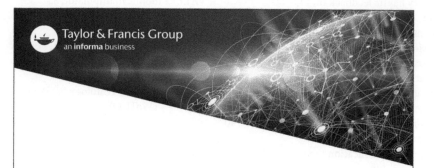

9 780367 730222